How to Facilitate Meaningful Classroom Conversations across Disciplines, Grade Levels, and Digital Platforms

FURTHER PRAISE FOR *HOW TO FACILITATE MEANINGFUL CLASSROOM CONVERSATIONS*

"In a moment when dialog has never been more important, Michael Sherry has written a book that provides teachers—across grade levels and subjects—the tools for promoting and sustaining meaningful classroom discussion. Drawing on rich examples from real classrooms, each chapter builds on the previous to develop a complex picture of how classroom discussions fail and succeed in an array of contexts. Teachers will find this book engaging, accessible, and full of practical solutions grounded in a robust theory and scholarship."—**Amanda Haertling Thein, associate dean for faculty and academic affairs, University of Iowa**

"*How to Facilitate Meaningful Classroom Conversations* offers teachers and teacher educators invaluable guidance on the complex dynamics of classroom dialogue and how to manage them productively across disciplines, settings, and topics. The book is an extraordinary accomplishment: it communicates sophisticated ideas about discourse, interaction, learning, and identity in an accessible, conversational manner; it grounds its exposition in vivid examples of real classroom discussions, thoughtfully analyzed; it offers readers dozens of practical activities and sensitive guidance on how to enact them; and it is beautifully written, at times even moving."—**Adam Lefstein, professor, Ben-Gurion University of the Negev**

"Mike Sherry has thought more deeply about discussion than anyone I know—and it shows in this book. He offers a clear vision of both the 'how' and the 'why' of classroom discussion. The book helped me see discussion in a new way, and it challenged me to reflect on how I can bring it to my own teaching. Any teacher, at any level or in any context, can learn from this book."—**Anne Elrod Whitney, professor of education, Penn State University**

"Sherry is expert at making visible the ways and reasons some traditional teaching practices hinder whole-group discussion, despite our best intentions to do the opposite. Rooted in transcripts from real classrooms—across grade levels, subject areas, and teaching contexts—this book offers teachers detailed support for achieving higher-quality classroom talk with their students. This book will be a go-to resource for me and the teachers I teach!"—**Carlin Borsheim-Black, associate professor of English language and literature and co-author of *Letting Go of Literary Whiteness: Antiracist Literature Instruction for White Students***

How to Facilitate Meaningful Classroom Conversations across Disciplines, Grade Levels, and Digital Platforms

Michael B. Sherry

ROWMAN & LITTLEFIELD
Lanham • Boulder • New York • London

Published by Rowman & Littlefield
An imprint of The Rowman & Littlefield Publishing Group, Inc.
4501 Forbes Boulevard, Suite 200, Lanham, Maryland 20706
www.rowman.com

6 Tinworth Street, London, SE11 5AL, United Kingdom

Copyright © 2021 by Michael B. Sherry

All rights reserved. No part of this book may be reproduced in any form or by any electronic or mechanical means, including information storage and retrieval systems, without written permission from the publisher, except by a reviewer who may quote passages in a review.

British Library Cataloguing in Publication Information Available

Library of Congress Cataloging-in-Publication Data

Names: Sherry, Michael B., 1978– author.
Title: How to facilitate meaningful classroom conversations across disciplines, grade levels, and digital platforms / Michael B. Sherry.
Description: Lanham : Rowman & Littlefield, [2020] | Includes bibliographical references. | Summary: "This book provides a coherent framework, concrete examples, and a collection of practical ideas for encouraging and sustaining meaningful classroom conversations"— Provided by publisher.
Identifiers: LCCN 2020012616 (print) | LCCN 2020012617 (ebook) | ISBN 9781475855036 (cloth) | ISBN 9781475855043 (paperback) | ISBN 9781475855050 (epub)
Subjects: LCSH: Communication in education. | Classroom management. | Interpersonal communication—Study and teaching. | Interaction analysis in education.
Classification: LCC LB1033.5 .S53 2020 (print) | LCC LB1033.5 (ebook) | DDC 371.102/2—dc23
LC record available at https://lccn.loc.gov/2020012616
LC ebook record available at https://lccn.loc.gov/2020012617

To Anne and Isabelle

Contents

Acknowledgments		ix
1	Two People Talking by Themselves?	1
2	Transforming Recitations into Dialogic Discussions	16
3	Organizing Student-Led Dialogic Discussions	39
4	Facilitating Disciplinary Dialogic Discussions	59
5	Inviting Out-of-School Cultural Practices into Dialogic Discussions	79
6	Developing Dialogic Discussions over Time	104
7	Designing Dialogic Online Discussions	128
8	Listening to the Silence in Difficult Dialogic Discussions	151
Appendix A Key Terms		167
Appendix B Classroom Examples		173
Appendix C Activities for Promoting Dialogic Discussions		218
References		225
About the Author		237

Acknowledgments

This book would not have been possible without the support of many people, most of all Dr. Anne Lawrence: you have taught me more about dialogue, research, and writing than I can ever express—thank you for always listening to my soul's voice. Thanks to Dr. Joan Kaywell for blazing the paths, including the one that led me here. Thanks to those who have provided feedback on this work along the way, especially Dr. Karen Ames, Dr. Mandie Dunn, Dr. Amanda Haertling-Thein, Dr. Mary Juzwik, Dr. Brett Merritt, Dr. Martin Nystrand, Dr. Peter Smagorinsky, and Dr. Anne Whitney. Thanks to Carlie Wall and the others at Rowman & Littlefield for their patience. And thanks to all the teachers and students who allowed me to join their conversations, and who struggle day after day to stay in meaningful dialogue with one another.

1

Two People Talking by Themselves?

I stood before my eighth graders, a dog-eared copy of Shakespeare's Romeo and Juliet *in hand. The students, seated in a horseshoe of desks around the perimeter of the room, waited quietly, some leaning forward attentively, others slumped in their seats.*
   "So yesterday we were talking about monologue," I said. "What did we say a monologue was?"
   Miriam shot a hand into the air. I nodded to her. "One person talking by themselves?" she responded.
   "Right!" I smiled, and Miriam sat back in her seat contentedly. "So today we're going to talk about dialogue. What is a dialogue?" I looked around the room expectantly. When no one volunteered, I call on one of the slumpers, leaning on his hand and trying not to make eye contact. "John?" Without lifting his head, John swiveled toward me. Seconds passed. Finally, I prompted him. "If a monologue is one person talking by themselves, then a dialogue *is . . . ?"*
   "Two people talking by themselves?"

Does this scene seem familiar? Many prospective and practicing teachers have imagined themselves leading a discussion of a beloved text, with students circled around the conversation like a conspiratorial campfire. Many readers of this vignette have recognized Miriam, an obedient responder, in some of their own students and expressed their frustration with students like John, a more resistant one. Some readers may also identify with these students, remembering their own hopeful hesitance or rebellious resistance as students encountering this familiar question-and-answer routine. Yet most teachers sense that this kind of exchange is not the ideal they envisioned. It is not really a discussion. "People talking by themselves" is not a real dialogue.

WHAT IS A DIALOGIC DISCUSSION?

So what is a "dialogic" discussion? Teachers and researchers past and present disagree.[1] The Socratic Seminar, a whole-class discussion activity that takes its name from the teacher depicted in Plato's fourth-century *Dialogs*, differs from the book-club style discussions of Literature Circles, first practiced in the 1980s[2] (see chapter 3 for more on these different classroom discussion activities). Seventeenth-century literary salons differ from twenty-first-century online discussion forums. Talk in a history class may differ from how teachers and students discuss science.[3] Across these examples, there are similarities and differences that help to make some important distinctions. Multiple people participate in a conversation—they "take a turn" in the company of others.[4] But not all conversation is **dialogic**: sometimes turns in a conversation seem unrelated, as people talk past each other rather than addressing others and responding to what they have already written or said (think of some political debates or talk shows!).

> **Take a Turn**
> What is (or isn't) a discussion to you? Make a list of features you associate with classroom discussions (or the lack thereof).

The Greek word *dialogos* comes from roots meaning "to speak through."[5] In this sense, all language is "dialogic," drawing on previous uses by others that echo in any word. Even John's retort in the vignette above makes cleverly ironic use of Miriam's previous phrase "talking by themselves." But while this classroom conversation might be dialogic, in this sense, it is not what most people think of as a **discussion**, in which participants engage in a shared inquiry, using others' contributions to build meanings together (even if they disagree).

Below is a list of qualities used to describe a discussion. These are drawn from prior research[6] and compiled over the years from teachers across grade levels, academic disciplines, and school contexts:

- Multiple participants (not just the teacher) contribute.
- Participants draw on relevant examples to address a shared focus.
- Participants build on what others have said or written.
- Participants consider, and even take on, other points of view.
- Participants make meaning together that they couldn't have made separately.
- Participants contribute in certain shared ways, but they can also be themselves.

Not all of these may seem essential to you. Some of these qualities may seem difficult or impossible within a particular grade level or content area, or within the context of particular schools, classrooms, curricular standards, or online course management systems. Upon reflection, you may realize that discussion is not appropriate for what you want to accomplish with students. If so, you've already begun to consider an important lesson of this book: the reasons for holding a discussion, and what makes a good one, depend on the context—the nature and purposes of the activity, the cultural experiences of the participants, the subject matter of the discussion, and the learning environment (including technological tools and platforms) for discussion. But if discussion does seem right for you, please read on.

WHY DO DISCUSSIONS MATTER?

In the following excerpt, US first-grader Guillermo had just recounted his story about wrestling practice to teacher Jessica Davis, who knelt by the easel where she had written it on a large piece of chart paper. Guillermo's classmates, seated in a semicircle on the floor in front of the easel, offered revision suggestions for a sentence about doing warm-up neck rotations.

1. TONISHA: What does "like this" mean?

2. MS. DAVIS: Oh, so you're saying a reader might not know what "this" refers to?

3. GUILLERMO: Well, I did say we go side to side.

4. TONISHA: You already said it up here,

5. but down here. *(Points to the end of the sentence)*

6. JOEY: Maybe you could make it longer.

7. MS. DAVIS: So we're saying we don't know how you go "side to side."

8. I wonder if he could cross out "like this" and add a detail to explain.

9. GUILLERMO: Okay. *(Picking up pen)*

10. JOEY: Hey, maybe he could put an arrow!

In this brief excerpt, three students, as well as Ms. Davis, participated in a discussion of Guillermo's writing, a story about an out-of-school hobby important to him that became central to this lesson. Ms. Davis explained that, "I truly believe that when you listen to children, they in return will listen to you. . . . This is also a way

> Notice how Ms. Davis reflects and amplifies what students have said. How does it make you feel as a student when someone responds this way to you?

that I show my students respect." In this discussion, speakers drew on specific examples that had already been said and written to offer ideas about how best to realize Guillermo's explanation of neck rotations that "go side to side, like this." They shared a focus on revising Guillermo's story. Ms. Davis's "we" at line 7 suggested that they were in it together, even if their ideas differed. As she described this lesson afterward, "Everyone feels comfortable to participate . . . and they all have the opportunity to do so. The teacher acts more as a facilitator to the students' discussing."

Much prior research has suggested that when students get to talk—to be active contributors—and to learn from one another (not just the teacher), they are more likely to learn and remember.[7] Through discussion, students can begin to see how their own familiar ways of talking outside of school might be adapted to the classroom,[8] and how they might find their voices in academic conversations.[9] Studies have also shown that discussions can improve students' ability to use evidence and make arguments[10]:

citing what others have written or said is a literacy skill valued across disciplines. Discussions can also help students learn to communicate and think in ways particular to historians, scientists, or members of another disciplinary community.[11] According to some researchers, discussions in which students learn to build on what others have said, and to consider points of view other than their own, are essential to participation in a literate, democratic, and peaceful society.[12]

The opposite is also true.

Classroom conversations can convince students that they have little to learn from school or one another, that their home language practices are not welcome, that the loudest voice wins the argument, and that academic discourse is as mystifying and alien as the views of anyone who disagrees with them. No wonder then that teachers and students might avoid attempts at whole-class discussion like the hapless exchange in the vignette that began this chapter.

Yet outside the classroom, dialogue has never been more important. From climate change summits or peace talks among neighboring nations, to clashes between rival ethnic groups or political party mudslinging, to workplace conversations or a traffic stop on a dark street, we must learn to bring our own and others' words into relationship with integrity or suffer the consequences. What to do?

WHY DO DISCUSSIONS SUCCEED . . . AND FAIL?

This book presents a dialogic approach to classroom conversations across grade levels, activities, subject areas, and technological platforms. Each chapter adds another layer to this approach, introducing new concepts and offering additional tools for teachers seeking to promote and sustain meaningful class discussions. And in order to understand this approach, each chapter also takes a closer look at why discussions fail.

In the same US first-grade classroom described above, a nearly identical lesson six months later produced much different results. As before, Ms. Davis had just written Hunter's story about his hockey game on the chart paper and invited students seated around the author to offer their revision suggestions.

1. MS. DAVIS: Adriana, what do you think?

2. ADRIANA: The "i" has to be capitalized?

3. MS. DAVIS: Come and point to what "i" needs to be capitalized.

4. ADRIANA: *(Stands up, walks to the chart paper,*

5. *points to "i" in "it" at the beginning of the second line)*

6. MS. DAVIS: *(Reading the whole sentence aloud)* Oh.

7. "I am at my hockey game and it is almost time for me to play."

8. *(Standing to address the class)* When do we have capital letters in our writing?

9. *(Various students raise their hands.)*

10. MACKENZIE: *(Leaning forward with her hand raised high)* OH!

11. MS. DAVIS: Remember, what's one place that we need to have a capital letter?

12. Mackenzie?

13. MACKENZIE: Beginning and the end of a sentence,

14. when you start a new sentence.

15. MS. DAVIS: Okay, is this the beginning of a sentence?

16. CLASS: NOOO!

Though the activity was nearly identical, this conversation differed from the previous one in Ms. Davis's classroom. There, students and their teacher drew on relevant examples of what had already been written or said to explore different possibilities for revision of Guillermo's story.

> How might Adriana feel at this point?
>
> How else could Ms. Davis have responded to Adriana's seemingly "wrong" answer?

Here, the emphasis was on previously discussed capitalization rules and getting the one right answer. In that first excerpt, the class was a "we," and each person's contribution was valued. In this exchange, Adriana's hesitant idea was singled out as an error by a unanimous chorus, a public humiliation perhaps made worse because this student was also an English Language Learner. And what if Adriana's answer wasn't "wrong" at all, but rather an attempt to suggest a possible revision: "I am at my hockey game. ~~and~~ It is almost time for me to play"? As Ms. Davis reflected later, "I feel like this is being disrespectful to Adriana because I'm not really understanding where she's coming from and listening to her idea and her point of view."

It serves no one to blame Ms. Davis or her students (or ourselves, for who among us has not participated at some point in a scene like this one?). Instead, we might consider that attempts at dialogue like the one above often succeed or fail at one of several levels:

1. **Genre:** expectations for talk and behavior related to the type of activity and to the social context in which a conversation occurs
2. **Academic Discipline:** expectations for talk and behavior about certain kinds of subject matter, or in communities who study those subjects
3. **Culture:** expectations for talk and behavior in communities in which people participate outside the social situation in which the conversation occurs
4. **Tool:** the medium, device, platform, or other technology used by participants in the conversation

One might think of these four levels—with their corresponding initials, G, A, C, T—as the DNA of discussions. For example, one way to understand the excerpt above is via genre: in this second excerpt, Ms. Davis and her students participate in a classroom talk genre called **recitation** that has persisted for over a century in American schools. In this pattern, the teacher poses questions in quick succession that review or test what students have learned, as Ms. Davis does in lines 8–16.

Because there is usually one right answer, and the teacher evaluates students' responses after each turn, this routine can cause some students who agree to "play the game" (like Adriana) to respond uncertainly—with a question mark in their voices.[13] Others, like Mackenzie, play along with teachers in the back and forth of recitation so that "we can tell that they know that *we* know that *they* know what *we* know!"[14] But some students may be unwilling to risk a wrong answer, which might be face-threatening. And some (like John, in the opening vignette) may simply resist being forced to say what the teacher is already thinking—the equivalent of a classroom "Jedi mind trick." If teachers and students can explicitly recognize classroom talk patterns associated with activity genres that may discourage student participation, like recitation, they can perhaps work to transform them. Likewise, they can choose to employ other patterns of talk that promote whole-class, dialogic discussion.

However, education research has also described the remarkable consistency and persistence of the recitation question-and-answer routine, across disciplines and grade levels, since the early twentieth century.[15] Some researchers have even suggested that this "teaching game" is *the* dominant genre, or type of talk found in classrooms.[16] Moreover, studies have found that while many English teachers and students recognize recitation as constraining classroom conversation, they nevertheless reinforce this pattern through their participation.[17] For these teachers, recitation may be the seed, as well as the worm, in the apple. Through patterns of talk, teachers and students create, assume, impose, resist, and reinforce not only classroom routines, but also classroom identities.

For example, why did Ms. Davis and her students, so clearly capable of and thoughtful about dialogic discussion in the first lesson, slip into recitation during the second one? What did this permit Ms. Davis to accomplish as a teacher? Who did it allow Mackenzie—or Adriana—to become as a student? To understand why attempts at dialogic discussion succeed or fail, it is equally important to examine how patterns of talk, and the teacher and student identities those patterns can imply, might align or conflict with who they are or want to be within the culture of the classroom, as well as in cultural communities beyond it.

Cultural communities also include those associated with a particular academic discipline: expectations of a successful discussion in English language arts might be both similar to and different from those for a discussion in science. For Ms. Davis, an elementary teacher, these disciplinary overlaps and distinctions might be more regularly visible. But

> **Take a Turn**
> Why do you think recitation has persisted for so long?
>
> What pros and cons might this routine have for teachers and students?

school subjects also matter if a high school student has come from a math classroom with one set of expectations to an English class with another.

This book also addresses how whole-class discussions fail or succeed because of non-human elements beyond social patterns of talk or cultural identity associations. These elements include the tools used in learning environments, like the setup of desks in a classroom or the interface of a course management system (or a teleconference call). How was conversation in Ms. Davis's lessons affected, for example, by the fact that these excerpts took place with students seated on the floor in a circle, and involved a handwritten text of the student's story transcribed on a flipchart? How would this lesson have unfolded differently if students had sat at their desks with the story written on the board? Or at separate computers, reading from their screens?

Finally, this book examines elements that bring these four parts of "discussion DNA" into dynamic, living relationship, such as the temporal sequence of events within a lesson or an academic year, as well as beyond the classroom. Across space and time, these and other aspects of the more-than-human world can suggest something to participants, for better or for worse, about a place and their place in it—in a class, in a school, in the larger world. These ecological elements further illuminate ways in which dialogue depends not only on individuals, but also on emergent and collective forces, like a flock of birds wheeling against the evening sky.

HOW MIGHT ONE USE THIS BOOK?

What good would a book on discussion be without opportunities for readers to participate? One such opportunity, which you may have already noticed in this chapter, is presented by the dialogue boxes that invite you to "take a turn," considering a question related to the content as it unfolds. The end of each chapter also includes prompts for teachers' further reflection related to a particular aspect of whole-class discussions, as well as ideas for discussion activities to explore with students. Key terms from each chapter, appearing for the first time in bold font, are listed and defined in a glossary at the back of the book. In addition to key terms, the back of the book also includes a complete list of the discussion activities featured in each chapter.

Another opportunity for reader participation (and a major part of each chapter) is provided by the examples—written transcripts of actual classroom talk during lessons in different classrooms, grade levels, and subject areas. As in the excerpt from Ms. Davis's class, these conversations are presented as transcripts. Readers new to this genre might approach these examples like a play script, with the names of characters, italicized stage directions, and numbered lines meant to help keep track of the participants' roles, their verbal and nonverbal interactions, and the turn-by-turn sequence of their unfolding conversation. Try reading them aloud, alone or with others.

As you will have noticed, the examples in each chapter appear with annotations: questions and explanations meant to aid your reflection on what is happening (and how and why) at particular moments in the transcribed conversation. To aid in this, the appendixes include a table that shows the topic/genre, grade level, and academic discipline from which the examples in each chapter are drawn.

Like a double-helix, each chapter builds on concepts and examples from the previous ones, adding increasing complexity to how one might understand why whole-class discussions succeed or fail in different contexts—widening concentric circles, ripples in a pond. For this reason, you may wish to read the chapters consecutively. However, because they each address a particular aspect of whole-class discussions, each chapter could also be read separately, and readers with a specific interest may prefer to dive in or jump around.

Chapter 2 begins with a closer look at recitation and how language-level moves might help to avoid or transform that common classroom conversation genre. Chapter 3 examines how other genres of activity shape opportunities for dialogue, particularly small-group, student-led discussions. Chapter 4 moves beyond the individual classroom, attending to how discussions may differ by academic discipline. Chapter 5 focuses on how out-of-school cultural experiences can influence teacher and student participation in discussion. Chapter 6 addresses patterns in discussions over time within and across lessons. Chapter 7 considers discussions in online forums. And chapter 8 addresses discussions of personal, controversial, and even traumatic issues in the classroom.

REFLECTIONS FOR TEACHERS

1. Review the bulleted list of qualities that characterize discussions (or your own list, if you generated one in response to the first "Take a Turn" prompt above).
   a. Which of these is (most) important to you? Why?
   b. Choose one or more of these features: in your experience, what can a teacher do to encourage this type of participation?
2. Recall a lesson during which you participated as a teacher or as a student in an attempt at whole-class discussion. What do you think made that discussion succeed or fail?
3. Consider the same lesson, but this time from another point of view (as a student or as the teacher). What, if anything, does this change about your reflection on whether and how the discussion succeeded or failed?
4. Reread the first excerpt from Ms. Davis's class:
   a. What do you notice?
   b. What do you wonder about?
   c. With which participant do you especially identify? Why?
   d. Pick a line that stands out to you: what is important about this moment?
   e. If you could tell this teacher one thing, what would it be?
   f. How, if at all, would you revise this interaction, and why? Rewrite the transcript or rehearse alternatives with other readers, and reflect on your reasons for making these revisions.
5. Reread the second excerpt from Ms. Davis's class:
   a. What do you notice?
   b. What do you wonder about?
   c. With which participant do you especially identify? Why?
   d. Pick a line that stands out to you: what is important about this moment?
   e. If you could tell this teacher one thing, what would it be?
   f. How, if at all, would you revise this interaction, and why? Rewrite the transcript or rehearse alternatives with other readers, and reflect on your reasons for making these revisions.

6. What experiences, if any, have you had with recitation as a student?
7. What experiences, if any, have you had with recitation as a teacher?
8. In reflecting on their experiences as students, teachers often remember recitation as a mostly negative practice (for example, as one that created a reluctance to participate for fear of getting the wrong answer). Yet, most teachers also recall implementing recitation at some point in their own classrooms. Why do you think this might be?

EXPLORATIONS WITH STUDENTS

1. Ask students (on their own, in groups, or as a class) to list, draw, or role-play what they think makes a good discussion.
    a. Compare students' responses to the bulleted list of qualities that characterize discussions (or your own list, if you generated one in response to the first "Take a Turn" prompt, above). What is similar or different, and why?
    b. Choose one or more of the similarities or differences between students' reflections on what makes a good discussion and your own: present both reflections to students and ask them to consider why they are similar or different.
2. Begin with a list of features that characterize a good discussion (the bulleted list in this chapter, your own list, or a synthesis of your own and students' ideas from the previous exploration question) in one side of a three-column table. With students, brainstorm practices that might help to encourage good participation: What can teachers do? What can students do?

What makes a good discussion	What teachers can do	What students can do

CHAPTER SUMMARY

- Not all conversation is dialogic; not all dialogic discourse is discussion.
- Dialogic discussions involve shared inquiry, in which multiple participants build on one another's contributions to make meaning together (even if they disagree).
- Attempts at whole-class dialogic discussion can promote student participation . . . or discourage it.
- Discussions may be shaped by **G**enre, **A**cademic Discipline, **C**ulture, and **T**ools—the "DNA of discussions."
- Much of what passes for discussion is actually recitation, a persistent and prevalent teacher-led question-and-answer routine.

NOTES

1. M. C. O'Connor and S. Michaels "When Is Dialogue 'Dialogic'?" accessed January 2, 2010, http://proquest.umi.com.proxy1.cl.msu.edu/pqdweb?index=4&did=1339279201&SrchMode=3&sid=1&Fmt=6&VInst=PROD&VType=PQD&RQT=309&VName=PQD&TS=1262468378&clientId=3552&aid=1.

2. Harvey Daniels, *Literature Circles: Voice and Choice in the Student-Centered Classroom* (York, ME: Stenhouse Publishers, 1994).

3. M. B. Sherry, "Bringing Disciplinarity to Dialogic Discussions: Imaginative Entry and Disciplinary Discourse in a Ninth-Grade History Classroom," *Curriculum Inquiry* 46, no. 2 (2016): 168–95; W. C. Parker, "Listening to Strangers: Classroom Discussion in Democratic Education," *Teachers College Record* 112, no. 11 (2010): 2815–32; N. Mercer, L. Dawes, and J. K. Staarman, "Dialogic Teaching in the Primary Science Classroom," *Language and Education* 23, no. 4 (2009): 353–69; C. Chin, "Classroom Interaction in Science: Teacher Questioning and Feedback to Students' Responses," *International Journal of Science Education* 28, no. 11 (2007): 1315–46.

4. *The Oxford English Dictionary* traces the word *conversation* to French and Latin roots related to turns (of talk, of a plow in the field) and to dwelling in the company of others.

5. The Greek word *dialogos* comes from *dialegesthai* (dia = through, legein = speak).

6. M. Y. Kim and I. A. G. Wilkinson, "What Is Dialogic Teaching? Constructing, Deconstructing, and Reconstructing a Pedagogy of Classroom Talk," *Learning, Culture, and Social Interaction* 21 (2019): 70–86.

7. E.g., S. W. Freedman et al., *Inside City Schools: Investigating Literacy in Multicultural Classrooms* (New York: Teachers College Press, 1999); J. A. Langer, "Discussion as Exploration: Literature and the Horizon of Possibilities," in *Exploring Texts: The Role of Discussion and Writing in the Teaching and Learning of Literature*, edited by G. E. Newell and R. K. Durst (Norwood, MA: Christopher Gordon, 1992), 23–43; G. Ladson-Billings, "Toward a Theory of Culturally Relevant Pedagogy," *American Educational Research Journal* 32, no. 3 (1995): 465–91; C. D. Lee, *Culture, Literacy & Learning: Taking Bloom in the Midst of the Whirlwind* (New York: Teachers College Press, 2006); K. M. Losey, "Mexican American Students and Classroom Interaction: An Overview and Critique," *Review of Educational Research* 65, no. 3 (1995): 283–318.

8. M. B. Sherry, "Indirect Challenges and Provocative Paraphrases: Using Cultural Conflict-Talk Practices to Promote Students' Dialogic Participation in Whole-Class Discussions," *Research in the Teaching of English* 49, no. 2 (2014): 141–67.

9. A. Segal, I. Pollak, and A. Lefstein, "Democracy, Voice, and Dialogic Pedagogy: The Struggle to Be Heard and Heeded," *Language and Education* 31, no. 1 (2017): 6–25.

10. A. Reznitskaya and I. A. G. Wilkinson, *The Most Reasonable Answer: Helping Students Build Better Arguments Together* (Cambridge, MA: Harvard Education Press, 2017).

11. Sherry, "Bringing Disciplinarity"; Parker, "Listening to Strangers"; Mercer, Dawes, and Staarman, "Dialogic Teaching in the Primary Science Classroom"; Chin, "Classroom Interaction in Science."

12. Sherry, "Indirect Challenges and Provocative Paraphrases"; Parker, "Listening to Strangers."

13. J. D. Marshall, P. Smagorinsky, and M. W. Smith, "The Language of Interpretation: Patterns of Discourse in Discussions of Literature" (Urbana, IL: NCTE, 1995).

14. Nystrand et al., *Opening Dialogue: Understanding the Dynamics of Language and Learning in the English Classroom* (New York: Teachers College Press, 1997), 18.

15. A. N. Applebee et al., "Discussion-Based Approaches to Developing Understanding: Classroom Instruction and Student Performance in Middle and High School English," *American Educational Research Journal* 40, no. 3 (2003): 685–730; Ronald Gallimore, Stephanie Dalton, and Roland G. Tharp, "Self-Regulation and Interactive Teaching: The Effects of Teaching Conditions on Teachers' Cognitive Activity," *The Elementary School Journal* 86, no. 5 (1986): 612; J. Hoetker and W. Jr. Albrand, "The Persistence of Recitation," *American*

Educational Research Journal 6 (1969): 145–67; Nystrand et al., *Opening Dialogue*; V. T. Thayer, *The Passing of the Recitation* (Boston: D.C. Heath, 1928).

16. Bellack et al., *The Language of the Classroom* (New York: Teachers College Press, 1966).

17. J. S. Chisholm and A. J. Loretto, "Tensioning Interpretive Authority during Dialogic Discussions of Literature," *L1-Educational Studies in Language and Literature* 16 (2016): 1–32; T. Reynolds, "Understanding and Embracing Contradictions: An Exploration of High School English Teachers' Beliefs about Whole-Class Discussion," *Language and Education* 32, no. 4 (2018): 1–15.

2

Transforming Recitations into Dialogic Discussions

"Two people talking by themselves?" As John's retort hung in the air, students looked at me to see how I would respond.

I laughed. *"That's a good point, John! Sometimes when people are supposed to be having a dialogue, it seems like they're talking by themselves."* As I spoke, I walked across the room toward two other students who were whispering and giggling. *"In fact, we saw that happen in the play when Juliet talks to her parents. Have any of you ever felt like that? Turn to your partners and talk about a time when you were trying to have a dialogue with someone, and you felt like you were talking past each other."*

The previous chapter addressed the typical question-and-answer routine called recitation, a routine that teachers and students may associate with whole-class conversation—indeed, with what it means to be a teacher and a student—but one that researchers often address as the opposite of whole-class, dialogic discussion. This chapter examines recitation's troubled relationship to discussion, as well as whether and how this routine might in fact be a starting point for fostering dialogue.

HOW RECITATION WORKS AT THE LANGUAGE LEVEL

Consider the following example from a tenth-grade English language arts (ELA) classroom in a US Midwestern public school. The teacher had planned to review story elements like Exposition, Rising Action, Climax, Falling Action, and Resolution with a class of twenty-two tenth graders at a rural high school. The desks were arranged in a horseshoe, and the diagram below was written on the board.

1. MR. SCHULZ: So . . . what does this remind you of?

2. ASHLEY: A mountain.

3. SCHULZ: A mountain. Alrighty . . .

4. So could someone tell me what is the first part of a story?

5. Like what starts out a story usually?

How do you think the teacher feels at this point?

How might Ashley feel?

Compare your answers to your own experiences as teacher and student.

6. From here to here to here. *(Points to diagram on board)*

7. Yes?

8. KEN: A problem?

9. MR. SCHULZ: A problem? Okay . . . *(Writes on board)* Yes?

10. DIANA: A climax.

11. MR. SCHULZ: Climax. *(Writes on board)* That would be right up there.

12. JAMIE: The characters?

13. MR. SCHULZ: Okay. *(Writes on board)* The characters and problems and stuff—

14. what is that called . . . ? At the beginning of a story?

15. KELSEY: Introduction?

16. MR. SCHULZ: Introduction? Introduction's a word for it.

17. There's another word that starts with an "E." ...

18. The "ex_____" ... Go ahead?

19. ASHLEY: Exposition?

20. MR. SCHULZ: It's an exposition.

21. It's this thing when you're introducing the characters and other stuff,

22. so you're right when you say "introduction,"

23. but "exposition" is a better word for it if you want to get technical.

In the transcript above, you may have noticed that the teacher did most of the talking. In fact, he spoke at every other turn, falling into a recurring, three-part pattern (Table 2.1) that education researchers have dubbed **IRE/F**[1]: (1) The teacher asks or *initiates* a question, (2) a student *responds*, and (3) the teacher *evaluates* or *follows-up* on that student's response. This pattern appears in recitations across classrooms and grade levels, and you may remember it from the examples in chapter 1.

Table 2.1. The three-part pattern of IRE/F

IRE/F pattern	Chapter 1	Chapter 2
Initiate	TEACHER: What's one place that we need to have a capital letter?	TEACHER: What starts out a story usually?
Respond	STUDENT: When you start a new sentence?	STUDENT: A problem?
Evaluate/ Follow-up	TEACHER: Okay.	TEACHER: A problem? Okay.

The problem with the IRE/F pattern is that it immediately signals to students that they will be evaluated based on whether their responses match what the teacher expects: introduction may be a fine word, but "exposition is a better word for it if you want to get technical." This emphasis on getting to the one "right" answer (the one the teacher is thinking of) not only discourages further discussion, but it can also have a negative effect overall on students' literacy learning.[2] One reason for this might be that trying to get students to guess or recall the answer the teacher is searching for is unnecessarily difficult. One researcher has called IRE/F "a lecture in question form"[3]: for example, in the excerpt above, one alternative might have been for Mr. Schulz to simply list the story element names and definitions on the diagram before asking students to apply them to examples from their own experience. Yet because this pattern is so persistent across classrooms, disciplines, and grade levels, much prior research has focused on each of the three turns of IRE/F as opportunities to avoid or to transform recitation.[4]

HOW TO TRANSFORM TEACHER QUESTIONS

For example, questions initiated by the teacher during recitations tend to be **C-LOT questions:** *c*losed-ended, *l*ower-*o*rder *t*hinking[5]—that is, questions for which the teacher has an answer in mind, and students are expected only to recall or apply what they already know (see lines 4, 13, and 16 above). While they can be useful in some situations, C-LOT questions can also narrow the flow of conversation, blocking attempts at whole-class, dialogic discussions.

In contrast, teacher questions that invite multiple answers and encourage students to analyze, synthesize, or evaluate—questions that are *o*pen-ended and require *h*igher-*o*rder *t*hinking (**O-HOT questions**)—are more likely to spark whole-class, dialogic discussions.[6] Table 2.2, below, summarizes this taxonomy of teacher questions and orders of thinking.

Rapid-fire C-LOT questions can leave little time for students, particularly English Language Learners (like Adriana, from chapter 1), to consider a question, possible answers, and their own ideas and interests.[7] And when teachers attempt to use C-LOT questions to lead students to the right answer

Table 2.2. Functions of teacher questions that can promote or discourage dialogic discussions

O-HOT	*Open, higher-order thinking* "What made you think that?"	*Open, lower-order thinking* "When you read this, what did you think?"	
	Closed, higher-order thinking "At this part, what does the author want you to think?"	*Closed, lower-order thinking* "Did this part make you think A or B?"	C-LOT

(see lines 16–17 above), students may rely on other factors, like the teacher's tone of voice and emphasis[8] (because, as Table 2.2's C-LOT quadrant suggests, one alternative is often marked as the preferred one by the phrasing of the question). It is also worth noting that student questions tend to be more open-ended and more likely to lead to whole-class, dialogic discussion[9] (as in chapter 1, when Tonisha asked Guillermo, "What does 'like this' mean?").

> Notice how the teacher speaks at every other turn in the above dialogue, and students' turns are hesitant and short—sometimes just one or two words. Who is doing most of the work? What are students learning?

HOW TO TRANSFORM TEACHER FOLLOW-UPS

When teachers' follow-ups to students' responses evaluate them as right or wrong, they tend to suppress extended student participation by implicitly sending the discouraging message that there is a single, correct answer that students must produce.[10] Often, hands go down as students sense that the teacher is hunting for a particular answer. In lines 13–19 of the transcript above, ellipses (. . .) indicate those painful pauses when the teacher was waiting for an answer and no one volunteered. Except the crickets. And tumbleweeds.

Alternatively, studies have found that if teachers postpone or share with students the opportunity to follow-up on each speaker's response (e.g., "Would anyone like to disagree with that?"), they may encourage further dialogue.[11] This kind of follow-up uses a move called **uptake**, in which a subsequent speaker quotes or refers back to what someone has already said, which can encourage student participation.[12] Follow-ups that use uptake may include quoted words and employ pronouns like "this/that" and "I/you/he/she/it"; they may even

> **Take a Turn**
> Recall a lesson in which you've participated as a teacher or a student. How would you categorize the questions during that lesson?

take the form of a follow-up question (as in my personal favorite, "What makes you think that?", a question that encourages further thinking in

Table 2.3. Functions of uptake (with examples) that can promote further discussion

Quoting/Paraphrasing	"*You* said *that* . . ."
	"Are *you* saying *that* . . . ?"
Elaborating	"*I* believe *that* because . . ."
	"What makes *you* think *that*?"
Clarifying	"*I* didn't understand *that*."
	"What did *she* mean by *that*?"
Agreeing/Disagreeing	"I agree with *his* point *that* . . ."
	"Would *anyone* like to disagree with *that*?"

almost any situation). In addition to quoting or paraphrasing, teacher follow-ups that invite students to elaborate, clarify, and disagree can promote dialogic discussion.[13] Of course, students can also use these kinds of follow-ups to build on what others have written or said.[14]

At a language level, questions and comments that involve uptake disrupt the pattern of IRE/F: instead of simply moving on to another student's answer (as in lines 3–4 and 9–10 of the transcript above), a teacher follow-up like, "What makes you think that?" or "So you're saying that . . ." can probe for the roots of a student's response and invite more explanation.

Uptake also signals implicitly to students that what is taken up by the next speaker is important—especially if that person is the teacher. Using uptake can model for students how to quote or paraphrase others' words for one's own purposes, an important literacy skill. But when a teacher takes up a student's response, it can also imply that students' responses are important enough to merit a follow-up—that the teacher was paying close enough attention to take up what that person just said. This makes a change from IRE/F, in which an unexpected answer can be met with a dismissive follow-up like Mr. Schulz's "Alrighty" or the more typical, "Anyone else?" before the teacher moves on to the next question or respondent.

Take a turn
Recall a time when your response to a teacher's question was met with a dismissive follow-up. How did that feel? What would you say to that teacher now? How do you wish that teacher had responded?

Although they sometimes play along with the familiar script of IRE/F, students may prefer dialogic discussions to recitation.[15] Perhaps you've experienced firsthand that moment as a teacher or a student when everyone tries to avoid making eye contact to avoid being called on. In some cases, student resistance to recitation can be more overt. Unfortunately, when teachers get unexpected or resistant answers from students, they often follow-up with more C-LOT questions and dive deeper into IRE/F. Adriana's unexpected answer in chapter 1 produced this reaction from Ms. Davis, and Ashley's answer did the same with Mr. Schulz in the recitation excerpt above. Instead of retrenching in recitation when students don't provide the "right" answer (or when, like John from the opening vignette, a student seems to be intentionally resistant), teachers can capitalize on that moment to transform the genre of the activity.

HOW TO TRANSFORM THE GENRE

The **genre** is the type of communication appropriate to a social situation, and the rules, roles, relationship, and possible responses it entails. Any classroom activity proposes such rules, roles, relationships, and possible responses, sometimes through explicit instructions, and sometimes implicitly, through the setup of the desks in the room and the moves people make along the way as they participate. Notice the word *proposes*: students (like John) can still reinterpret, resist, or refuse to participate. However, repetition reinforces these rules, roles, relationships, and possible responses, both during an activity and when that activity recurs over time within and across lessons and classrooms. If recitation appears across classrooms, disciplines, and grade levels, it is no wonder that teacher and students readily recognize this teaching genre.

Genres of activity in a classroom, involving roles like teacher and student, may differ from the genres for a sports practice or theater rehearsal, involving roles like coach and player or director and actor, even when the participants in these contexts are the same people. Teacher and student or coach and player may experience different (implicit) expectations for how to speak, act, and relate to one another. Prior experiences can also evoke a genre, particularly if participants recognize contextual clues that suggest a genre of activity in which they have participated before.

Recitation implicitly suggests a genre in which the teacher is the expert who will ask questions (to which she already knows the answer) in order

Transforming Recitations into Dialogic Discussions   23

to test students' knowledge. Students often recognize this genre as soon as they begin to hear the IRE/F pattern. However, they do not always accept it. Consider the following excerpt from a homework review of textbook questions in a US Midwestern ninth-grade suburban history classroom:

    1. MR. WEBER: What was the Schlieffen plan?

    2. BECCA: Um . . .

    3. MR. WEBER: Yeah, Becca?

    4. BECCA: *(Reading from book)* "It called for holding action against Russia."

This first exchange seemed headed for IRE/F: the teacher, Mr. Weber, posed a closed-ended, lower-order thinking question that asked students to recall the textbook description of the WWI event that they had read about for homework. A student, Becca, responded compliantly by reading the "right answer" word-for-word from the book. Luckily, other students spoke up, unexpectedly disrupting the IRE/F sequence.

    5. PENNY: I didn't really understand that.

    6. AMY: Yeah, I didn't remember that at all.

    7. MR. WEBER: Okay, that's what it says in the book, right?

    8. And then, while they're holding action,

    9. just holding the line against Russia. On the East.

    10. They've got this. *(Drawing on board)* There's Russia.

    11. We've got Germany here, and we've got Belgium here.

    12. Alright, and they decide they want to hold this line against Russia.

    13. But while they're doing it, they want to start marching into Paris, France.

    14. After that they go over and attack Russia. Does that help?

Mr. Weber followed up on these unexpected contributions with an attempt to clarify by drawing a map on the board and describing the interactions among the three countries it depicted. While this follow-up moved further from the IRE/F sequence, it wasn't a significant departure from the genre of recitation-style activity: a homework review in which the teacher tests students' knowledge of the chapter reading, providing clarification when necessary. However, students' responses to his question offered another opportunity for transforming the genre of the activity.

> Notice that, like many teachers, Mr. Weber's initial response is to give an explanation—a mini-lecture—that reasserts his authority. What other moves could he have made?

14. MR. WEBER: After that they go over and attack Russia. Does that help?

15. BECCA: No.

16. PENNY: Well, yes.

17. AMY: But what are the three . . . ?

18. OLIVIA: Yeah, what are the three little bubbles?

19. PENNY: Yeah, what are the rocks?

20. STUDENTS: *(Laughing)*

21. MR. WEBER: Rocks? *(Pointing to map)* Germany, Belgium, France.

Despite Mr. Weber's attempts to clarify, students' responses made it clear they had not understood the map explanation. Or perhaps they were resisting a return to the recitation genre. Though their responses, particularly their laughter, might seem disrespectful, it is worth noting that laughter often accompanies this type of unexpected behavior—when someone breaks the implicit rules of a social situation, we "crack up." Instead of reading that laugher as impertinence and reasserting one's authority, a teacher can use that moment as a **pivot**—a signal that can help people shift from one genre to another.[16] In this case, another student's unexpected question provided that pivot for Mr. Weber:

> **Take a turn**
> Recall a moment when there was nervous laughter in your classroom as a student or a teacher. What expectations were broken? How did others respond?

22. SHIRIN: Question: when they go through all those places,

23. do they, like, try to get them to go with them?

24. Or are they, like—?

25. MR. WEBER: Are they trying to ask people to go with them? Is that what you're—?

26. SHIRIN: Kind of, yeah.

27. MR. WEBER: I don't know if they were necessarily trying to gain military strength

28. through grabbing people up as they went.

29. But say there was another country's army marching through Talbott.

30. What impact would that have on Talbott if tens of thousands of soldiers

31. . . . . it'd be kind of weird?

Shirin's question about the German army's march toward France through Belgium prompted Mr. Weber to pose an open-ended, higher-order thinking question: one that invited multiple right answers and asked students to evaluate the impact of the Schlieffen plan. That is, Shirin's closed-ended query allowed Mr. Weber's O-HOT question, pivoting the frame from reviewing homework answers to imagining a contemporary, hypothetical version of the historical event: what impact would an occupying army have on students' hometown of Talbott? Students went on to consider multiple perspectives on this imagined invasion:

Laughter again: In the following excerpt, Mr. Weber's comment brings home the surprising concreteness of the army's impact. But perhaps it also breaks down his role as the authoritative teacher, recasting him as a collaborator rather than an evaluator.

37. CHASE: They'd screw everything up.

38. MR. WEBER: I couldn't even imagine how bad Glen Road would be.

39. STUDENTS: *(Laughing)*

40. ELLA: Oh my god!

41. AMY: We'd have to, like, walk everywhere.

42. MR. WEBER: They'd have to eat something, right?

43. LAURA: Yeah, they'd take all our food!

44. MR. WEBER: They'd take all our food. They'd take a lot of our stuff . . .

45. And here they are, just marching through.

46. And say they were trying to get to *[the neighboring town of]* Burch:

47. would it be our fault that we were in between?

48. GARY: Yeah, I would—

49. BECCA: No, because we just happen to be there.

50. MR. WEBER: And what impact would it have on all of us if these people were violent?

51. Would you want to stay here?

52. STUDENTS: No!

53. TOM: I'd fight them.

54. MR. WEBER: So it did have a very profound impact on the people of Belgium,

55. a very important impact. That will later factor into the war.

In response to Mr. Weber's question, students imagined the impact on the roads, the food stores, and the security of their hometown of Talbott if an army marched through on the way to the neighboring town of Burch, elaborating together a hypothetical scenario that paralleled the historical event. The shift from recitation-style homework review to dialogic discussion was not merely the result of Mr. Weber's O-HOT question: the genre for this activity differed from the implicit rules, roles, relationships, and possible responses available to students during the initial homework review.

Instead of testing them on their recall of the textbook definition of the Schlieffen plan, Mr. Weber positioned students as co-creators of an imagined, hypothetical scenario, with equal insider knowledge of the potential impact of an invading army on their hometown and the option to disagree with one another (and with him!) about how citizens might respond to that invasion. The complete transcript of this lesson excerpt in chapter 4 (Table 4.1) shows the shifts from the recitation genre to dialogic discussion, including the pivotal moment in which Shirin's question and Mr. Weber's follow-up began to transform the genre of activity. Note that, while Mr. Weber was instrumental in promoting and supporting the genre for this new activity, this transformation could not have happened without students. In other words, it was **emergent**: no one person was responsible for defining the genre's rules, roles, relationships, and possible responses.

TRANSFORMING TEACHER-STUDENT ROLES

Some research has suggested that IRE/F can be useful to reestablish what the class already knows so that subsequent discussion can build on this foundation.[17] Yet national studies have also found that teachers ask far more C-LOT questions and spend more instructional time overall on IRE/F than on dialogic discussion.[18] Why? Perhaps because such questions seem to allow a teacher to maintain "control" of the conversation, and thus fit in with what may be a sense of the traditional teacher's role in contemporary Western culture as one that requires that person to maintain order and be the most knowledgeable person in the room. The IRE/F pattern, in which the teacher often participates at every other turn, certainly affirms this role, establishing the teacher as the center of the interaction (see Figure 2.2, below).

Other environmental factors often conspire to reinforce this role: classrooms, class sizes, and curricular expectations may suggest—or assume—that the teacher will be a central figure delivering content to students. Yet Mr. Weber managed (with students' help) to pivot from a genre in which he was the center of the interaction to one in which their shared inquiry was the center. Together, they tried to understand a historical event by investigating a hypothetical scenario to which they all had equal access by virtue of its local and imaginary qualities. As Mr. Weber put it, "We had some people, you know, she's thinking about the army, thinking about the march, and I could hear them all talking about it, and I'm thinking *Right now, I need to relate them to something* . . . that was a conscious effort

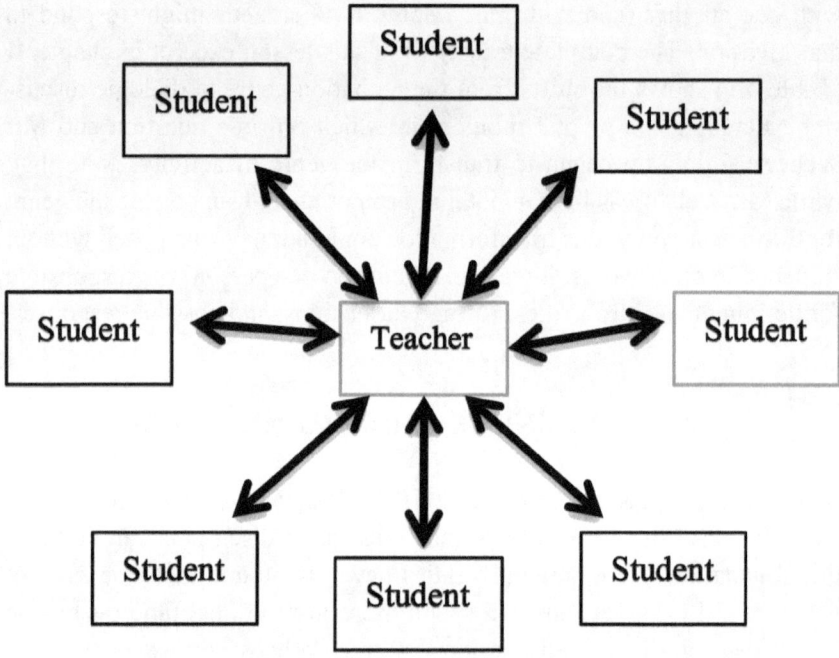

Figure 2.2. The teacher as the center of the interaction during IRE/F.

on my part to say, 'Let's talk about something we all know.'" Figure 2.3 suggests the subtle but significant change in this interaction.

You may notice that, although the diagram now centers on a shared inquiry rather than the teacher, the arrows do not connect the participants directly. From a language-level perspective, one might argue that, although they elaborated the hypothetical scenario together, there was still relatively little uptake by students of what others had written or said. Nevertheless, they seemed to have a better (and a more enthusiastic!) grasp of the Schlieffen plan than they had from the initial answer to the textbook question review. What began with C-LOT questions and IRE/F ended in dialogic discussion that suggested deeper understanding of the historical event.

In short, teachers may be able to transform recitation and include opportunities for dialogic discussion, even on the spur of the moment, by changing the nature of teacher questions and follow-ups. However, these language-level moves are not inherently "dialogic." They depend on the genre or implicit expectations of the roles, relationships, and responses

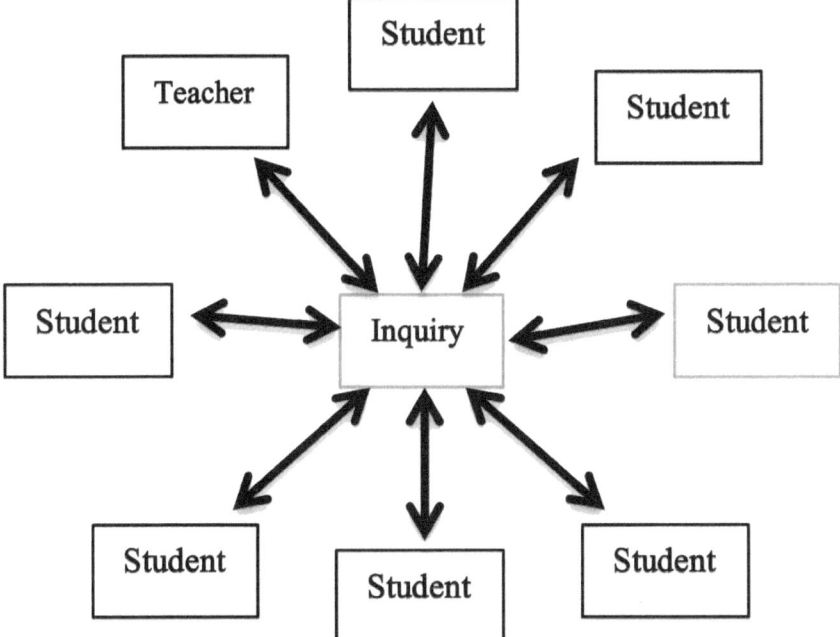

Figure 2.3. Recitation revised: Inquiry at the center of the interaction.

available to participants in a social interaction occurring in a particular context. Student responses, including seemingly disruptive behavior (often accompanied by laughter), may enable teachers to pivot from recitation to other activities that allow for dialogic discussion. Below is a list of activities that follow easily from just such a pivotal moment.

ACTIVITIES FOR TRANSFORMING RECITATION INTO WHOLE-CLASS, DIALOGIC DISCUSSION

1. **Think-Pair-Share:** Have students stop and write a response (or prepare one for homework and bring it to class); students then pair with a partner and discuss what they wrote before engaging in a whole-class discussion.
   Rationale: Getting to share with one person is less intimidating; there is more individual accountability.

Variations:
- Partners must choose one topic or question to put forward to the group.
- Pairs meet with another pair to discuss, then choose one topic or question to put forward to the group.

2. **Most Important Passage/Idea:** Having read a text (and/or written about it), students choose what was for them the most important passage or idea from that text; in the margin next to this passage/idea, they write why they chose it. Students can then share with a partner and/or the class.
   Rationale: Choosing an important passage encourages engagement with specific moments of the reading (take it to the text! J) and evaluation in relation to one's own experiences/principles.
   Variations:
   - Each member of a group of four reads his or her chosen passage *without* explaining why he or she chose it. When all members have shared, anyone can begin conversation by responding to *someone else's* passage. Only once someone else has taken up your passage can you explain your own choice.
   - Combine with Think-Pair-Share: partners must discuss and debate/choose one important passage; groups of four must debate/choose one important passage.

3. **Silent Discussion:** Having written a response (or brought a written response to class), students pass their responses to the right. After reading a classmate's response, they write back to that person underneath it. Repeat as many times as necessary, then return to original author for review and discussion.
   Rationale: Having to read silently and respond increases engagement with the writer's ideas and allows responder to be more selective (and maybe more honest/intimate) about his or her response.
   Variations:
   - Small groups exchange reading responses in this way and then discuss.
   - Author writes a question below the original response; each subsequent responder also ends with a question for the next reader.

4. **Discussion Mapping:** Students write down ideas (on a note card or sticky note) and then post them on a wall or board. During or after

this posting process, students can begin to group their responses next to other similar ideas (e.g., about the same topic, character, event, or passage).
Rationale: Writing down ideas and posting them holds everyone accountable. Arranging them in relation to one another encourages uptake, as students consider how ideas are related.
Variations:
- Students can use different colored note cards or sticky notes for different foci (e.g., blue for one topic, character, event, or passage and yellow for another) or for different kinds of responses (to agree/disagree, to provide an example, to pose a question, etc.).
- Students can add a second round of written posts once the original notes have been mapped into categories.

5. **Participation Stems:** Either before or after reading and responding to a text, students receive a list of question/response stems (as a handout or bookmark) that they can use during discussion (e.g., "I'd like to respectfully disagree with ____ because . . ." and "I have an example of what we're talking about: it's ____").
Rationale: This teaches students *how* to participate in discussion (since these participation stems don't come naturally to everyone!).
Variations:
- Have students invent their own stems.
- Design different sets of participation stems for different genres.

6. **Speed-Dating:** After reading a text and writing responses, teacher (or each student) selects line or passage from each writer's response (these can be printed in advance or written on a note card at beginning of class). Each class member chooses one of these lines or passages (not his or her own). Arrange desks in two rows facing each other (if the classroom is already in rows, this can easily be done with students in front/behind or across the aisle). Pairs read their lines or passages to each other and discuss, attempting to bring them into relationship, for one or two minutes. At end of time, place lines or passages face down on desk, then shift seats to face a new partner (e.g., all students in a row move down one seat; the last person moves to the front of the line).
Rationale: Emphasizes the value of the responder's line or passage; allows students to engage with and relate specific ideas from

classmates' texts. High-energy but intimate; everyone talks in pairs, under cover of everyone else talking at the same time.
Variations:
- Have students keep their lines or passages when they shift to the next seat, but they must bring their line or passage into relationship differently with each new partner.
- Instead of lines or passages, teacher or student puts one topic or idea from the reading on a card.
- Instead of switching seats, students dialogue electronically with their partner (via text, email, or online message board).

7. **Draw from the Basket:** Having read and responded to a text, students each write on a slip of paper one topic or question they would like to pursue further (they may also list one vocabulary word or idea about which they felt confused or uncertain). These slips of paper are collected in a "basket"; teacher(s) draw them out one by one (or sort through and choose) to generate discussion.
Rationale: Students are more likely to pose authentic, open-ended questions, more likely to choose topics they truly want to discuss, more likely to ask about what confuses them if it will remain anonymous.
Variations:
- Use more specific guidelines for basket contributions: have students write down one thing they liked, one thing they found frustrating, one thing they didn't understand, one question, one application to classroom teaching/their own student experience, and so on.
- Instead of adding to a physical basket, student can add ideas to a collaborative online space: a class message board, shared document, social network, or discussion forum.

8. **Imagined Dialogue:** Having read and responded to a text, students imagine a dialogue between that text (or the author of that text, or a character from the text) and other stakeholders (these could be other texts or authors already read in class, other characters, or other generic roles—teacher, parent, student, etc.). This dialogue can be elaborated with a group and even enacted; voice of the original text or author must be tied to specific evidence from the original text.

Rationale: Invites students to dramatize different points of view/ responses to the text; a great way to bring different readings into relationship.

Variations:
- Require students to give voice to different parts of the same text.
- Have one or more students sit in a "hot seat" to respond "in role" as a character, author, text, or part of a text while the rest of the class asks questions.

9. **Notice/Question/Interpret:** Having read and responded to a text, students answer three rounds of questions (What is one thing you notice? What is one question you have? What is one interpretation you can make?). These can be answered individually and/or with partner(s). After each round, students can share answers with a partner or the class.

Rationale: Students gradually discover patterns, connecting reading strategies to writing/preparation for discussion.

Variations:
- Have students complete a K-W-L chart. (What do they *k*now? What do they *w*ant to know? What have they *l*earned by the end of the discussion?)
- Have students narrate their thinking about the text while reading aloud (to a partner or to the class), before discussing why they responded this way.
- Have students add logographic cues to the text (smiley faces, exclamation points, question marks, etc.), and then discuss why they added these.

10. **Scaled Response or "Four-Corners" Discussion:** In response to a question or statement about a text they have read, or another shared focus, students decide where to position themselves on a scaled response (e.g., strongly disagree/disagree/agree/strongly agree; or always/often/sometimes/never), writing down an explanation for why they have chosen this position for now. Then students raise hands to show who shares the same position before discussing what they chose and why.

Rationale: All students are accountable for choosing a position in relation to the focal issue; the positions are relative, encouraging students to connect their perspectives to those of others and to recognize differences.

Variations:
- Have students find one or more people who share their position, or who hold a different position, with whom they can discuss their answers before opening to whole-group discussion.
- Have students move to physical locations in the room assigned to each position (e.g., "Everyone who chose 'strongly agree,' please go to this corner of the room") and discuss with the other students who chose that position before opening to whole-class discussion.

REFLECTIONS FOR TEACHERS

1. On your own or with a group, reread (or reenact) the transcript of Mr. Schulz's class conversation. What moments, if any, might have provided opportunities to pivot from recitation to another activity that allowed for dialogic discussion? What else could Mr. Schulz have done differently?
2. Use the teacher question taxonomy in Table 2.2 to categorize questions during your own or someone else's lesson. For example, you might partner with a colleague or review a video recording from your own class.
3. Use Table 2.3 to categorize the functions of uptake during your own or someone else's lesson. For example, you might partner with a colleague or review a video recording from your own class.
4. Pay attention to how the genre of an activity or routine is presented during a class in which you participate as a teacher or a student. How are the rules, roles, relationships, and available responses defined? What is made explicit? What is left implicit?

Activity/Routine	What Is Explicit?	What Is Implicit?
Rules		
Roles		
Relationships		
Possible Responses		

5. Make a list of the genres of activity that tend to appear during a particular class in which you participate as a teacher or a student.
   a. What do you notice?
   b. Which genres (or variations on a genre) appear more often? Why?
   c. Which genres (or variations on a genre) appear less often (or not at all)? Why?
   d. Which genre(s) do you prefer? Why?
   e. Which genre(s) do others at your institution (students, teachers, colleagues, administrators) seem to prefer? How do you know? Why?

EXPLORATIONS WITH STUDENTS

1. Share (or enact) with students a transcript of a classroom conversation (perhaps one of those included in this book, one you invent, or one based on an actual conversation from your class). Ask students to comment on what they notice, what they like, what they don't like, and why.
2. Share with students a representation of the functions of different kinds of questions (see Table 2.2). The product you share might be created by you, by students (in groups), or by you and students, and it might take the form of a poster, handout, bookmark, or other object to which individuals or the class can refer during discussions.
3. Share with students a representation of the functions of different kinds of uptake (see Table 2.3). The product you share might be created by you, by students (in groups), or by you and students, and it might take the form of a poster, handout, bookmark, or other object to which individuals or the class can refer during discussions.
4. Introduce students to the concept of *genre* by referencing their experiences with books, music, film, or even clothing. In the age of algorithms that derive genres from one's online activity, students will most likely have much implicit knowledge of this concept (from an online music-sharing or video-streaming service). Connect *genre* to different types of classroom activities and patterns of talk (like

attendance, group work, peer review, discussion). What patterns do students notice? What genres do they like? Dislike? Why?

CHAPTER SUMMARY

- The teacher-led Q&A routine, called recitation, typically consists of three moves often abbreviated as IRE/F.
- Recitation can be transformed by changing the initiating first move of IRE/F: instead of C-LOT questions, teachers can ask O-HOT questions.
- Recitation can be transformed by changing the third move of IRE/F: instead of strictly evaluative follow-ups, teachers and students can use uptake to follow up on what others have already written or said.
- Transforming the genre by changing the rules, roles, relationships, and responses available to participants can also promote dialogic discussions.
- Student responses, even those that may seem disruptive, can be opportunities to pivot from recitation to other genres more conducive to student participation in whole-class, dialogic discussion.

NOTES

1. Courtney B. Cazden, "Classroom Discourse," in *Handbook of Research on Teaching*, vol. 3 (New York/London: Macmillan; Collier Macmillan, 1986), xi, 1037; H. Mehan, "'What Time Is It, Denise?': Asking Known Information Questions in Classroom Discourse," *Theory into Practice* 18, no. 4 (1979): 285–94; J. Sinclair and M. Coulthard, *Towards an Analysis of Discourse: The English Used by Teachers and Pupils* (Oxford, UK: Oxford University Press, 1975); G. Wells, *Dialogic Inquiry* (Cambridge: Cambridge University Press, 1999).

2. A. N. Applebee et al., "Discussion-Based Approaches to Developing Understanding: Classroom Instruction and Student Performance in Middle and High School English," *American Educational Research Journal* 40, no. 3 (2003): 685–730; Cambridge Primary Review Trust, "Dialogic Teaching," Evaluation Report and Executive Summary (London, UK: Education Endowment Foundation, 2017).

3. J. Lemke, *Talking Science: Language, Learning and Values* (Norwood, NJ: Ablex, 1990).

4. F. Hardman, "Embedding a Dialogic Pedagogy in the Classroom: What Is the Research Telling Us?," in *Routledge International Handbook of Research on Dialogic Education* (New York: Routledge, 2020), 139–51.

5. M. Nystrand et al., *Opening Dialogue: Understanding the Dynamics of Language and Learning in the English Classroom* (New York: Teachers College Press, 1997); M. Nystrand et al., "Questions in Time: Investigating the Unfolding Structure of Classroom Discourse" (Albany, NY: National Reseach Center on English Learning and Achievement, 2003).

6. M. B. Sherry, "How the Visual Rhetoric of Online Discussion Enables and Constraints Student Participation," *Journal of Adolescent & Adult Literacy* 61, no. 3 (2017): 299–310; Nystrand et al., "Questions in Time."

7. Courtney B. Cazden and E. Leggett, "Culturally Responsive Education: Recommendations for Achieving LAU Remedies II," in *Culture and the Bilingual Classroom: Studies in Classroom Ethnography* (Rowley, MA: Newbury House Publishers, 1981), viii, 248 p.

8. Nystrand et al., *Opening Dialogue*.

9. Nystrand et al., *Opening Dialogue*.

10. Nassaji and Wells, "What's the Use of 'Triadic Dialogue'? An Investigation of Teacher-Student Interaction," *Applied Linguistics* 21, no. 3 (2000): 376–406.

11. M. S. Aukerman, "When Reading It Wrong Is Getting It Right: Shared Evaluation Pedagogy among Struggling Fifth Graders," *Research in the Teaching of English* 42, no. 1 (2007): 56–103.

12. J. Collins, "Discourse Style, Classroom Interaction, and Differential Treatment," *Journal of Reading Behavior* 14 (1982): 429–37; Nystrand et al., *Opening Dialogue*.

13. Nystrand et al., *Opening Dialogue*; S. Michaels et al., *Accountable Talk Sourcebook: For Classroom Conversation That Works*, 1st ed., vol. 3 (Pittsburgh, PA: Institute for Learning, University of Pittsburgh, 2012); M. B. Sherry, "Indirect Challenges and Provocative Paraphrases: Using Cultural Conflict-Talk Practices to Promote Students' Dialogic Participation in Whole-Class Discussions," *Research in the Teaching of English* 49, no. 2 (2014): 141–67.

14. L. B. Resnick, C. O'Connor, and S. Michaels, "Classroom Discourse, Mathematical Rigor, and Student Reasoning: An Accountable Talk Literature Review" (Pittsburgh, PA: Pittsburgh Science of Learning Center, 2007).

15. A. Reznitskaya and M. Glina, "Comparing Student Experiences with Story Discussions in Dialogic versus Traditional Settings," *The Journal of Educational Research* 106, no. 1 (2013): 49–63.

16. D. Holland et al., *Identity and Agency in Cultural Worlds* (Cambridge, MA: Harvard University Press, 1998).

17. G. Wells, "Reevaluating the IRF Sequence: A Proposal for the Articulation of Theories of Activity and Discourse for the Analysis of Teaching and Learning in the Classroom," *Linguistics and Education* 5, no. 1 (1993): 1–37; M. P. Boyd and D. Rubin, "How Contingent Questioning Promotes Extended Student Talk: A Function of Display Questions," *Journal of Literacy Research* 38, no. 2 (June 1, 2006): 141–69, https://doi.org/10.1207/s15548430jlr3802_2.

18. Nystrand et al., *Opening Dialogue*; Cambridge Primary Review Trust, "Dialogic Teaching."

3

Organizing Student-Led Dialogic Discussions

"In fact, we saw that happen in the play when Juliet talks to her parents. Have any of you ever felt like that? Turn to your partners and talk about a time when you were trying to have a dialogue with someone, and you felt like you were talking past each other."

In response to my question, students erupted into conversation. I walked around the room, past each group of four with their desks squared against one another so that two facing pairs were seated side by side. Reaching Miriam and John's group, I paused to listen.

"So what are we supposed to be doing?" asked John.

Miriam repeated to John the question I had posed to the class, "When you were talking with someone, have you ever felt like you were talking past each other?"

"With my dad. I'm like 'Dad, check this out,' and he's like 'Yeah, that's great.' But I can tell he's not really listening. But then he tells me to do something, and he's like, 'Why don't you listen to me?'" John sighed, slumping back in his seat.

Miriam nodded, "Yeah, that's a good example." Turning away from John, she cast a sidelong glance at me where I stood listening nearby. "Is that right?"

The previous chapter examined how teachers might transform recitations into whole-class discussions. While changing teacher questions and follow-ups in order to disrupt the IRE/F pattern and transform the recitation genre can invite dialogic discussion, alternatively, teachers can begin with a completely different activity genre. This chapter explores other attempts to transform the rules, roles, relationships, and responses available to students (and some accompanying pitfalls) in order to encourage dialogic discussions.

For example, instead of a whole-class conversation led by the teacher, dialogic discussions can emerge from small-group conversations among students, like the one in the vignette above. Such conversations can encourage dialogic discussion not only because a small group allows more opportunities to participate without the social pressure of speaking in front of a larger group, but also because students can learn to manage their own conversations.[1] However, teachers may worry that, without guidance, student conversations will be "off-task" or unproductive. Moreover, students may simply reproduce talk patterns that resemble teacher-led recitation: in the exchange above, Miriam appears to assume the role of the teacher, initiating a question, eliciting a response from John, and then following up with an evaluative comment. How can teachers encourage small-group and student-led dialogic discussions?

The primary goal of this chapter is not to promote a single answer to this question or to explain how best to implement a particular small-group discussion activity genre. Rather, the goal is to show how genres of classroom activity for encouraging discussion can explicitly cast students in roles that differ from those they might assume during recitation or other similar teacher-led classroom talk genres. Please see the end of the chapter for further resources on these and other genres that attempt to transform the rules, roles, relationships, and responses available to students in ways that can encourage dialogic discussion.

AN EXAMPLE OF STUDENT-LED DISCUSSION: LITERATURE CIRCLES

What might a small-group discussion look like? How does it compare to whole-class discussion and recitation? And what might go wrong? To begin to address some of these questions, consider the following excerpt from a Literature Circle discussion. A **Literature Circle**[2] is a routine or recurring activity genre in which small groups of students who are reading the same text (that might be different from the one read by another group) take turns playing roles with particular responsibilities as they participate in regular conversations about the section of the text they have agreed to read for that meeting.

In the excerpt below, four suburban seventh-grade ELA students discussed *The Outsiders* by S. E. Hinton, in which rival gangs clash, resulting in (spoiler alert!) tragedy for the main characters. The students sat with their desks facing one another in a small group separate from the rest of the class.

> How do students' responses compare to those in Mr. Schulz's class from chapter 2? to conversations in a class from your own experience?

1. KATIE: Okay. Had Johnny not died,

2. do you think he would still continue to be a Greaser after all that happened?

3. RICK: Okay. I think Johnny would have gone on to be someone,

4. and he would have traveled.

5. Because when he was talking to Pony in the hospital,

6. he just said that he didn't want to die, there was so much he hadn't seen.

7. So I think he would have traveled and become something.

8. ASHLEY: Yeah, he didn't realize what he didn't have when he was a Greaser,

9. but I think he would still be a Greaser just because of his situation.

10. He couldn't not be a Greaser,

11. but I think the whole experience would have changed him.

12. KATIE: He was loyal to his buddies.

13. So he would still be a Greaser,

14. he just wouldn't be as violent.

15. JEN: Yeah, and also it was him and Pony who were always saying,

16. "Will we still have time to make something of ourselves?"

17. So I think he would go out and do something

18. because his family wasn't very caring.

19. So I think he would help himself do something.

20. KATIE: It's been said that Darry wanted to die,

21. but do you think he robbed the store so that—

22. ASHLEY: Oh! *(Raises hand)*

23. KATIE: —he would die?

24. ASHLEY: No, I think he robbed the store out of grief that Johnny was dead.

25. So I don't think he robbed the store because he wanted to die.

26. RICK: Yeah, I think so much was going on at that moment that he had to do

27. something to take his mind off it: so robbing the store. But it was said way

28. earlier in the book that Greasers weren't supposed to get caught, if they got

29. caught they were on their own. But I'm not sure if he wanted to get caught on

30. purpose or if he just slipped up . . .

Notice that, in the excerpt above, students' responses were longer, more detailed, and less hesitant than in the excerpt from Mr. Schulz's class. Instead of single-word responses, students spoke in paragraphs. They referred to events and even to specific lines from the text. And they did this without teacher prompting at every other turn.

In this and other student-led activity genres, the rules, roles, relationships, and responses available to a participant differ from those in other social interactions in the classroom, like recitation. For example, Literature Circles makes students responsible for choosing the focus and directing the conversation, explicitly casting them in roles that allow for collaborative inquiry (see Figure 3.1, below).

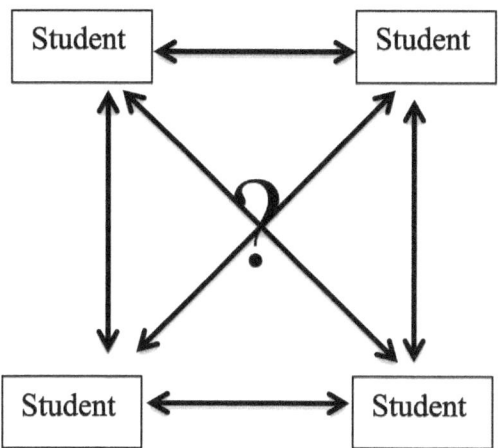

Figure 3.1. Literature Circles recasts students' roles in classroom conversation.

While this diagram is a symbolic representation, one way that teachers can begin to change the genre of the activity is through literally transforming the physical space. In the example above, and in the opening vignette, students sit in small groups facing one another, rather than in rows facing the teacher. This arrangement, like other language-level features of a genre, can suggest implicitly to students that their small-group interactions are important.

However, changing genres includes challenges. Rearranging desks is usually not enough to encourage productive small-group discussions. Additionally, you may have noticed that, in the excerpt above, a single student (Katie) seemed to ask most of the questions. Moreover, her questions, at lines 3 and 18, were closed-ended, yes/no questions that could have produced minimal answers if posed by a teacher. But they didn't. As in the opening vignette, even C-LOT questions can invite dialogic discussion when the genre of the activity casts students in roles that encourage this kind of participation. How does this happen?

Take a turn

How are the desks arranged in a classroom in which you participate as a teacher or a student? What does this arrangement suggest about the kinds of interactions that will occur?

HOW TO ENCOURAGE STUDENT-LED DISCUSSIONS: PREPARATION AND SELF-EVALUATION

Unlike some of the activities suggested in chapter 2, Literature Circles depends on explicit preparation (see Table 3.1, below for sample response stems to share with students). This chart might be used in conjunction with video models, or with transcripts like the ones in this chapter, to help students (and teachers) begin to learn how the Literature Circles genre works.

Table 3.1. Sample participation stems associated with each Literature Circles role and purpose

Literature Circles Role (during discussion)	Purpose and Participation Stems
Discussion Director	Managing <u>participation</u> in discussion
—makes sure everyone contributes —makes sure class norms are upheld —makes sure that all ideas are both supported and challenged	"I'd like to hear from _____ on this topic." "Is that really the best way for us to _____?" "Does anyone want to agree/disagree?"
Questioner	Managing the <u>quality</u> of discussion
—asks follow-up questions that help elaborate and deepen interpretations of the text —makes sure the group sets goals for reading and manages time during discussion activities	"Can you give us an example?" ("Take it to the text!") "How much should we read for next time?" "Are we ready to move on to the next step?"
Summarizer	Managing the <u>direction</u> of the discussion
—keeps a record of the group's discussion —points out connections among group members' comments	"Like last week, today we've talked about _____." "How does what _____ just said relate to what you've been saying?"
Citation Manager	Managing the <u>possibilities</u> for discussion
—makes sure that all members of the group are prepared with notes/responses —points out particular moments of the text (or related materials to support or provoke further discussion)	"What was one part of the text you marked for us to talk about?" "What did you think of this: _____?"

These are just a few of the typical roles teachers can offer to students during Literature Circles. This genre requires students to prepare for a conversation by assuming a role with particular responsibilities and possibilities. That role can give purpose to students' reading and can guide their participation in discussion, as they practice particular strategies or skills associated with certain ways of analyzing and talking about texts (e.g., Citation Manager selects important passages for group discussion). In this way, Literature Circles resemble other genres that teach not only *with* discussion, but also *for* discussion,[3] teaching students *how* to participate by explicitly recasting their roles, their relationships to the text (or another focus of collaborative inquiry), and the available ways of responding. A list of routines that similarly transform students' (and the teacher's) roles in whole-class or small-group discussion appears at the end of this chapter.

On the other hand, there are indications in this excerpt that these students have not completely departed from a recitation genre. Consider Ashley's response at line 22. Despite her obvious enthusiasm—she wants to answer the question before Katie has finished asking!—Ashley raises her hand, a move associated with participation in whole-group, teacher-led activity genres like recitation, rather than in Literature Circles. Additionally, although students give longer, more detailed, and more personal answers, they each respond to the initial question posed by Katie, the Discussion Director, with little uptake, other than "yeah," of the previous speaker's contributions (somewhat like Miriam, in the vignette at the top of this chapter). These moments arise from **genre contact**: aspects of another, related genre appear during an activity that may evoke a different, even contradictory set of rules, roles, relationships, and available responses.[4] With help, students might learn to spot these moments and improve their small-group discussions using a reflection tool like the one in Textbox 3.3.

Along with preparation before discussion, groups can use regular evaluation to revise, personalize, and improve their participation in dialogic discussion. This is not to suggest that all Literature Circles or small-group discussions must at all times demonstrate or avoid a particular talk pattern. Within genres of music, film, and even clothing style, not all of the things that belong to a category have exactly the same features. Nevertheless, you can probably recognize the difference between examples that

> **TEXTBOX 3.3.**
> **REFLECTION TOOL FOR LITERATURE CIRCLES GROUPS**
>
> ___ For this meeting, we read to _____.
> (If not, please explain; if this is the first meeting, write down what you plan to have read for next time.)
>
> ___ All group members had prepared by _____
> _____.
> (If not, please explain; if this is the first meeting, discuss how you will prepare and write down your ideas here.)
>
> ___ This time, the following people filled these roles:
> Discussion Director_____
> Questioner_____
> Citation Manager_____
> Summarizer_____
>
> ___ All members made sure these roles were fulfilled:
> _____   _____
> _____   _____
> (Group member signatures)
>
> ___ This time, the Summarizer represented our work by _____
> _____.
> (Please attach to this sheet, if possible.)
>
> ___ We discussed how our work could be improved, and our goals for next time are
> _____
> _____.

belong to musical genres such as popular and classical, or to film genres like romantic comedy and horror. Likewise, the genre for any activity is flexible, but students can nevertheless learn to identify the difference between recitation and dialogic discussion genres. However, over time, talk patterns become more established, and so students' prior experiences with well-established genres can color their experiences with new ones. Moreover, students may encounter genres like recitation outside the classroom: IRE/F, or variations on this pattern, can appear in other contexts;[5] for example, in broadcast journalism, interviewers often ask leading, C-LOT questions.

Ashley's hand-raising and the lack of uptake in the excerpts above are not meant as criticisms of Literature Circles or of these middle schoolers' enactment of it. Rather this analysis is meant to suggest the power of genre to implicitly shape participants' sense of the rules, roles, relationships, and possible responses available during classroom activities. Recall the second excerpt in chapter 1 from Ms. Davis and her first graders, who slipped easily into recitation following Adriana's comment. Even by first grade, many students may have had far more experience with school activities that frame conversation as a sequence of disconnected responses directed by (and to) a central authority. It is no wonder, then, that students (and teachers) may struggle with more dialogic activity genres. Student-led activity routines can disrupt the IRE/F pattern and the recitation frame, but without explicit preparation, continuing guidance, and regular self-evaluation on how and why their talk patterns shape participation in this routine, students may fall back on other familiar patterns.

AN EXAMPLE OF STUDENT-LED DISCUSSIONS: PEER REVIEW

Consider another example of a common classroom activity genre that provides opportunities for dialogic discussion by casting students in a role traditionally reserved for the teacher: peer review. In the following excerpt from peer review in a college-level writing classroom, three students sit facing one another to discuss one writer's draft of a personal narrative assignment, based on guidelines furnished in a handout.

Peer Review Guidelines

Expectations: What is it you hope to gain from peer review today?
Plans: What practices might help you or your classmates attain those expectations?
Procedure: For this peer review, groups of three will follow these steps:

1. Author: sets expectations; reads/explains narrative aloud
2. Peers: write comments using rubric; share *praise/questions*
3. Author: asks *questions/responds* to peer comments
4. Peers: make *suggestions/respond* to author questions

Have you received comments about . . . ?	Member 1 ☑	Member 2 ☑	Summarize those comments for yourself below.
Focused: includes events and interpretations that together relate to the purpose of the story			
Active, Vivid: uses active verbs, concrete nouns, and vivid details to convey the "scenes" of the story			
Voice: selection of purpose, details, and words creates consistent and relatable narrator and is appropriate to purpose			
Coherent: events and interpretations are related in an authentic, well-paced order consistent with the purpose and voice of the story			

Reflection: Now that you've received some comments, how will you address them when you revise your work?
Evaluation: Were your expectations met today? Why or why not?

1. MARK: So what are we supposed to do?

2. KELSEY: We're each supposed to read our paper

3. and get comments from the other people.

4. And then talk about it.

5. TINA: Yeah, the author reads

6. and then stays quiet while the other two talk,

7. and then she gets to talk again at the end.

8. MARK: Okay, so who goes first?

9. TINA: I will if you want.

10. KELSEY: Okay.

11. TINA: "Sometimes a lesson takes a long time to learn. When I was a freshman—"

12. MARK: Wait, aren't you supposed to tell us what you want us to look for?

13. TINA: Oh yeah! Um, I'm not sure.

14. I guess when I wrote it I had one story in my mind

15. but toward the end I kind of ran out of gas.

16. So if you have any ideas about that.

17. And whatever else you notice. Organization. Grammar.

18. Really anything is fine.

19. KELSEY: Okay.

20. TINA: Okay, so I'll start over. *(Reads)* So now I'll be quiet and you two can talk.

21. MARK: Well, I have a comment, but it's not about the end.

22. KELSEY: Go ahead. I think that's okay.

23. MARK: I think the first sentence should be taken out.

24. It sounds like a cliché.

25. KELSEY: I agree, but then you can't just start with "When I was a freshman . . ."

26. MARK: Why not?

27. KELSEY: Well, aren't we supposed to start with the action?

28. MARK: I guess.

29. KELSEY: I mean a lot of the examples we looked at started in the middle of action.

30. MARK: Well, it could start when she gets to the professor's office.

31. TINA: But do you need the background?

32. Sorry, I know I'm not supposed to—

33. I just thought a reader would need to know what happened earlier in the—

34. MARK: —Well could she—you—could you put some of that stuff into the first scene,

35. kind of like a flashback?

36. TINA: I guess so.

37. KELSEY: I kind of disagree—

38. MARK: But you were the one arguing for starting with the action!

39. KELSEY: —because, yeah, but I think that might be confusing for—

40. TINA: —So I guess I'm going to cut the first line,

41. but leave the background?

42. MARK: Whatever.

Some readers of this conversation have suggested that students might have been better off with a teacher facilitating, or at least reinforcing guidelines for participation: for example, students seem uncertain about when the author can speak, and initiate a false start before recalling that the peer review guidelines begin by asking the writer to set expectations for the focus and format of peer feedback. Moreover, in this excerpt Mark and Kelsey seem to ignore Tina's request for help with her ending (line 21) and impose their vision of her narrative's opening; their disagreement leaves her uncertain (lines 31–33, 40) about what revisions to make.

On the other hand, the genre of peer review, like Literature Circles, puts students in charge of negotiating the focus of their collective inquiry. If one purpose of using this genre was to help students learn to participate in collaborative discussion about writing, then there were also many positive moves. For example, Mark and Kelsey did not focus exclusively on language-level correction of Tina's grammar, a common pitfall of peer review. Instead, they discussed the rhetorical effect of her opening on a reader (lines 31–41), exploring alternatives to a generic first line that intersected with a technique modeled in class (lines 27–29). Their disagreement, though potentially confusing, also showed how the text might affect audiences differently, leaving the final decision to Tina, as the text's author. If we interpret overlapping talk as a sign of engagement[6] rather than disorder, then these students might be understood as enthusiastically discussing an open-ended, higher-order thinking question—what contextual information does a reader need (and when) to understand a narrative scene?

ORGANIZING STUDENT-LED DIALOGIC DISCUSSIONS TAKES TIME AND REQUIRES RISK

Even with thorough guidelines and opportunities for reflection and self-evaluation, student-led discussion activities like Literature Circles and peer review may produce conversations like the ones above, which exhibit some features that teachers may find positive and others that may seem negative. Students may cite textual examples, anticipate reader responses, and demonstrate increased engagement. But they may also go off-task, interrupt one another, or stall out at a superficial level, particularly at first. They may even reproduce talk patterns associated with recitation or other familiar genres, and with different (and even conflicting) purposes through genre contact.

Sadly, students may resist engaging with student-led, dialogic discussion because of the risk it involves. To ask honest, O-HOT questions, to give authentic, personal answers, and to admit what they don't know—these are risks that recitation and other "schoolish" genres[7] do not require of students. This unwritten contract with teachers may be one reason students put up with recitation:[8] "I'll answer your test questions if you promise not to make me work too hard or reveal too much."

Though it may be challenging for teachers to introduce a genre in which we relinquish control and let students experiment and make mistakes, such opportunities may help students learn *how* to participate in dialogic discussions of literature and writing. Further, they may help students to reimagine school as a place where such discussions can happen. As a college-student participant in Literature Circles once said to me, "This is the first time I ever enjoyed reading a book for school, because I got to talk about what *I* wanted to talk about, rather than what *you* [the teacher] wanted me to talk about." Their experiences with class activity genres over time can shape students' and teachers' vision of what it means to "do school"—and of what it means to be a student or a teacher.[9]

ACTIVITIES FOR FOSTERING STUDENT-LED DIALOGIC DISCUSSIONS

1. **Fishbowl:** Having read and responded to a text, at least three (or more) designated students start a conversation about the text; others listen and take notes, generating questions. At end of time, a new group (or the other half of the class) replaces the old one. Repeat as necessary.
   Rationale: Students get to perform and to reflect on the quality of their discussions.
   Variations:
   - "A Walk in the Park": Students who are in the fishbowl get to walk around the room as they discuss.
   - "Tag-Team": Students can "tag-in" to the discussion by tapping someone in the fishbowl who then retires to the sidelines to reflect/observe.
2. **Structured Debate:** Students choose or are assigned to different positions on a debatable topic; having prepared to defend that position, one or more students present their ideas to the opposing side (and/or to other evaluators) in a sequence that may include parts like opening arguments, rebuttals, cross-examinations, and closing statements.

Rationale: Students are encouraged to practice disagreement that is civil and structured by relationships among ideas (rather than only by "sides").

Variations:
- Students rotate into speaking positions: for example, debate begins with a pair who each get a turn before others take a turn or tag in.
- Three groups take turns arguing one side, then another (as well as playing the role of evaluator for the other two groups as they debate).

3. **Socratic Seminar:** Having prepared in advance, one or more student leaders pose O-HOT discussion questions to a group; other students respond in ways that may correspond to particular roles or to agreed upon class norms (e.g., talk to one another, not just to the discussion leader; don't interrupt; use examples and evidence; ask follow-up questions).

    Rationale: Despite its name, Socratic Seminar differs from Plato's *Dialogues* in which Socrates leads others through logical steps in a way that is not particularly dialogic.[10] In this activity, students practice generating O-HOT questions, using uptake, and evaluating the discussion.

    Variations:
    - Combine with fishbowl, so that half the class participates in seminar while the other half evaluates, and then switch.
    - Have each student call on the next person to avoid designating one leader.

4. **Complex Instruction:**[11] Students receive a "group task" that asks them to create something in response to a problem, question, or other prompt. Creating this product requires all students' input, but students each have different responsibilities associated with a role detailed in advance and in the "group task" materials: Team Captain, Resource Manager, Recorder/Reporter, Facilitator.

    Rationale: Based on twenty years of work in classrooms by math education researcher Dr. Elizabeth Cohen, this approach to group work attempts to preserve equity by making tasks "group worthy"—everyone's participation is necessary, and responsibility must be shared; roles in this activity genre are associated with task processes rather than discrete academic skills.

Variations:
- After creating their group product, students can share with, and respond to, other groups.
- "Gallery Walk": Once groups have each created a product, students rotate around the room, stopping in front of each group's product to discuss it with their own group.
- "Peer Response Parade": During a gallery walk, each student writes one or more comments and leaves them near the other group's product (for example, stuck on a wall near the relevant part of a poster presentation, or typed as marginal comments on a digital document). After returning to their own product, a group reviews the comments and then responds during subsequent whole-class discussion to questions and trends in the comments.

5. **Response Roles:**[12] Before or during a discussion, students receive assigned response roles with accompanying participation practices and/or conversation stems: for example, Problem Poser, Devil's Advocate, Theme Spotter, Evidence Assessor, Synthesizer.

Rationale: Teaches students *how* to participate in discussion, providing practice in archetypal academic roles associated with scholarly inquiry.

Variations:
- Add other roles that correspond to the values and practices appropriate to inquiry about a particular topic or academic discipline (e.g., in discussing a historical event, a "Period Perspective" on how stakeholders at the time might have viewed an issue differently).
- Add other roles that correspond to values and practices for civil discussions (e.g., an "appreciator" who tracks and compliments insightful or useful comments; an "anti-judge" who monitors respectful responses).
- Have students invent their own list and labels for class discussion roles with more and less serious options (e.g., an "illustrator" who relates visually, a "six-word wonder" who offers a new perspective or a synthesis in six words or less).

REFLECTIONS FOR TEACHERS

1. Use the table below to list your thoughts about student-led discussions. For a teacher and for a student, what might be easy, enjoyable, helpful, and productive about using a small-group discussion genre in a classroom in which you currently participate in one of those roles? What might be difficult, distasteful, confusing, and unproductive?

Thoughts on Student-Led Discussions	+	–
For a Teacher		
For a Student		

2. Compare the transcript from Mr. Schulz's class to the transcript of a Literature Circle discussion, above. What evidence can you find of what students in each class have learned?
3. Consider a student-led activity in which you have participated as a teacher or a student. How were the roles students assumed in that activity similar to or different from the roles of teacher and student in more traditional, teacher-led activities like recitation? Why might this be?
4. Consider a student-led activity in which you have participated as a teacher or a student. What guidelines (if any) were provided regarding students' roles, relationships, and potential responses during discussion? What opportunities for reflection did the activity include? How well did this preparation and evaluation support students' dialogic discussions?
5. Consider that, during a student-led activity like Literature Circles or peer review, your role as teacher may at times involve contributing only your silence (or at most, listening in). What might be welcome/challenging about that for you? Why?

EXPLORATIONS WITH STUDENTS

1. Having introduced students to the concept of *genre,* have them identify genres and associated rules, roles, relationships, and possible

responses (using the table below) in activities or routines both in and outside the classroom (e.g., at sports practice, theater rehearsal, the grocery store, the dinner table). Why are the expectations different?

Activity/Routine in Class	Activity/Routine Outside Class
Rules	
Roles	
Relationships	
Possible Responses	

2. Ask students to recall their experiences with group work and discussion: What worked well? What was problematic or difficult? Why? Use these reflections to generate a list of practices to encourage and to avoid, and roles that might help.
3. Using a video model or transcript (from your own or another's class, or from this book), discuss with students the triumphs and challenges of a student-led discussion. What worked well? What was problematic or difficult? Why? Use these evaluations to generate a list of practices to encourage and to avoid, and roles that might help.
4. During each week or month of a school year or semester, introduce students to another role and related discussion practice (e.g., Questioner) and spend time modeling, practicing, discussing, and evaluating what "good" or "bad" participation in that role might look like.
5. Discuss with students the unwritten expectations teachers have of students, and students have of teachers, that might apply to whole-class and small-group discussions.

CHAPTER SUMMARY

- As an alternative to teacher-led recitation or to whole-class conversations, small-group, student-led activity genres can also promote dialogic discussion.
- Student-led activity genres like Literature Circles or peer review often succeed by explicitly (re)defining the rules, roles, relationships, and responses available to participants.
- Student-led discussions often succeed by providing guided opportunities for pre-discussion preparation and post-discussion reflection and self-evaluation.
- Fostering effective student-led discussions in small-group activity genres can take time and may mean risks for students and teachers as they depart from traditional roles.

NOTES

1. J. D. Marshall, P. Smagorinsky, and M. W. Smith, "The Language of Interpretation: Patterns of Discourse in Discussions of Literature" (Urbana, IL: NCTE, 1995).

2. Harvey Daniels, *Literature Circles: Voice and Choice in the Student-Centered Classroom* (York, ME: Stenhouse Publishers, 1994).

3. W. C. Parker and D. Hess, "Teaching with and for Discussion," *Teaching and Teacher Education* 17 (April 2001): 273–89.

4. G. S. Morson and C. Emerson, *Mikhail Bakhtin: Creation of a Prosaics* (Stanford: Stanford University Press, 1990); M. Bakhtin, *Problems of Dostoevsky's Poetics*, trans. C. Emerson, *Theory and History of Literature*, vol. 8 (Minneapolis: University of Minnesota Press, 1984).

5. John C. Heritage and Andrew L. Roth, "Grammar and Institution: Questions and Questioning in the Broadcast News Interview," *Research on Language & Social Interaction* 28, no. 1 (January 1995): 1, https://doi.org/Article; W.-M. Roth and R. Gardner, "'They're Gonna Explain to Us What Makes a Cube a Cube?' Geometrical Properties as Contingent Achievement of Sequentially Ordered Child-Centered Mathematics Lessons," *Mathematics Education Research Journal* 24 (2012): 323–46.

6. D. Tannen, *Talking Voices: Repetition, Dialogue, and Imagery in Conversational Discourse*, vol. 2, *Studies in Interactional Sociolinguistics* (Cambridge; New York: Cambridge University Press, 2007).

7. A. E. Whitney, "In Search of the Authentic English Classroom: Facing the Schoolishness of School," *English Education* 44, no. 1 (2011): 51–62.

8. A. Lefstein, "Changing Classroom Practice through the English National Literacy Strategy: A Micro-Interactional Perspective," *American Educational Research Journal* 45, no. 3 (2008): 701–37.

9. J. Snell and A. Lefstein, "'Low Ability,' Participation and Identity in Dialogic Pedagogy," *American Educational Research Journal* 55, no. 1 (2018): 40–78; M. B. Sherry, G. Dodson, and S. Sweeney, "Improvising Literate Identities: Comparing Cultural Roles and Dialogic Discourse in Two Lessons from a US Elementary Classroom," *Linguistics & Education* 50 (2019): 36–45.

10. E. Matusov, *Journey into Dialogic Pedagogy* (New York: Nova Science Publishers, Inc., 2009).

11. Elizabeth G. Cohen, *Designing Groupwork: Strategies for the Heterogeneous Classroom* (New York: Teachers College Press, 1986).

12. S. D. Brookfield, *The Skillful Teacher: On Technique, Trust, and Responsiveness in the Classroom* (San Francisco, CA: Jossey-Bass, 2015); S. D. Brookfield and S. Preskill, *Discussion as a Way of Teaching: Tools and Techniques for Democratic Classrooms* (San Francisco, CA: Jossey-Bass, 2005).

4

Facilitating Disciplinary Dialogic Discussions

*M*iriam repeated to John the question I had posed to the class, "When you were talking with someone, have you ever felt like you were talking past each other?"

"With my dad. I'm like 'Dad, check this out,' and he's like 'Yeah, that's great.' But I can tell he's not really listening. But then he tells me to do something, and he's like, 'Why don't you listen to me?'" John sighed, slumping back in his seat.

Miriam nodded, "Yeah, that's a good example." Turning away from John, she cast a sidelong glance at me where I stood listening nearby. "Is that right?"

"What do you think?" I asked Miriam.

"C'mon," said John. "You know nothing's ever really 'right' in this class." He laughed ruefully. "I wish that were true in my next class."

"Not me," said Miriam. "I like when you know if it's right. If you show your work, of course."

Chapter 3 proposed that the rules, roles, relationships, and possible responses available during classroom conversations depend on the genre, or type of activity. We saw that, even in student-led, small-group discussions, students might import expectations from their prior experiences with certain commonly occurring repeated activities, like recitation—that prevalent and persistent IRE/F pattern typical of teacher-led Q&A. This chapter builds on the idea that prior experiences with other activity genres in classrooms might shape expectations for how speakers participate in conversations.

Even from one class period to the next, students experience varying expectations for how to participate (and why). For example, in the vignette above, Miriam and John imply that in English language arts, discussions may serve to generate multiple interpretations, while in another class the focus may be on reaching consensus, or on demonstrating how one arrived at the correct answer.

Chapter 4 addresses how classroom conversations in math and science may differ from those in history and English language arts, and what moves might support or inhibit students' participation in dialogic discussions that perform and promote disciplinary literacies[1]—principles and practices associated with meaning-making in particular academic and professional learning communities. This matters because if students' attempts to participate in certain ways are met with approval in one context and disapproval in another, they may be confused or discouraged. John prefers the flexibility of English language arts, while Miriam finds that discipline's uncertainty uncomfortable. In the extreme, students may come to feel that certain kinds of conversations include or exclude them, that they can or cannot belong to the cultural community of scientists or historians—that, "I'm not a math person" or "I just don't get English."

What may be especially challenging for students and teachers is that the expectations and purposes for disciplinary dialogic discussions can differ for reasons beyond the immediate social situation. The reasons for the rules, roles, relationships, and responses that are available may not be clear from the nature of the activity: for example, why might students be expected to draw on personal experiences during one conversation and to set aside subjectivity in another? What makes a keen observation in science different from a situated insight about history? The answers to these questions may relate to cultural values and practices associated with different academic disciplines that are often left implicit. What moves can teachers make to encourage students' participation in dialogic discussions that also help them learn to converse like scientists or historians?

DISCIPLINARY DISCUSSIONS IN SCIENCE: REVOICING

Consider the following example from a sixth-grade science classroom.[2] In this lesson, students were studying ratios by creating lemonade concentrates. Each student made one, recording the ratio of sugar and lemon juice, in preparation for adding them into a class graph. One student, Paulina, lost her concentrate ratio, recalling only that she had used two spoonfuls of sugar, and between ten and twenty-two spoonfuls of lemon juice. With the teacher Ms. Lynne's guidance, the class discussed what Paulina should do. Should she create a completely new concentrate or enter into the graph a ratio with her known sugar amount and an average of the possible missing lemon juice values? Some students argued that neither option would be Paulina's "real" first concentrate, but then Steven made the following comment:

1. STEVEN: . . . Um, but if she kept her, um, sugar

2. and used that

3. and then took her thing of ten to twenty-two

4. and then picked another number like halfway,

5. like Allison said,

6. and then made that her concentrate . . .

7. MS. LYNNE: So then you don't agree with Sarita that

8. if she *[Paulina]* picks a number halfway between

9. then that's not really making her first concentrate either?

> Both Steven and Ms. Lynne characterize other speakers' contributions during their turns. What potential benefits or pitfalls might this move entail?

Both Steven and Ms. Lynne **animated** other speakers, characterizing them by describing their words and actions:[3] Allison, Sarita, and Paulina became characters with particular positions and relationships. But whereas Steven simply repeated what Allison said, Ms. Lynne responded to Steven's suggestion using a particular kind of uptake called **revoicing** that not only repeats but also connects another's assertion to an inference,[4] often through a phrase like, "So you're saying that . . ."

Like other kinds of **metatalk**, or talk about dialogue as it unfolds,[5] revoicing can serve two important purposes. First, it can prompt the speakers to agree or disagree with the proposed animation and inference, encouraging further participation. Second, it can bring different perspectives into dialogue: in this excerpt, Steven had not explicitly disagreed with Sarita, but he and the class could now consider these two positions in dialogic relationship. In this science classroom, revoicing encouraged students to participate in defining and theorizing, based on evidence, as well as to clarify the processes that had led to those definitions and theories.

Although such practices may also appear in humanities classrooms, defining and theorizing based on evidence gathered through replicable processes may be especially appropriate to science and math. While revoicing can be used for other purposes, and can even block further discussion if a teacher intervenes after every turn to repeat what students have said, this technique can encourage dialogic discussions that also include disciplinary purposes and practices associated with science and math.

DISCIPLINARY DISCUSSIONS IN MATH: REVOICING

Unfortunately, disciplinary purposes and practices are often left implicit, especially in classroom activity genres like recitation. The following example from a first-grade geometry lesson in a suburban Midwestern school illustrated the (missed) opportunity such conversations can present:[6]

1. MS. KOHL: Think of one of the shapes that we talked about this week.

2. Who can think of a shape?

3. Student A?

4. STUDENT A: A Granny Smith.

5. MS. KOHL: *(Laughing)* A Granny Smith?

6. Is that a shape?

7. STUDENTS: No!

8. MS. KOHL: That's an apple.

As in the excerpt from Ms. Davis's first-grade writing lesson in chapter 1, here Ms. Kohl and her other students slipped into IRE/F, disdaining Student A's answer. Yet there was no explanation of what defines a shape and why a Granny Smith cannot be one. While some students seemed to know that the answer was wrong, they may not have understood the implicit, disciplinary reasoning that made it so.

What follows is an imagined revision of the same exchange,[7] in which Ms. Kohl revoiced Student A's response in ways that made that disciplinary reasoning explicit:

1. MS. KOHL: Think of one of the shapes that we talked about this week.

2. Who can think of a shape?

3. Student A?

4. STUDENT A: A Granny Smith.

5. MS. KOHL: *(Laughing)* A Granny Smith?

6. Are you saying that you see angles and curves—

7. maybe even symmetry—

8. in an apple,

9. which is something that we find in our everyday lives?

10. STUDENT A: Yeah, round,

11. kind of like a circle.

12. MS. KOHL: You're saying that a Granny Smith is kind of like a circle.

13. What about a Granny Smith is not like a circle?

14. STUDENT A: It has lumps.

15. MS. KOHL: Okay, so a Granny Smith apple may not be perfectly round.

16. "Perfectly round" is one of the defining features of a circle

17. listed on our chart.

This animation and revoicing of Student A suggested a much different vision of that student: instead of treating the response like an obvious error, Ms. Kohl assumed Student A had made a disciplinary connection. Can you think of a time when this did or didn't happen in a classroom you have participated in as teacher or student?

18. So even when we're not in school, we're thinking like mathematicians

19. when we compare geometric shapes, like circles,

20. with ordinary things, like apples.

21. Can you remember a time when you thought like a mathematician

22. outside of school

23. by seeing a geometric shape in an ordinary thing?

In this imagined revision, Ms. Kohl used the formulation "you're saying that" (lines 6, 12) to animate Student A and take up the answer "a Granny Smith." Instead of assuming that answer was wrong, Ms. Kohl used revoicing to connect that answer to an inference that made disciplinary reasoning explicit: a Granny Smith has features of a geometric shape (lines 6–9). This inference invited Student A back into the conversation to confirm that a Granny Smith is "round, kind of like a circle" (lines 10–11). Through a subsequent chain of inferences, this imagined exchange transformed IRE/F, through revoicing, into an opportunity to induct students into disciplinary processes of defining a geometric shape (and theorizing how that concept might apply to ordinary things). Student A's answer, instead of being denigrated, was honored as an example of "thinking like a mathematician outside of school" (lines 21–22). Instead of cueing the other students to IRE/F, as she did in the original exchange, Ms. Kohl asked a question in this version (lines 21–23) that pivoted to another activity genre in which students would draw on their own experiences to generate further examples, elaborating on the defini-

> Here, Ms. Kohl revoiced Student A's answer in a way that introduced a definition implicit in the response, but that Student A did not actually say. What might be beneficial or problematic about this?

> **Take a turn**
> Think of a time when you participated as a student in a whole-class discussion in another discipline than the one in which you feel most comfortable. What, if anything, about the discussion genre contributed to your feelings of discomfort?

tion of a geometric shape and the process of thinking like a mathematician by seeing geometric shapes as both like and unlike ordinary things.

Revoicing, itself, is not a disciplinary practice, nor is it an inherently positive technique for fostering dialogic discussion. As the original excerpt from conversation in Ms. Kohl's math class demonstrates, repeating what students have already said can easily be used to humiliate and silence them, rather than to identify and encourage the ways they are already participating in scientific or mathematical conversations.

DISCIPLINARY DISCUSSIONS IN HISTORY: IMAGINATIVE ENTRY

Whereas revoicing may be especially useful to promote dialogic discussions that include the kind of defining, theorizing, and clarifying of processes expected by disciplinary communities in science and math, the following example showcases a technique that may be more appropriate to dialogic discussions in history and literature classrooms. This excerpt comes from the same suburban ninth-grade history classroom featured in chapter 2. Recall that, in Mr. Weber's class, students had been reviewing questions about a textbook chapter they had read for homework the night before. Though students had found the "right" answer from the textbook to the homework question about the Schlieffen plan ("it called for holding action against Russia"), they expressed confusion about this WWI initiative by the Germans. After a failed attempt to explain by drawing a map on the board, Mr. Weber used a student's question about the German army's invasion of Belgium as an opportunity to pose a hypothetical scenario based on the historical event: if another country's army marched through students' hometown of Talbott, what impact would that have?

22. SHIRIN: Question: when they go through all those places,

23. do they, like, try to get them to go with them?

24. Or are they, like—?

25. MR. WEBER: Are they trying to ask people to go with them? Is that what you're—?

26. SHIRIN: Kind of, yeah.

27. MR. WEBER: I don't know if they were necessarily trying to gain military strength

28. through grabbing people up as they went.

29. But say there was another country's army marching through Talbott.

30. What impact would that have on Talbott if tens of thousands of soldiers

31. . . . . it'd be kind of weird?

Mr. Weber's question pivoted students from a recitation-style review of textbook homework questions to a whole-class discussion in which students imagined different perspectives on this hypothetical/historical scenario:

37. CHASE: They'd screw everything up.

38. MR.WEBER: I couldn't even imagine how bad Glen Road would be.

39. STUDENTS: *(Laughing)*

40. ELLA: Oh my god!

41. AMY: We'd have to, like, walk everywhere.

42. MR. WEBER: They'd have to eat something, right?

43. LAURA: Yeah, they'd take all our food!

In chapter 2, this example illustrated how, with students' help, a teacher transformed recitation (teacher-led Q&A about what students had already read) into whole-class discussion. Here, Mr. Weber's hypothetical question bears further examination as an attempt to foster not only dialogic but also disciplinary discussion about the implications of the historical event.

How does Mr. Weber's question resemble the disciplinary move made by science teacher Ms. Lynne and math teacher Ms. Kohl? One might argue that, in taking up Shirin's question and casting students as figures in a "what if" scenario, Mr. Weber performed a similar revoicing of the inquiry and animation of students, asking them to hypothesize about a hypothetical situation based on their own experience. However, whereas subsequent conversation in science and math might focus on defining and theorizing, or clarifying methods, Mr. Weber's history class had a different disciplinary purpose and practice.

When teacher and students imagine themselves into a hypothetical situation based on past events, they engage in **imaginative entry**.[8] Imaginative entry can invite students to empathize with historical figures,[9] like the people of Belgium during the German invasion. In this way, they can not only begin to understand the historical event in a context beyond a textbook, but they can also imagine different perspectives within the "historical problem space":[10] How would an occupying army affect roads? food stores? Would people feel threatened? be enlisted? What might have happened next? Or differently?[11] In this way, a historical event like the Schlieffen plan can seem less like a foregone conclusion—an "it" that "was" ("It called for holding action against Russia"). Rather, it can be an opportunity to see the past as full of contingent possibilities, and to see history as an attempt to synthesize multiple perspectives based on understandings of a sequence of events in context—to "think like a historian."[12]

Consider another excerpt that occurred later in the same lesson from Mr. Weber's suburban ninth-grade history class:

64. MR. WEBER: So when they are—they have the Schlieffen plan—

65. they start setting up these wars, battles.

66. And they decide on . . . on a different type of battle.

67. What's that type?

68. TOM: Trench warfare.

69. MR. WEBER: Trench warfare.

70. So this is—what if all of a sudden

71. we decided we were going to take it out to the football field and

72. we were going to get into a battle with Mr. Abbott's fourth hour?

As in the previous example, in which a textbook question about the Schlieffen plan opened into discussion of the hypothetical invasion of Talbott, this excerpt began with a closed, lower-order thinking (C-LOT) question that produced a minimal, two-word response from Tom. However, Mr. Weber's subsequent open-ended, higher-order thinking (O-HOT) question asked students to imagine themselves in another contemporary hypothetical scenario based on historical events, pivoting again to an imaginative entry activity.

In the ensuing discussion, he and students imagined what it would be like, hypothetically, if they dug a hole in the field and fenced it for protection in order to continue the battle against the rival class. As in the previous excerpt, in which students considered the possible impacts of an army's invasion, this dialogic discussion drew students into imagining the details of trench warfare:

78. MR. WEBER: What would it be like when we're in there?

79. ERICA: Wouldn't they like see, if they're running, wouldn't they like see there's a hole?

80. MR. WEBER: Okay, they would see the hole, but how would they get over to us?

81. ERICA: Um run.

82. CHELSEA: Run and climb.

83. LAURA: Jump.

84. TOM: Dig.

85. MR. WEBER: Would there be any—

86. AMY: Couldn't we just shoot them before they got over anyways?

87. STUDENTS: *(Laughter)*

88. AMY: I'm dead serious.

89. MR. WEBER: No, Amy, you are dead serious, go ahead and say it again.

90. STUDENTS: *(Laughter)*

91. AMY: They probably wouldn't be able to get over anyways

92. because if we're just like sitting there

93. we could probably just like shoot them before they could get over a fence.

94. TOM: What if they had guns too?

Imagining "what would it be like when we're in there" became a shared inquiry focus, promoting dialogic discussion. Students imagined different possibilities, proposing details that collaboratively supported, challenged, and elaborated an emerging account of trench warfare.

> 106. MR. WEBER: So let's think about it: what would it be like if we're in the trenches?
>
> 107. How would it feel?
>
> 108. TOM: Boring.
>
> 109. MR. WEBER: Boring.
>
> 110. BECCA: I would feel claustrophobic. Because they're like right on top of you.
>
> 111. MR. WEBER: Alright.
>
> 112. PENNY: Yeah but they're—
>
> 113. AMY: But you'd kind of feel powerful.
>
> 114. PENNY: —because they couldn't get to you.
>
> 115. AMY: Yeah, I'd feel safe.
>
> 116. MR. WEBER: Okay, you would kind of feel safe, sometimes.
>
> 117. BECCA: Hiding in a hole?

Notice how the pronouns and verbs changed as the conversation continued: instead of referring to what "they decided" about an abstract "it" that "was" (lines 66–67), the class had moved to using "we" and "would/could" (lines 78–86) and finally to "you/I" and "are" (lines 110–17). Table 4.1 (below) shows that similar shifts in verb tense and pronoun use also occurred in the previous discussion of the Schlieffen plan and the imagined invasion of students' hometown.

These shifts in verb tense and pronoun use suggested that the events under discussion had become more present and personal as students identified with different perspectives in the hypothetical/historical scenario. These discussions were not only dialogic, but also disciplinary, as students participated in a shared inquiry into an event, attempting to elaborate an account that included different perspectives, much like historians might do.

Table 4.1. Shifts in verb tense and pronoun use during dialogic, whole-class discussions of the Invasion of Talbott/Belgium and of Football/Trench Warfare. (Verbs are underlined and pronouns bolded.)

Present tense and "they"	SHIRIN: Question: When **they** go through all those places, do **they** like try to get them to go with **them**? Or are **they**, like—? MR. WEBER: Are **they** trying to ask people to go with **them**? Is that what **you're**—? SHIRIN: Kind of, yeah.	64. MR. WEBER: So when they are—**they** have the Schlieffen plan, **they** start setting up these wars, battles. And **they** decide on . . . on a different type 65. of battle. What's that type? 67. TOM: Trench warfare. 68. MR. WEBER: Trench warfare. So this is—
Conditional Mood and "We"	MR. WEBER: Well, I don't know **they** were necessarily trying to gain military strength through grabbing people as **they** went. But say there was another country's army marching through Talbott. What impact would that have on Talbott if tens of thousands of soldiers . . . it'd be kind of weird? PENNY: Um people would maybe follow **them**? MR. WEBER: Okay. PENNY: To see where **they're** going? MR. WEBER: Some might follow **them**? AMY: Maybe freak out? MR. WEBER: What kind of impact would it have on the roads? PENNY: A lot! MR. WEBER: On traffic? STUDENT: Well, **they'd** break **them**. STUDENT: **They'd** screw everything up. MR. WEBER: I couldn't even imagine how bad Glen Road would be. STUDENTS: *(Laughter)* STUDENT: Oh my god! AMY: **We'd** have to, like, walk everywhere. MR. WEBER: **They'd** have to eat something, right? LAURA: Yeah, **they'd** take all **our** food! MR. WEBER: **They'd** take all **our** food. **They'd** take a lot of **our** stuff	68. what if all of a sudden **we** decided **we** were going to 69. take it out to the football field and **we** were going to get into a 70. battle with Mr. Abbott's fourth hour? . . . 79. ERICA: Wouldn't **they** like see, if **they're** running, wouldn't **they** like see 80. that there's a hole? 81. MR. WEBER: Okay, **they** would see the hole, but how would **they** get **us**? 82. ERICA: Um run. 83. CHELSEA: Run and climb. 84. LAURA: Jump. 85. TOM: Dig. 86. MR. WEBER: Would there be any— 87. AMY: Couldn't **we** just shoot them before they got over anyways? 88. STUDENTS: *(Laughter)* 89. AMY: I'm dead serious. 90. MR. WEBER: No, Amy, you are dead serious, go ahead and say it again. 91. STUDENTS: *(Laughter)* 92. AMY: **They** probably wouldn't be able to get over anyways because if

	MR.WEBER: And here **they** <u>are</u> just marching through, and say **they** <u>were</u> trying to get to [*the neighboring town of*] Burch: <u>would</u> it be **our** fault that **we** <u>were</u> in between?
	93. **we**'re just like sitting there we could probably just like shoot them before
	94. **they** could get over a fence.
	95. TOM: What if they had guns too?
Conditional/ Present Tense and "You"/"I"	GARY: Yeah, **I** <u>would</u>—
	BECCA: No, because **we** just <u>happen</u> to be there.
	MR.WEBER: And what impact <u>would</u> it have on all of **us** if these people <u>were</u> violent? Would **you** <u>want</u> to stay here?
	STUDENTS: No!
	TOM: **I'**<u>d</u> fight them.
	106. MR. WEBER: It would be tough to hide. So think about it: what would it
	107. be like if we're in the trenches? How would it feel?
	108. TOM: Boring.
	109. MR. WEBER: Boring.
	110. BECCA: **I** would feel claustrophobic . . . they're like right on top of **you**.
	111. MR. WEBER: Alright.
	112. PENNY: Yeah but they're—
	113. AMY: But **you'**d kind of feel powerful.
	114. PENNY: —because they couldn't get to **you**.
	115. AMY: Yeah, **I'**d feel safe.
	116. MR. WEBER: Okay, **you** would kind of feel safe, sometimes.
	117. BECCA: Hiding in a hole?
Past Tense and "They"	MR.WEBER: So it did have—it <u>did</u> have very profound impact on the people of Belgium, a very important impact. That <u>will</u> later <u>factor</u> into the war.
	BECCA: Wait, so what <u>was</u> the impact? Negative?
	MR.WEBER: I would say there <u>was</u> a lot of negative impact of that.
	AMY: But some positive: **they** <u>were</u> safe.
	SHIRIN: No, not really.
	MR.WEBER: You <u>don't</u> necessarily <u>know</u> **these** people <u>are</u> trying to protect **you**, right?
	BECCA: **They** <u>could</u> be, like, protecting you . . .
	202. MATT: You're probably going to run out of ammo.
	203. MR. WEBER: No **they** <u>did</u> have supplies and they did have ammo. But, I
	204. mean, food and bullets, it takes a whole lot more than that to live
	205. comfortably. At least for me. So this was probably not the best place . . . .

Like revoicing, imaginative entry has its dark side. Asking students to imagine themselves into scenarios based on historical and literary events—even hypothetical or fictional ones—may be disturbing. As the past becomes more present and personal, it may also become more threatening, hurtling students into the middle of a situation that seemed safely distant.[13]

Choices made by historical or literary figures that seemed inevitable suddenly carry the weight of responsibility, as Amy perhaps began to realize in the football field/trench warfare discussion above. In contrast, imaginative entry may also risk trivializing the gravity of an event or slipping into presentism, if students unwittingly apply their own perspectives, instead of empathizing with historical ones, as they imagine themselves into a historical or a literary narrative.

> **Take a turn**
> Return to your memory of the discussion you recalled in the previous "take a turn" prompt (about your student experience of a discussion in a subject area outside your comfort zone). Imagine yourself into the role of the teacher. What might that person have thought or felt? What would you, as teacher, have done differently?

WHAT DOES IT MEAN TO "DO DISCIPLINARY"?

Chances are good that, in reading these examples, you've asked yourself, "Is that really the best example to define and theorize discussing like a scientist?" Perhaps, in imagining yourself in these classroom scenarios, you thought, "If I were the history teacher, I would do it differently." If so, you are surfacing cultural assumptions, values, and practices associated with what it means to participate in an academic discipline like history, language arts, math, or science. Disciplinary principles and practices are dynamic and contested: fields change over time, and even subject matter experts disagree about how knowledge is made in their disciplines. These are ongoing scholarly conversations.[14] Moreover, people may have different visions of what classroom conversations in those subject areas should look like and cultural notions of what it means to be a teacher or student of these disciplines that can change expectations for participation in whole-class, dialogic discussions.

In the face of such shifting complexity, we might as teachers be tempted to (over)simplify the "rules" for students or to simply give up. "I can barely get them to participate at all, much less to talk like a scientist or think like a historian." But perhaps through disciplinary dialogic discussions, students might glimpse what it means to participate in a scholarly conversation or to be a part of a disciplinary cultural community. They may recognize in that way of communicating a set of values and practices that appeals to them, that belongs to them, or to which they could one day belong.

ACTIVITIES FOR PROMOTING DISCIPLINARY DIALOGIC DISCUSSIONS

1. **Experiences/Patterns/Explanations (Science):** Having encountered a scientific phenomenon (e.g., how shadows form or how cold soda can freeze after being opened), students first share *experiences* (verifiable observations about the phenomenon), then identify *patterns* (repetitions and contrasts in those observations), and finally generate *explanations* (theories and models that account for the patterns in their observations).
   Rationale: Charles "Andy" Anderson has suggested that, whereas "school science" often provides many explanations with limited opportunities for students to participate in authentic experiences and to generate patterns, "scientists' science" relies on a large number of *experiences* to generate reliable and accurate *patterns* as a solid foundation for disciplinary *explanations*. By involving students in shared inquiry about their experiences and the patterns they notice, teachers can induct them into scientific discussions.
2. **"How (Else) Do You Know?" (Math):** Given a math problem, students first solve and then discuss the answer to the problem. However, rather than simply evaluating their solutions, a teacher can invite students to discuss how they know if an answer is correct, whether the problem could be solved differently, and why one procedure might be preferable to another.

Rationale: Because even machines can perform basic computation, standards for math now require students to develop mathematical reasoning, demonstrating their conceptual knowledge by explaining how they arrived at an answer, what other ways a problem might be solved, and how they know if an answer is correct. Like mathematicians, students explore whether an answer can be reached, and/or justified, by other (perhaps more efficient) means.

3. **Time Travel Tickets (History):** Students each receive contextual information (e.g., a role-card, letter, ticket, passport, picture, or other cultural artifact) about a historical figure and that person's role in an event (e.g., the sinking of the RMS *Titanic*—see https://titanicorlando.com/visit). During and after a detailed review or re-enactment of the event, students contribute to discussions about how their characters experienced the event differently, and why.
Rationale: Receiving contextual information about a historical figure encourages students to identify and empathize with a particular perspective on a past event; as these different perspectives come into relationship through discussion, students engage in disciplinary thinking by comparing, contrasting, debating, synthesizing, and evaluating different historical accounts.

4. **Alternate Endings (English Language Arts):** On their own or in small groups, students compose alternate endings to a story. Afterward, they discuss how and why their endings are different from, yet still justified by, the original text.
Rationale: Endings depend on story features like plot, character, and point of view, as well as stylistic features, including voice and genre. Students must "read like writers" as they use these disciplinary concepts to create their endings and explain their decisions.

REFLECTIONS FOR TEACHERS

1. Review the national standards for a particular subject area (or another public description of shared values and practices) that pertain to discussions or to classroom talk. Then review a similar set of standards or description of expectations for discussions in another

subject area. Which attitudes and practices are similar or different across these academic disciplines? Why might that be?
2. Reflect on your expectations for whole-class discussions in your classroom, or one in which you've participated as teacher or student, and try to describe how you would like students to participate. You might even list specific practices or attitudes you would like students to exhibit. Then, consider this list in light of a particular subject area: which of these practices and attitudes (if any) are disciplinary—that is, associated with thinking and acting like a scientist, mathematician, historian, or member of another professional community? How might even shared attitudes and practices (e.g., listening to others with an open mind) have different purposes from one subject area to another?
3. Given your answers to the previous question, what guidelines (if any) have you given, or would you like to give, to students about how to participate in disciplinary dialogic discussions (in which class members engage in shared disciplinary inquiry, building on what others have written or said to make meanings together, even if they disagree)? What might students find beneficial or confusing about those guidelines, given their experiences with classroom talk in other subject areas?
4. Identify a time in your own experience as a student when you felt either especially at home or especially alienated from the content during classroom conversation. What cultural expectations for participation in a particular discipline might have contributed to those feelings?
5. Find a colleague or classmate with a strong preference for another subject area, and discuss your answers to these questions with that person. How do your (disciplinary) expectations for classroom talk differ, and why? How do the participation guidelines you give (or might give) to students compare? How are your own experiences of dis/comfort with disciplinary conversations similar and different?
6. On your own or with a colleague, review one of the transcripts from this chapter. What do you find familiar/foreign/intriguing/repellent about how that conversation unfolded? What, if anything, might that feeling have to do with disciplinary preferences? How do you

think a comparable conversation might have unfolded differently in another subject area?

EXPLORATIONS WITH STUDENTS

1. Have students write or talk about their experiences with expectations for whole-class discussions in different subject areas. For them, what is a "discussion" in each subject area?
2. Have students complete the following table on their own or together (with you) as a class in order to describe how dialogic discussions might compare across disciplines:

How do class discussions (in which we build on one another's ideas to figure things out) differ across subject areas?		
Subject Area	Purpose (why we do it)	Practices (what we do)
Math		
Science		
History		
English Language Arts		

3. What similarities and differences do students notice? How do they explain the differences? How do they feel about these comparisons?
4. Ask students to circle words in the following list that match their own attitudes, values, or preferences. Then, have them consider (on their own, in groups, or with you as a class): How might these concepts align or conflict with particular subject areas? How might they shape whole-class discussions in those academic disciplines?

Objective	Choices	Realistic	Observation	Personal	Consensus
Contextualized	Generalizable	Facts		Perspectives	Concrete
Individual	Reflection	Cause/Effect	Behavior	Measurable	Interpretation
Abstract	Culture	Empathy	Experiences	Evidence	Processes
Symbolic	Disagreement	Situated	Enduring	Impressions	Constraints

CHAPTER SUMMARY

- Whole-class, dialogic discussions in different academic disciplines may have different purposes and may value different ways of participating; these disciplinary cultural differences may be left implicit.
- In math and science, revoicing may be used not only to promote dialogic uptake of what others have said, but also to encourage students to theorize or to clarify a procedure, both disciplinary moves.
- Imaginative entry may be used in history and English classrooms both to promote dialogic discussion and to encourage disciplinary skills like historical empathy and synthesis of different perspectives.

NOTES

1. P. Prior, "A Microhistory of Mediated Authorship and Disciplinary Enculturation: Tracing Authoritative and Internally Persuasive Discourses," in *Writing/Discplinarity: A Sociohistoric Account of Literate Activity in the Academy* (Mahwah, NJ: Lawrence Erlbaum Associates, 1998), 215–46; R. C. Lent, *This Is Disciplinary Literacy: Reading, Writing, Thinking, and Doing . . . Content Area by Content Area* (Thousand Oaks, CA: Corwin, 2016); Elizabeth B. Moje, "Responsive Literacy Teaching in Secondary School Content Areas," in *Meeting the Challenge of Adolescent Literacy: Research We Have, Research We Need* (New York: Guilford, 2008), 58–80; K. E. Pytash and L. Ciecierski, "Teaching from a Disciplinary Literacy Stance," *Voices in the Middle* 22, no. 3 (2015): 14–18.

2. M. C. O'Connor and S. Michaels, "Aligning Academic Task and Participation Status through Revoicing: Analysis of a Classroom Discourse Strategy," *Anthropology & Education Quarterly* 24, no. 4 (1993): 318–35.

3. Erving Goffman, "Footing," in *Forms of Talk* (Philadelphia: University of Pennsylvania Press, 1981); Erving Goffman, *Frame Analysis: An Essay on the Organization of Experience* (Boston: Northeastern University Press, 1986).

4. O'Connor and Michaels, "Aligning Academic Task."

5. C. Edwards-Groves and C. Davidson, "Metatalk for a Dialogic Turn in the First Years of Schooling," in *Routledge International Handbook of Research on Dialogic Education* (New York: Routledge, 2020), 125–38.

6. A. M. Lawrence and S. Crespo, "IRE/F as a Cross-Curricular Collaborative Genre of Implicit Argumentation," *Theory into Practice* 55, no. 4 (2016): 1–12.

7. Lawrence and Crespo, "IRE/F as a Cross-Curricular Collaborative Genre."

8. L. Levstik, "Any History Is Someone's History: Listening to Multiple Voices from the Past," *Social Education* 61 (1997): 48–51; L. Levstik and K. C. Barton, *Researching History Education: Theory, Method, and Context* (New York: Routledge, 2008); L. Levstik and K. C. Barton, *Doing History: Investigating with Children in Elementary and Middle Schools* (New York: Taylor & Francis, 2001); K. C. Barton, "Students' Ideas about History," in *Handbook of Research on Social Education*, ed. L. Levstik and C. A. Tyson (New: Routledge, 2008), 239–58.

9. J. Kohlmeier, "'Couldn't She Just Leave': The Relationship between Consistently Using Class Discussions and the Development of Historical Empathy in a 9th Grade World History Course," *Theory and Research in Social Education* 34, no. 1 (2006): 34–57; Sarah Brooks, "Historical Empathy as Perspective Recognition and Care in One Secondary Social Studies Classroom," *Theory & Research in Social Education* 39, no. 2 (Spring 2011): 166–202.

10. A. Reisman, "Entering the Historical Problem Space: Whole-Class Text-Based Discussion in History Class," *Teachers College Record* 117, no. 2 (2015): 1–44.

11. G. S. Morson, "Sideshadowing and Tempics," *New Literary History* 29, no. 4 (1998): 599–624; N. Welch, "Sideshadowing Teacher Response," *College English* 60, no. 4 (1998): 374–95.

12. National Center for History in the Schools, "Historical Thinking Standards," University of California (Los Angeles: National Council for History Standards, 1996), http://nchs.ucla.edu/Standards/historical-thinking-standards-1; S. Wineburg, *Historical Thinking and Other Unnatural Acts: Charting the Future of Teaching the Past* (Philadelphia: Temple University Press, 2001).

13. Simone Schweber, *Making Sense of the Holocaust* (New York: Teachers College Press, 2004); G. S. Morson, *Narrative and Freedom: The Shadows of Time* (New Haven: Yale University Press, 1994).

14. A. N. Applebee, *Curriculum as Conversation: Transforming Traditions of Teaching and Learning* (Chicago: University of Chicago Press, 1996).

5

Inviting Out-of-School Cultural Practices into Dialogic Discussions

"With my dad. I'm like 'Dad, check this out,' and he's like 'Yeah, that's great.' But I can tell he's not really listening. But then he tells me to do something, and he's like, 'Why don't you listen to me?'" John sighed, slumping back in his seat.

Miriam nodded, *"Yeah, that's a good example."* Turning away from John, she cast a sidelong glance at me where I stood listening nearby. *"Is that right?"*

"What do you think?" I asked Miriam.

"C'mon," said John. *"You know nothing's ever really 'right' in this class."* He laughed ruefully. *"I wish that were true in my next class."*

"Not me," said Miriam. *"I like when you know if it's right. If you show your work, of course."*

From where I stood listening, I asked John and Miriam, *"So are you saying that people often talk past each other in families?"*

Miriam nodded, *"Yeah, in my family, sometimes everyone talks at once and it's hard to—"*

John interrupted, *"Yeah, when my older brothers are home and everyone's talking at the dinner table—forget about it! I can't get a word in edgewise!"*

Chapter 4 addressed the idea that students' experiences in other classrooms might shape expectations for how they participate in conversation. Talk in those other classrooms might differ, not only because of different genres, or types of activity, but because of different cultural expectations associated with other academic disciplines, like history, language arts, math, or science. Those academic disciplines have shared values, purposes, and practices that may differ—for example, to reach consensus about a solution or to generate multiple interpretations of a text. Students unfamiliar with those implicit, disciplinary cultural expectations might struggle to participate. Likewise, communities in which students participate outside of school have different cultural values and practices associated with discussions. How teachers recognize, welcome, and address students' prior experiences with conversations outside the classroom may also shape whole-class dialogic discussions, for better or for worse.

For example, in the vignette above, John interrupts Miriam to describe conversations in his family. Whereas John's interruption might be an effective strategy during a large, male-dominated family dinner-table conversation characterized by fast, simultaneous, overlapping talk, it may be less welcome in a small-group classroom discussion. Moreover, how fast people respond on the heels of another speaker may depend not only on effectiveness in a social situation like a family dinner, but also on cultural expectations related to pacing and pausing in conversation: in some cultures, most people talk fast and interrupt frequently; in others, long pauses between speakers is common and interruptions are rare.[1] Failure to meet these cultural expectations may be considered rude, despite the fact that they are often left implicit and usually cannot be inferred from the immediate social situation.[2]

This chapter addresses how students' home and out-of-school language practices in roles associated with age, ethnicity, gender, and other aspects of cultural identities might affect their participation in dialogic discussions. Those language practices may conflict with the conversational style of other students or with the expectations of classroom activity genres; yet to discourage them might also mean marginalizing some students. How can teachers support and guide students' use of out-of-school cultural language practices during classroom conversations in ways that encourage dialogic discussions?

To identify such practices may be hard for teachers, because those cultural roles stem from interactions beyond the immediate social context or even from apparent genre contact with other classroom activities. Moreover, it is important to avoid essentializing: for example, it would be a mistake to assume, based on John's exchange with Miriam, that all students from big families will be "high talkers," or that boys are more likely to interrupt than girls. However, teachers who recognize and welcome students' home and out-of-school cultural language practices can promote dialogic discussions—conversations in which students may dialogue not only with their classmates, but also with multiple ways of talking, thinking, and being beyond the classroom.

AN EXAMPLE OF A CULTURAL LANGUAGE PRACTICE: AVOIDING DISAGREEMENT

Consider the following excerpt from a tenth-grade English language arts lesson in an urban Midwestern school as an example of how students might respond to an invitation to discuss a controversial issue. Teacher Tamara Jefferson had asked students in her fourth-hour class to compose entries in their writing journals in preparation for reading Sophocles's *Antigone*. In this Greek tragedy, the title character decides to bury her brother, despite the fact that Theban law decreed by her uncle, King Creon, forbids the interment of traitors. Ms. Jefferson asked students to relate the events of the story to a present-day dilemma: Should a doctor or nurse remove life support from a suffering or terminally ill patient, despite possible legal consequences? Reflecting on this lesson, Ms. Jefferson explained, "I know a lot of students—I hear that all the time they have loved ones in the hospital, loved ones who, you know, have been sick and possibly on life support. It's a real topic to them. So I wanted to bring them something that they could possibly relate to in the twenty-first century, but also I could connect it back to Antigone." However, while students engaged enthusiastically with the topic, they did not take up one another's perspectives in dialogic discussion:

1. KAYLA: I don't think . . . I don't think he should
2. because then he go'n' lose his job,
3. and it's all over, and he probably never go'n' get a doctoring job again.
4. MS. JEFFERSON: Right. Okay. Okay. Go ahead.

5. GARRETT: Um, it's not like I would follow the law, but in my mind, like,

6. following the law, it's like, kind of like my own personal belief that

7. if I push my ways on other people that, like, change their beliefs,

8. maybe in their religion or something, that they can't do that or something.

9. So it would be kind of like me pushing my ways on other people.

10. MS. JEFFERSON: Okay. Good point. Montana?

11. MONTANA: Basically I would say that I would follow my conscience,

12. but it would be toward, like, rather than just up and pulling the plug,

13. I would try to go through whatever, try to find whatever loopholes I could,

14. try to find existent family members, or whatever.

15. I would basically work around the system before I made anything decisive,

16. and if that didn't work, yes, I would pull the plug just to stop the suffering.

17. MS. JEFFERSON: Okay. Derek?

This activity genre, in which students first wrote and then shared their opinions on a provocative moral issue, succeeded in producing student responses from different perspectives: Kayla pointed to the professional consequences of breaking the law (lines 1–3), and Garrett and Montana to the role of religion and moral conscience (lines 6, 11). But while several more students subsequently shared responses, there was no uptake of classmates' viewpoints.

Although multiple speakers voiced a variety of opinions, and the tone of this activity remained positive and harmonious, nevertheless, the conversation exemplified what researchers who study conversations might call **non-collaborative disagreement**: speakers did not engage directly with differing perspectives voiced by other participants.[3] As a result, they did not take up opportunities to challenge thinking or change minds.

In a later reflection, Ms. Jefferson herself noted her fourth-hour students' difficulty with disagreeing in ways that cited other conversational turns: "There's a blanket statement over here, and then we go over there, and it does not connect to anything that was said over here. But in sixth hour . . . they know how to bring that person's thoughts and ideas in before they make the next comment. . . . Here, I haven't yet had a chance to get them to build on one another's conversation." For Ms. Jefferson, it was not enough that her students expressed different opinions on the subject. She wanted them to explicitly relate their perspectives to others, as her sixth-hour class had learned to do.

Based on your reading of previous chapters, you have probably noticed or wondered about conversational moves made by Ms. Jefferson that may have contributed to her students' non-collaborative disagreement. First, Ms. Jefferson had asked students simply to share their journal entries, an open invitation, but one that perhaps prompted students to report rather than to discuss their perspectives. Second, while the fourth-hour students had journaled on ethical dilemmas and shared their entries with the class in previous lessons, Ms. Jefferson had not yet, in the fourth hour, explicitly modeled classroom disagreement about passionately felt positions, in which students explored differences of opinion by referencing others' views. Third, during the conversation, Ms. Jefferson inadvertently impeded discussion by employing IRE/F. For example, after each turn, she responded with "Right," "Good point," and "okay" (lines 4, 10, and 17).

These "follow-ups" did little to take up students' ideas, and their appearance after each turn suggested that Ms. Jefferson would evaluate all students' answers. Like the initial instructions for the journaling activity, such evaluative follow-ups did not produce the lively debate Ms. Jefferson had envisioned, a dialogic discussion characterized by **collaborative disagreement**, in which students would reference others' contributions while disagreeing with those positions.

Additionally, cultural expectations beyond the immediate social situation or the implicit rules, roles, relationships, and available responses of the classroom activity genre may have influenced students' participation. In schools, teachers and students may avoid disagreement because of the *content* it often accompanies: controversial topics during classroom discussions may promote disagreement because such topics often relate to differences associated with age, class, ethnicity, gender, race, sexual orientation, or other deeply held aspects of cultural identity and practice.[4] In this case, students like Garrett may have been reluctant to disagree more explicitly in ways that might "push my ways on other people that, like, change their beliefs, maybe in their religion or something." While teachers might address students' reluctance regarding controversial *content* by offering explicit guidelines, modeling collaborative disagreement, and encouraging self- and whole-class evaluation of discussion practices (see chapter 2), the *form* of disagreement may also have different cultural meanings for some students.

Some cultures see disagreement as an inherently negative and potentially hostile interaction, or at least a breakdown of the social situation. In Ms. Jefferson's fourth-hour class, more than half the students (including Garrett and Montana, in the excerpt above) had grown up in European American middle-class households in the US Midwest—contexts in which speakers may avoid explicit disagreement, according to some researchers.[5] Perhaps you're thinking: "Wait a minute! I grew up in just such a household, and we had no trouble disagreeing!" Not all members of cultural communities may share the same attitudes. Regardless, Ms. Jefferson's fourth-hour students were noticeably reluctant to disagree directly.

In contrast, other cultures view disagreement as a positive and even a sociable interaction—as a means of bringing different perspectives to a

> **Take a turn**
> Is it easy or hard for you to disagree with others, based on your age, ethnicity, gender, race, or sexual orientation? What does disagreement mean for the cultures in which you participate?

shared inquiry, or even as a way of playfully engaging together in a shared cultural practice.[6] For example, African American culture includes several practices in which members of a group engage in call-and-response "battles" to test their verbal and performative prowess: through rapping, dancing, playing music, and playing the Dozens (a collaborative game in which players trade mock insults that attempt to poetically outdo the previous turn).[7] These interactions are playful, not aggressive: speakers often challenge each other indirectly, and repeat others' words and actions with an ironic twist, a pattern researchers of African American Language (AAL) have also identified in oral and written argumentation by scholars, politicians, and other preeminent public figures from Zora Neale Hurston and Dr. Martin Luther King Jr. to President Barack Obama and Oprah

Winfrey.[8] As in the previous example, not all members of a cultural community necessarily share familiarity with a given practice: not all people who are African Americans speak AAL or engage in this kind of ironic revoicing, nor are all students who prefer playful disagreement likely to be African American.

You might recall, from the opening vignette of previous chapters, John's provocative repetition of Miriam's phrase "people talking by themselves"—an indirect critique of a classroom activity which, despite its focus on dialogue, initially appeared to be teacher-dominated. Uptake of what others have already said and done makes these indirect criticisms and provocative repetitions dialogic.[9] As such, teachers might draw on students' experiences with this cultural disagreement practice to promote dialogic discussion that encourages collaborative disagreement, as Ms. Jefferson did with her sixth-hour class in the excerpt that follows.

AN EXAMPLE OF A CULTURAL LANGUAGE PRACTICE: ENCOURAGING DISAGREEMENT

This whole-class discussion occurred midway through Ms. Jefferson's sixth-hour class's unit of study on John Hersey's *Hiroshima*. In a previous lesson, the class had discussed the maxim "All's fair in love and war" in preparation for writing a position paper about "fairness" and the US's atomic bombing of Japan. Unsatisfied with what she had found to be simplistic reactions from students in the previous activity, Ms. Jefferson planned in this lesson to compare the bombing of Hiroshima to the terrorist attacks of September 11, 2001. She hoped to draw on a relevant, contemporary experience to help students better understand an unfamiliar historical one, and by provoking debate over this controversial comparison, to encourage students to define and defend their positions on the Hiroshima bombing before writing position papers.

To begin, Ms. Jefferson asked a student to recall what the class had previously discussed:

1. MS. JEFFERSON: So what did we say this idea of "All is fair in love and war" actually means?

2. What does that quote mean, Franklin? What did we say that was?

3. FRANKLIN: Like if you're in a war, you can go to any extent.

4. MS. JEFFERSON: So Franklin said if you're in a war you can go to any extent.

5. If it gets to the point where you need to drop an atomic bomb,

6. then that's fair.

7. If it gets to the point, similar to 9/11 here,

8. where you take a plane and you crash into the Trade Center . . .

9. then that's also fair.

> Ms. Jefferson juxtaposes a historical example that might seem far from students' experience with a contemporary one that is closer.

Ms. Jefferson's initial query seemed to be a closed, lower-order thinking (C-LOT) question that asked students to simply recall a definition as a means of reopening whole-class discussion of the maxim, "All's fair in love and war." But her response to Franklin introduced the controversial comparison with which she had planned to spark disagreement and complicate students' thinking about the bombing of Hiroshima. And instead of following up with "Right" or "Okay," she responded explicitly to Franklin's words, demonstrating to students not only that what Franklin had said was important, but also how to take up others' words in order to disagree collaboratively.

Additionally, Ms. Jefferson used moves associated with the African American cultural language practice described above, moves that may have been important given the high proportion of African American students in her sixth-hour class. By referring to Franklin in the third person (line 4), she indirectly addressed other listeners and invited them to respond.[10] This **indirect challenge** resembled a playful "battling" technique whereby a participant invites response from the audience by referring ironically to another's words in the third person. Ms. Jefferson's third-person address also avoided directly challenging Franklin in a way that might quickly have shut down any further debate by creating a pattern in which the teacher evaluated each student's opinion (as her use of "Right" and "Okay" had established in the fourth-hour excerpt).

Second, Ms. Jefferson did not simply repeat Franklin's answer. Instead, she provocatively revoiced Franklin's response in a way that evoked the call-and-response of battling or the verbal sparring of The Dozens. Ms. Jefferson's **provocative paraphrase**, a technique in which speakers turn others' words back on them through wordplay, subtly challenged Franklin's assertion by repeating his "if . . . then . . ." phrasing but also provocatively juxtaposing part of what he had said with another example: If it was fair for American forces to go "to any extent" in bombing Hiroshima, then was it fair for terrorists to do the same in attacking an American landmark? This provocative paraphrase implicitly modeled for students how to disagree with another's position by ironically pairing it with a counterexample, a technique that also resembled one from The Dozens, in which speakers "top" the previous turn by adding a new, usually ironic, twist. This use of an indirect challenge and a provocative paraphrase to reinterpret and to playfully challenge another's opinion also demonstrated that it was possible to disagree collaboratively during this activity.

It is worth noting another part of Ms. Jefferson's response: she pretended to misunderstand while also teasingly exaggerating Franklin's comment, attributing to him a position with which she knew (from a previous lesson) he disagreed—a move she called, "playing devil's advocate." Students' responses below suggest that they recognized Ms. Jefferson's response to Franklin as ironic—that she was pretending to mistake his opinion in order to promote further disagreement and discussion. Participants in rap battles and in The Dozens often use ironic, provocative paraphrases of others' words as a means of promoting disagreement that is playful, sociable, and collaborative.[11]

HOW STUDENTS TOOK UP A
CULTURAL DISAGREEMENT PRACTICE IN DISCUSSION

Indeed, Ms. Jefferson's initial response to Franklin seemed to inspire similar contributions to the discussion from students:

5. MS. JEFFERSON: If it gets to the point where you need to drop an atomic bomb,

6. then that's fair.

7. If it gets to the point, similar to 9/11 here,

8. where you take a plane and you crash into the Trade Center . . .

9. then that's also fair.

10. FRANKLIN: Well no . . . but . . . if they bomb us then—

11. RICHARD: —If they bomb us, and then we bomb them back,

12. then they can't say nothin' 'cause it's fair.

13. MS. JEFFERSON: So you're saying this is more of a retaliation.

14. If someone does something to me,

15. then I should have the right to do the same thing to them.

16. Or even if I do something bigger and better than what they did to me,

17. then that makes it right. Okay.

18. BRIAN: What's interesting is that, they bombed Pearl Harbor,

19. which was a naval base, but we bombed a city.

Like their teacher, first Franklin and Richard, then Brian, disagreed with a previous speaker. This disagreement was collaborative because it first addressed what that person had said and then coupled his or her point with a counterexample. Both Franklin and Richard provocatively paraphrased Ms. Jefferson's "If . . . then . . ." statement by pairing it with a new twist: Unlike the 9/11 attacks, Franklin and Richard suggested, the Hiroshima bombing had been provoked by the bombing of Pearl Harbor ("If they bomb us . . . then we bomb them back").

Brian indirectly challenged this "eye-for-an-eye" comment and provocatively paraphrased its "they/we" structure by pointing out that, like the 9/11 attacks (and unlike Pearl Harbor), the Hiroshima bombing involved a civilian city. Ms. Jefferson responded much as she had the first time, pretending to misunderstand Franklin and Richard's comments as extending to revenge on a larger scale: Was it fair to retaliate if the retaliation was bigger than the initial attack? Students not only disagreed, but did so collaboratively, using indirect challenges and provocative paraphrases to oppose others' positions. These moves resembled the cultural conflict talk practices described above: none of the speakers explicitly challenged the others, but each ironically criticized another's position implicitly by taking up part of it and connecting it with a contradictory example.

INVITING OTHERS BACK INTO DISCUSSION

Notice that, in provocatively paraphrasing Franklin's response above, Ms. Jefferson also drew him back into the discussion, encouraging him to defend his position. This tactic reappeared as conversation continued:

20. MS. JEFFERSON: No reason to kill innocent people.

21. Wait, but Kevin said they deserved it!

22. KEVIN: They did.

23. RICHARD: I just want to say something.

24. MS. JEFFERSON: Okay. Wait a minute. Let's let Kevin make his point

25. and then you can make yours.

26. Okay, Kevin. So they bombed us, they deserved it.

27. KEVIN: They shouldn't have killed Americans. For no reason.

Kevin's position is inflammatory. But instead of silencing or ignoring it, Ms. Jefferson invited him back into the conversation. What are some pros and cons of this move, in your opinion?

In response to Brian's comment about bombing civilians, Ms. Jefferson paraphrased it in a way that connected with a previous, contradictory comment by another speaker, Kevin. As she had done in responding to Franklin, Ms. Jefferson not only paired this previous speaker's point with Brian's but explicitly named Kevin as that speaker; although the comment was not addressed directly to Kevin, it drew him back into conversation, producing a response. Ms. Jefferson used the cultural conflict talk technique of indirectly challenging another speaker in order to elicit a response as a means of inviting that speaker back into the whole-class discussion to defend his position. Given the intolerant nature of Kevin's position, calling him out by name (albeit indirectly) in order to revisit this position may have been especially important.

Once Ms. Jefferson had modeled it, students also took up the practice of indirectly challenging another speaker to draw him back into conversation. Immediately afterward, Richard made a similar indirect challenge to a previous speaker by making a third-person reference to what Brian had already said:

28. RICHARD: You see how Brian was saying that we bombed a city?

29. But when we bombed them,

30. their military was underground.

31. So who else was there to bomb?

Like Ms. Jefferson, Richard paired Brian's assertion with another example in order to disagree with Brian's counterargument about bombing civilians. And like Ms. Jefferson, Richard also explicitly challenged Brian (though indirectly, in the third person) as the source of that argument, drawing him back into conversation to defend his perspective. Not only did Richard make use of what Brian had said, an example of collaborative disagreement, but he also used the same kind of indirect challenge that Ms. Jefferson had to call Brian out by name.

In response to being named, Brian squared off with Richard in several successive exchanges:

32. BRIAN: There was no point to build the bomb.

33. RICHARD: But we did build it,

34. so what's the point in making it sit there and not use it?

35. BRIAN: What's the point in using it?

36. RICHARD: To kill. So they know who's boss.

37. BRIAN: But if we bomb them,

38. we just had to rebuild them and pay them back for it.

Although they clearly disagreed strongly with each other, both Richard and Brian repeated parts of the other's points. Their responses included increasing repetition, not only of words, but also of sentence

> Brian seemed to think the US paid reparations to Japan after Hiroshima, which it did not. Do you agree with Ms. Jefferson's decision not to intervene? What are the pros and cons of that decision?

structures ("What's the point in . . . ?" in lines 34–35, and "But we . . ." in lines 33, 37). That is, their disagreement was increasingly collaborative, spurring each of them to attend more closely to what the previous speaker had said. Moreover, their use of provocative paraphrasing to turn the other's words back on him increasingly resembled the staccato exchanges of battling and The Dozens. While Ms. Jefferson had been instrumental in initiating and modeling practices for collaborative disagreement earlier in the discussion, she became less present as student participation increased.

Ms. Jefferson noted the importance of this discussion for students like Richard in a later interview, after students had written their position papers on the phrase "All's fair in love and war":

> Richard definitely said "Oh yeah," you know, "that makes sense because at first I was thinking, you know, they bombed us, oh well, but now I don't think it is fair for those civilians to lose their lives, you know, like in the Pentagon and the World Trade Center because—uh, I can kind of see that." And by the responses, I could definitely tell that they were thinking about the issue beyond surface level. . . . All we got at first was "Oh well! They shouldn't have bombed us." But now it's like "Well, was it really necessary? Why did we build the bomb at all?" . . . Usually, I'm always playing devil's advocate; now I have someone to help me!

According to Ms. Jefferson, the perspective of Richard (and perhaps that of other students) on the bombing of Hiroshima and the phrase "All's fair in love and war" changed after this whole-class discussion from an "eye-for-an-eye" position to more complex responses that questioned various aspects of the event. Ms. Jefferson's comment suggests that using indirect challenges and provocative paraphrases to promote collaborative disagreement may have been effective in destabilizing the initial positions taken by students like Richard.

The nature of these positions, which sometimes included intolerant, ill-informed, and potentially offensive ideas, might seem to call for more direct intervention on the part of the teacher. But such an intervention might have produced a different result, quashing discussion and perhaps eliciting resistance from students. As Ms. Jefferson wrote in a post-lesson reflection:

> I planned to do this by modeling and . . . probing them to connect their ideas. In order to do this, I used student responses by connecting them to

probing questions. I also believe that "sociable language" during this time was another great way for students to understand, and this "relaxed" language allowed me to push them further and draw the entire class . . . in on the intriguing comment.

For Ms. Jefferson, using strategies that evoked the playful, collaborative disagreement of an African American cultural form of conflict talk allowed her to "push them further" in a "relaxed" way, implicitly encouraging students to consider multiple counterarguments as they took up and responded to others' perspectives, rather than evaluating each student's comment with "Right" or "Okay," as she had done in the fourth-hour discussion presented above.

Indeed, other students now joined the conversation to criticize the position expressed in Brian's last statement and to juxtapose it again with 9/11-related American policy:

39. GLORIA: Why? It doesn't seem to me like, and I don't understand why . . .

40. In Iraq, they kinda did mess it up, too, 'cause they were fighting us.

41. So why shouldn't they help rebuild it if we got to rebuild it?

42. EBONY: Like when they crashed into the Trade Center,

> Like Brian, Gloria and Ebony voiced misinformed ideas: that US opponents in the Iraq War were responsible for the 9/11 attacks. Should Ms. Jefferson have responded differently? If so, why? How?

43. they didn't come and clean up our [unintelligible].

44. Why are we cleaning up their stuff?

45. GLORIA: Like, what she said, it's not like they asked for our help. . . .

46. MS. JEFFERSON: I think this debate—I think this debate is very . . . is very much needed. . . .

47. When you write this essay,

48. I want you to keep in mind this idea of "All is fair in love and war."

In response to Brian's point that the Hiroshima bombing would only require American efforts to rebuild the city after the war, Gloria and Ebony entered the discussion, juxtaposing Brian's point with events from the Iraq War and the 9/11 attacks: Why should the United States pay to rebuild after Hiroshima when no such gesture was made after 9/11? Although this argument was based on factual errors—for example, the United States did not help to rebuild after the bombing—Gloria and Ebony took up part of Brian's assertion about rebuilding to disagree collaboratively.

By offering a counterexample that called Brian's point into question, they used provocative paraphrasing. In addition, Ebony imitated the form of Gloria's comment (lines 42–44), following an example with an ironic rhetorical question. The use of ironic rhetorical questions was a device that had already appeared in conversation (lines 31, 34, 35). Further, the use of irony in these rhetorical questions resembled Ms. Jefferson's ironic responses in which she pretended to misunderstand previous comments in order to indirectly challenge them (lines 7, 13, 21).

The above transcript illustrates this and other regularities in language use that increasingly appeared over the course of this whole-class discussion. As the transcript demonstrates, although speakers disagreed, they did so collaboratively, by referencing and reworking what others had said. This collaborative disagreement included practices that resembled those from African American cultural language practices like rap battling and The Dozens. Such practices also include indirect challenges and provocative paraphrases. As the discussion progressed, speakers used indirect challenges to call out others by name, bringing them back into the conversation to defend their positions. They also used parallel phrases/sentence structures, including ironic rhetorical questions.

As the transcript shows, the discourse of the whole-class discussion can be divided into sections that suggest a progression of increasing regularities in language use, from general similarities in formulation at the beginning to strong parallels in phrases/sentence structures toward the end. These increasing regularities suggest that, during the discussion, participants attended more and more closely to what others had said, even as they elaborated on different perspectives. In short, as the discussion progressed, not only did participants disagree, and disagree collaboratively, but also the dialogic reworking of others' words intensified as the differences in their interpretations were amplified. What is also significant is that the devices they began to use more regularly ("if . . . then . . ." propositions; citation of other speakers; juxtaposition of counterexamples; and ironic, rhetorical questions) were not only techniques that resembled The Dozens, but also argumentative practices valued by academic communities, which are central to ELA curriculum.

DIALOGUE AT THE INTERSECTION OF CULTURES

Disagreement is just one aspect of class discussions that may be influenced by students' experiences with cultural language practices outside of school. However, disagreement is an example of a practice that may be influenced by intersecting and even conflicting expectations related to age, class, ethnicity, gender, and perhaps other aspects of students' cultural identities.

For example, some might argue that, by evoking students' cultural experiences with out-of-school experiences like battling and The Dozens, Ms. Jefferson may have encouraged male students like Franklin, Richard, Brian, and Kevin, but perhaps discouraged female students (though others, including Gloria and Ebony, might disagree![12]). And what about members of other cultural groups for whom conflict talk, even when collaborative, seems more perturbing than playful? Rather than replacing one set of exclusive norms with another, teachers might utilize a variety of activity genres that invite students' out-of-school cultural language practices into classroom conversation.

Ms. Jefferson, an African American woman, felt conflicted at first about using what she called "sociable language," despite its obvious success at engaging students. Initially, she tried to maintain more formal discourse, which she associated with the role of an English teacher: "Everyone has this idea of what the 'good teacher' role is. And so did I, you know, I really did, I wanted to present myself in a [certain] way." But because students saw through her attempts to play the "good teacher," Ms. Jefferson later changed her mind about using AAL practices: "They thought that I was playing a role, and I was. . . . And I just went home one night, I was like 'that's not who I am.' . . . I know that that's probably not a lot of people's technique . . . but I find that they're more responsive to me when I'm that way."

Ms. Jefferson's experience points to the challenges of using cultural language practices to invite students into whole-class dialogic discussions. Perhaps, like she did, you have doubts: will using "sociable language" undermine your authority with students? Or you may wonder, could another teacher, who was not African American, have had the same success with tapping into this cultural language practice? The answers to these questions will depend on context. Yet teachers might reflect on their own cultural expectations for participation in whole-class discussions, and consult with students about their experiences and preferences as they collaborate, over time, to create a shared classroom culture of dialogic discussion practices.

ACTIVITIES FOR INVITING OUT-OF-SCHOOL LANGUAGE PRACTICES INTO DISCUSSION

1. **Discussion Channels:** During a discussion, students are encouraged to switch between different "channels" with explicitly different expectations about when and how to participate: for example, whole-class discussion with certain formal constraints and pair or small-group conversations in which informal language practices are welcome.
   Rationale: Students become aware of how different contexts, audiences, and activity genres (even during a classroom discussion) can shape the expectations for how they participate.
   Variations:
   - Instead of switching channels during discussion, specify a regular time before or after discussion for students' informal conversation about the same topic.
   - Create a "back channel" for interaction during a discussion: using an online forum, students can pose questions or make comments related to class content while the face-to-face activity is still unfolding; specify guidelines for this back channel discussion that invite informal, non-academic language while still maintaining relevance and civility.
2. **Panel Interview/Town Hall:** In groups or as a class, students choose characters (real or fictional) with different voices (e.g., of

different backgrounds or perspectives) to participate in a panel interview or "town hall" discussion of a particular topic.

Rationale: In performing the voices of different characters, students may bring not only different positions but also different ways of speaking into relationship. Care should be taken to avoid stereotypical representations of a particular cultural group: for example, preparation and evaluation of this activity could emphasize the specificity of characters and the authenticity of their contributions, based on source material.

Variations:
- Stage the interview as an informal "pop-culture panel" or talk show, welcoming more commentary and banter from panelists and audience members who "call in."
- Stage the interview as a formal panel of experts (from different perspectives or different disciplines), encouraging audience members to pose questions to be answered by more than one panelist.

3. **Poems for Multiple Voices:** Using models from Paul Fleischman's *Joyful Noise*[13] (or other examples), students work on their own or in groups to create "dialogue poems" in which two or more different voices appear in parallel columns that can be read together. Parallel lines are meant to sound in unison, while others go back and forth in complement or counterpoint. After writing their poems, students share and discuss.

Rationale: Because dialogue poems are less restrictive than other academic and even poetic genres, students can bring different voices and styles into the classroom (and into dialogue with one another). As students compose, perform, and listen to others' poems for multiple voices with different perspectives and styles, they note moments where those voices overlap, complement, diverge, and contrast.

Variations:
- Specify the voices (or contexts for those voices) that students must use in their poems (e.g., parents and children or from in- and outside the classroom).
- Specify the voices (or contexts for those voices) from a particular text or event that includes multiple cultural perspectives/contexts (e.g., different characters from a story, figures in a historical event, positions on a socio-scientific issue).

- Specify that the voices students use must be their own, from different contexts: How does their voice overlap, differ, or even conflict with the voice of the person they are writing to? How would their voices change from one situation to another? What do those voices have to say to one another?

4. **Multi-Genre Discussion:** On their own or in groups, students can contribute to a discussion using a variety of modes, including nonverbal (e.g., write a comment on a sticky note, draw a picture, create a skit or human tableau).

   Rationale: Based on the premises that students learn through different means[14] and that expressing their learning in multiple forms will provide a richer, more compelling experience for an audience,[15] this approach allows students to participate in ways that are easiest for them, drawing on their home and out-of-school communication practices, and provides the class with an engaging variety of contributions related to the topic at hand.

   Variations:
   - Specify the genres that students can or must use to contribute: for example, since school contexts typically favor writing and speaking, consider limiting students to drawing or enacting their responses (followed by verbal explanations, if necessary) in order to push them beyond their comfort zones.
   - Encourage or require subsequent participants to take up or add to ideas, images, gestures, or words that others have contributed; for example, if one student or group has drawn a gesture of refusal, ask others to incorporate this image into their responses.

5. **Audience Participation:** During whole-class discussion, invite students to speak to audiences (real or imagined) beyond their immediate classroom community.

   Rationale: Research has suggested that student writers should be encouraged to craft school assignments for "authentic audiences" beyond the classroom.[16] Speakers might similarly be encouraged to participate in classroom discussions with out-of-school audiences in mind.

   Variations:
   - Invite actual audience members from different cultural groups in your local community to attend (or even participate in) a whole-class discussion in your classroom.

- Ask students to imagine multiple audiences from different backgrounds or perspectives as they participate in whole-class discussion; invite them to consider how they might appeal to or involve those audiences.

REFLECTIONS FOR TEACHERS

1. In a *New York Times* article on culturally responsive pedagogy, author Matthew Lynch proposes that, "Before seeking out knowledge about the cultures of the diverse students that they will be teaching, educators must first investigate their own heritage, upbringing, and potential cultural and racial biases." Consider how your own cultural background might affect your participation in discussion:
    a. To what cultural groups do you belong? You might consider common cultural markers like age, ethnicity, gender, nationality, race, or sexual orientation.
    b. What do you know about conversational customs in these cultural groups?
    c. What resources might you consult to learn more about cultural expectations for conversation among those groups?
    d. How does your own conversational style conform with or depart from those expectations?
2. Consider how cultural background might affect the participation of one or more of your students (or classmates) in whole-class discussion:
    a. To what cultural groups does the person/people belong?
    b. What do you know about conversational customs in these cultural groups?
    c. What resources might you consult to learn more about cultural expectations for conversation among those groups?
    d. How does the conversational style of the person/people seem to conform with or depart from those expectations?
3. Given your responses to the previous questions, how might your own conversational style and expectations for participation in discussion compare to those of others? Make a list of conversational moves that you and your students/classmates might understand differently (e.g., you might begin with pacing, overlapping talk, and disagreement and also consider nonverbal moves like posture and

eye contact). What do these differences suggest to you about explicit guidelines a teacher might provide for students?
4. The University of Pittsburgh houses a series of classrooms built to reflect the cultural values and contributions of different nationalities (see https://www.nationalityrooms.pitt.edu/). Acknowledging that a single example may not be representative of a culture, what does the setup of each of these rooms suggest to you about different cultural expectations for classroom conversation? What do you think about the setup of your own classroom (or one in which you participate as a teacher or a student)? In what ways are your students' expectations for classroom conversation based on the classroom environment?
5. Recall or imagine a time when whole-class discussion of a controversial cultural topic went well or poorly in your classroom as a teacher or a student. Apart from the content, how might the form of the discussion have contributed to its success or failure? For example, disagreement may be more challenging for some speakers because of age, ethnicity, gender, race, or sexual orientation.

EXPLORATIONS WITH STUDENTS

1. Invite students to consider how their participation in cultural groups outside the classroom might affect their participation in whole-class discussion:
    a. How would you describe conversations among people in your family?
    b. How would you describe conversations among people of your age?
    c. How would you describe conversations among people of your ethnicity?
    d. How would you describe conversations among people of your gender?
    e. How would you describe conversations among people of your nationality?
    f. How would you describe conversations among people of your race?
    g. How would you describe conversations among people of your sexual orientation?

h. To what other cultural groups (groups with shared interests, values, and practices) do you belong? How would you describe conversations among people of those groups?
   i. How do your answers above compare to how conversations occur in classrooms?
2. Invite students to consider a particular aspect of conversational style (e.g., pacing, volume, overlapping talk, length of turns, frequency of turns, audience participation, storytelling, irony/joking, questioning, and active listening).
   a. Based on your experiences in our classroom, how would you describe this aspect of our conversations?
   b. Based on your experiences outside our classroom, how does the way you participate compare to how others participate?
   c. What (if anything) about this aspect of conversation makes it easy or hard to participate in our class?
   d. What (if anything) could you or others do to make it easier to participate in our class?
3. Invite students to recall or imagine a time when whole-class discussion of a controversial cultural topic went well or poorly in your classroom (or another classroom). Apart from the content, how might the form of the discussion have contributed to its success or failure? For example, disagreement may be more challenging for some speakers because of age, ethnicity, gender, race, or sexual orientation.
4. On your own or with students, find examples of conversations in the media or popular culture (e.g., panel interviews, political debates, talk shows). How are the rules, roles, relationships, and possible responses in these conversations similar to or different from those in classrooms?

Conversation in Class	Conversation in Media/Pop Culture
Rules	
Roles	
Relationships	
Possible Responses	

5. On your own or with students, find examples of conversations in online spaces. How are the rules, roles, relationships, and possible responses in these conversations similar to or different from those in face-to-face situations?

Conversation in Online Forum	Conversation in Face-to-Face Situation
Rules	
Roles	
Relationships	
Possible Responses	

CHAPTER SUMMARY

- Students' participation in whole-class discussion may differ based on their prior experiences with cultural language practices outside the classroom.
- Not only the content, but also the form of whole-class discussions (e.g., those forms in which speakers can disagree) can invite or discourage students' participation when it evokes cultural language practices.
- Not all members of a cultural group will share familiarity with a cultural language practice.
- Rather than merely replacing one set of assumptions and norms with another, teachers should reflect on their own cultural experiences with discussion and invite students to do the same as they collaborate to create a shared culture regarding classroom talk.

NOTES

1. D. Tannen, "'Don't Just Sit There—Interrupt!': Pacing and Pausing in Conversational Style," *American Speech* 75, no. 4 (2000): 393–95.

2. J. J. Gumperz, *Discourse Strategies* (Cambridge, UK: Cambridge University Press, 1982).

3. A. D. Grimshaw, *Conflict Talk* (Cambridge: Cambridge University Press, 1990); D. Tannen, *The Argument Culture* (London: Virago, 1998).

4. D. Hess, *Controversy in the Classroom: The Democratic Power of Discussion* (New York: Routledge, 2009); W. C. Parker, "Listening to Strangers: Classroom Discussion in Democratic Education," *Teachers College Record* 112, no. 11 (2010): 2815–32.

5. B. Johnstone, "Variations in Discourse: Midwestern Narrative Style," *American Speech* 65, no. 3 (1990): 195–214; J. Liska and V. Hazleton, "Deferential Language as a Rhetorical Strategy: The Case for Polite Disagreement," *Journal of Social Behavior & Personality* 5, no. 3 (1990): 187–98.

6. Deborah Schiffrin, "Jewish Argument as Sociability," *Language in Society* 13, no. 3 (September 1984): 311–35; M. B. Sherry, "Indirect Challenges and Provocative Paraphrases: Using Cultural Conflict-Talk Practices to Promote Students' Dialogic Participation in Whole-Class Discussions," *Research in the Teaching of English* 49, no. 2 (2014): 141–67; L. E. Jordan, "Social Construction as Tradition: A Review and Reconceptualization of the Dozens," *Review of Research in Education* 10 (1983): 79–101; W. A. Corsaro and T. A. Rizzo, "Disputes in the Peer Culture of American and Italian Nursery School Children," in *Conflict Talk: Sociolinguistic Investigations of Arguments in Conversation*, ed. A. D. Grimshaw (Cambridge: Cambridge University Press, 1990).

7. Geneva Smitherman, *Talkin and Testifyin: The Language of Black America* (Boston: Houghton Mifflin, 1977).

8. Z. N. Hurston, *Mules and Men* (Philadelphia: J. B. Lippincott Company, 1935); Henry Louis Gates, *The Signifying Monkey: A Theory of Afro-American Literary Criticism* (New York: Oxford University Press, 1988); Smitherman, *Talkin and Testifyin*; Geneva Smitherman, *Talkin That Talk: Language, Culture, and Education in African America* (New York: Routledge, 2000); G-J. Masciarotte, "'C'mon Girl': Oprah Winfrey and the Discourse of Feminine Talk," *Genders* 11 (1991).

9. Sherry, "Indirect Challenges"; Dale E. Peterson, "Response and Call: The African American Dialogue with Bakhtin," *American Literature* 65, no. 4 (1993): 761–65.

10. M. C. O'Connor and S. Michaels, "Aligning Academic Task and Participation Status through Revoicing: Analysis of a Classroom Discourse Strategy," *Anthropology & Education Quarterly* 24, no. 4 (1993): 318–35; Erving Goffman, *Forms of Talk*, University of Pennsylvania Publications in Conduct and Communication (Philadelphia: University of Pennsylvania Press, 1981); V. N. Voloshinov, "Reported Speech," in *Readings in Russian Poetics: Structuralist*

and Formalist Views, ed. L. Matejka and K. Pomorska (Cambridge, MA: MIT Press, 1971).

11. C. Mitchell-Kernan, "Signifying, Loud-Talking, and Marking," in *Rappin' and Stylin' out; Communication in Urban Black America* (Urbana: University of Illinois Press, 1972), 309–30; M. Morgan, "Conversational Signifying: Grammar and Indirectness among African American Women," in *Interaction and Grammar*, Studies in Interactional Sociolinguistics 13 (Cambridge and New York: Cambridge University Press, 1996), 405–34; Jordan, "Social Construction as Tradition."

12. Morgan, "Conversational Signifying"; Mitchell-Kernan, "Signifying, Loud-Talking, and Marking"; Teun A. Van Dijk, *Discourse as Social Interaction* (London: SAGE, 1997), 151–52.

13. P. Fleischman, *Joyful Noise: Poems for Two Voices* (New York: HarperCollins, 2013).

14. Howard Gardner, *Frames of Mind: The Theory of Multiple Intelligences*, 10th anniversary ed. (New York: BasicBooks, 1993).

15. T. Romano, *Blending Genre, Altering Style: Writing Multigenre Papers* (Portsmouth, NH: Boynton/Cook, 2000).

16. V. Purcell-Gates, N. K. Duke, and J. A. Martineau, "Learning to Read and Write Genre-Specific Text: Roles of Authentic Experience and Explicit Teaching," *Reading Research Quarterly* 42, no. 1 (2007): 8–45; P. Slagle, "Getting Real: Authenticity in Writing Prompts," *The Quarterly* 19, no. 3 (1997); N. K. Duke et al., "Authentic Literacy Activities for Developing Comprehension and Writing," *The Reading Teacher* 60, no. 4 (2006): 344–55.

6

Developing Dialogic Discussions over Time

John interrupted, "Yeah, when my older brothers are home and everyone's talking at the dinner table—forget about it! I can't get a word in edgewise!"

"Speaking of that, have you both had time to share?" I asked, raising my eyebrows and looking meaningfully at John.

"Oh, sorry," he said, turning back to Miriam.

I circled the room, checking in with each group. "This is your two-minute warning," I said, flashing two fingers at each pair of students.

Previous chapters have suggested that students' participation in classroom conversations might be influenced by their prior experiences with other classroom activity genres, with other academic disciplines, and with cultural expectations for out-of-school language practices. Across these contexts, time is an important factor. Moreover, activity genres are flexible: even the same activity can change over time as participants become more familiar with the rules, roles, relationships, and available responses (and with each other). This chapter asks how dialogic, whole-class discussions can change and develop over time.

THE POWER OF NARRATIVE

Because this chapter focuses on changes to the same activity across lessons in the same classroom, it draws on the concept of **narrative**, or the sequencing of related events over time.[1] Of course narratives—stories—are often the subject of whole-class discussions, especially in disciplines like literature and history. Moreover, we saw in chapter 4 that even in other subject areas like math and science, teacher and students often animate other speakers through a technique like revoicing ("So you're saying . . ."), casting them as characters in narratives of classroom events, even those of an unfolding discussion. And as chapter 5 suggested, how those narratives characterize students can also influence their participation:[2] a provocative paraphrase ("Wait, but Kevin said they deserved it!") can call a student back into the conversation to defend his position.[3]

The opposite is also true, as anyone knows who has experienced this as a teacher or student. There are negative effects to being characterized, repeatedly and collectively, as a "pushover," a "tough grader," a "teacher's pet," or a "problem student" over the course of a year. In the vignette above, the teacher's comment and pointed look implied that John hasn't given Miriam time to share. While this might be true, it is a characterization that connects with John's resistance earlier in the lesson, as well as his own narrative about being ignored by his father and not having time to speak at the family dinner table. Over time, narratives that emerge during whole-class discussions can intersect with how other events beyond the class period position students, potentially affecting not only the unfolding of classroom events, but also students' relationships to the teacher and to the subject matter,[4] as the following examples illustrate.

Take a turn

In your own experience as a teacher or a student, how have you been characterized by emergent storylines in class discussions over time? How was that characterization positive/negative? How (if at all) did it affect your relationship to the subject matter? How (if at all) did it intersect with your out-of-school identities?

"A WHOLE LOT OF STORIES TO TELL": HOW NARRATED EVENTS CAN SHAPE CLASSROOM EVENTS

Recall the lesson in Mr. Weber's ninth-grade history class during which two dialogic discussions emerged from imaginative entry activities in which students elaborated hypothetical scenarios based on historical events. In the first activity, students imagined a present-day invasion of their hometown of Talbott as a means of better understanding the past invasion of Belgium as part of the German army's WWI Schlieffen plan. In a second activity during the same lesson, students imagined digging a trench on the football field to engage in a war with a rival class, using this hypothetical situation to better understand historical events associated with trench warfare. Figure 6.1 (below) shows how changes in verb tense and pronoun use suggest the following patterns in these two interactions from the same lesson in Mr. Weber's ninth-grade Talbott history class.

First, a prologue using present tense and "they" (referring to the characters in the historical event) prompted the teacher to propose a fantastical "What if . . . ?" scenario about unlikely or unrealized events, using the conditional mood (as in, "what would it be like?"). That scenario sequenced events in a narrative that simultaneously invoked a historical past event and a hypothetical present event. In that hypothetical narrative,[5] speakers initially used conditional "would" and pronouns like "we" or "our" to position themselves in relation to the action. As the narrative progressed, the present tense also appeared, and speakers used "you" and "I." The narrative ended with a return to past tense and "they."

The patterns presented in Figure 6.1 were emergent: none were explicitly proposed or directed by a single participant.[6] Nevertheless, speakers in both discussions made coordinated shifts in verb tense and pronoun use that followed a similar progression from past to present tense and from "they" to "you/I" during both hypothetical narratives. Similarly, both examples contained conflicting but related details that suggested different perspectives on the historical/hypothetical events: in the first example, students imagined that the army's presence would inspire people to "follow them" and "freak out," to flee and to "fight them," and to feel threatened and "safe"; over the course of the second example, life in the trenches was described as "claustrophobic," "powerful," "safe," "cold," "hot," "with all your friends," "hungry," "tired," "trying to fight," "going to get sick," and "waiting." These shifts in verb tense and pronoun use suggest that, through the juxtaposition of historical and hypothetical events, the past may have become more present and personal for students.

Moreover, their first-person participation in the hypothetical narratives may have been encouraged by their disagreement about the nature of the

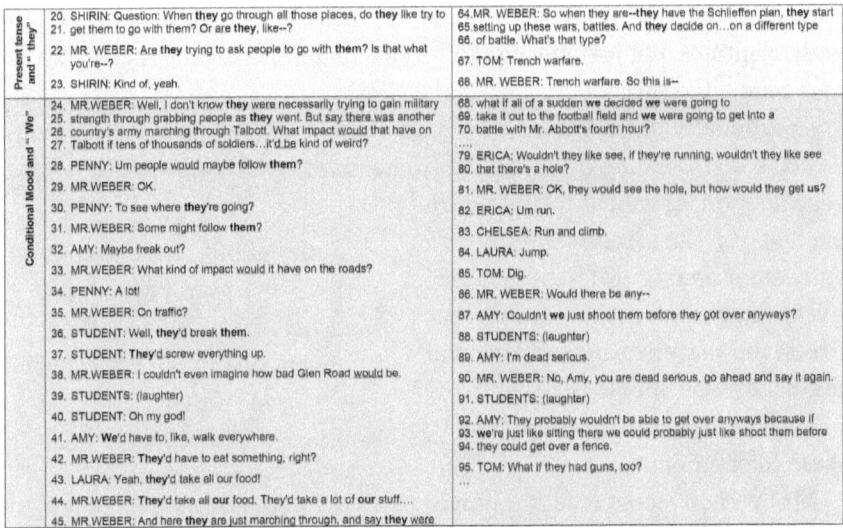

Figure 6.1. Shifts in verb tense and pronoun use during dialogic, whole-class discussions of the Invasion of Talbott/Belgium and of Football/Trench Warfare. (Verbs are underlined and pronouns bolded; shading indicates progression toward more present, personal uses of language.)

narrated event, as they imagined it from multiple "insider" perspectives rather than elaborating an authoritative account from a single, "objective" point of view.[7] Further, this disagreement seemed to exert an influence on subsequent turns in the discussion as speakers responded to different perspectives on the imagined events with contradicting phrases like "wouldn't they . . ." and "yeah but . . ." (lines 79–81, 87–95, 113–15). In both examples, the juxtaposition of events and of conflicting perspectives thus seemed to promote further discussion.

Additionally, the regularities of verb tense and noun/pronoun use suggested a coordination of the telling of the narrative among speakers. This coordination, as well as the influence exerted on the discussion by disagreement among different perspectives, suggested a relationship between the narrative interactions and the classroom activities. Figure 6.2 represents the relationship among these interactions:

> Think about a class in which you participate as a teacher or a student. What conventions have emerged over time in that classroom culture, without any one person ever defining them explicitly? How might this classroom culture relate to how students participate in whole-class discussion?

Mr. Weber recognized the power of narrative to engage students with history and encourage their participation in his class. "I want them to ask questions beyond the book. . . . US history is not in a red book that thick. There's a whole lot of stories to tell." In these examples, the juxtaposition of past and present and of narrative interaction and classroom activity produced positive results, but the examples that follow are not as successful. Next, I describe conversations in two subsequent lessons

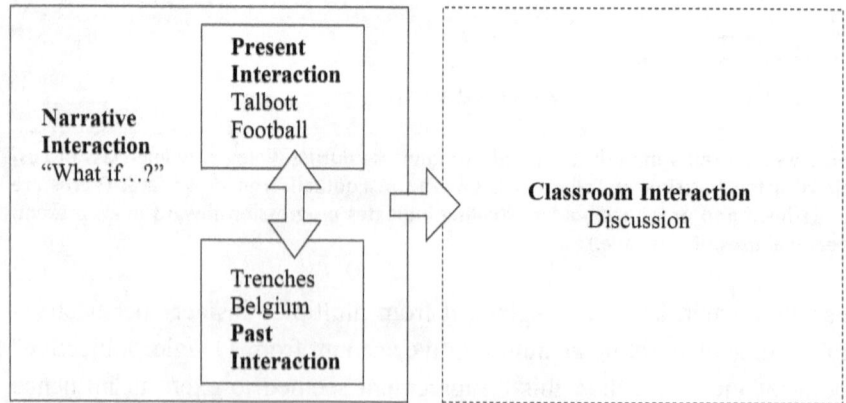

Figure 6.2. Relationship between narrative interactions and classroom interactions during Invasion of Talbott/Belgium and Football/Trench Warfare conversations.

that, while they contained features recognizable as belonging to the same activity genre, did not result in dialogic, whole-class discussions. Their similarities and differences compared to these first two examples are important to understanding the development of this emergent genre, as well as its relative success or failure at producing dialogic discourse.

THE STOCK MARKET CRASH: COLLAPSING INTO THE PAST

A second example from Mr. Weber's class occurred during a November lesson on the 1920s "Black Tuesday" US stock market crash. During the lesson, Weber intended to "begin the class by reminding the students of the [stock market simulation] game that we played over the past two days" and then "begin discussing the nature of the Great Depression, and some causes/effects in brief." However, Weber and his students soon departed from this "reminder" to attempt a clarifying explanation. A complete transcript appears in Figure 6.3 below, followed by description of the features of this interaction and the relationship between narrated events and the classroom activity.

This example began with a student question, and with an open-ended inquiry, rather than a query with a single right answer—both factors that usually prompt dialogic discussions[8]—about the stock market crash (line 1). In response to Victoria, Weber once again proposed a hypothetical scenario as a means of clarifying the historical event: "Say you guys together, you had most of the Rylant stock. Now in a real company . . ." (lines 8–9). However, this hypothetical scenario differed from the previous ones in animating students as figures in a generic reenactment of the historical event. Students were simply cast as buyers and investors in a typical stock market exchange. That is, there was no simultaneous comparison between a past event and a present context that might have been more familiar to students, and so little opportunity for them to contribute from their own perspectives.

The lack of relationships between students' contemporary experiences and the historical event being elaborated seemed to influence the subsequent classroom interaction. This influence can be seen in Matt and Whitney's responses (lines 23–32), which were short and hesitant. The brevity and tentativeness of these responses suggested that they were attempting

Authentic student question	1. VICTORIA: How are [stockbrokers] getting any money off of it? They're 2. just giving people help.
Hypothetical scenario about a past event that has already happened	3. WEBER: OK. Very good point. So it works like this. Uh, we're going to go 4. with Tom right here.... You owned a lot of Rylant stock [during the stock 5. market simulation game], right? 6. TOM: Yeah, me and Jon had like eight of them. 7. WEBER: Eight of them? So, in the very beginning though, we're just going 8. to start in the beginning. Say you guys together, you had most of the Rylant 9. stock. Now in a real company, a big company like Rylant, if you own the 10. majority of the stocks, in a situation like that, all of a sudden they start- 11. they're very interested in what you think, because when you own stock, 12. like,that certificate proves that you own part of that company. I-I think 13. you guys understood that as we went through it, right? You are buying 14. into that company. So if all of a sudden if you guys combined had like 15. fifty-one percent of it they're really interested in what you have in what 16. you have to say about Rylant Motors. 17. OK. So the problem we have here is that Tom starts taking partial 18. money from Matt because...Whitney is lending money to Matt.... Now, 19. Matt, you still have like zero dollars to your name, right? You don't have any 20. money, you just own that stock and the stock keeps going up, and you're 21. pretty happy about it. Now all of a sudden, Whitney, you need your money, 22. right? Because he owes you money. So what do you do?
Recitation	23. WHITNEY: Ask him to turn it in? 24. WEBER: You ask him for it. And Matt, Whitney comes up to you and says, 25. "Can I have my money please?" And what do you pay her with? 26. MATT: The stock? 27. WEBER: You could. Maybe. Whitney, do you want stock? You're a bank. 28. WHITNEY: No? 29. WEBER: You want money right? 30. WHITNEY: Yeah. 31. WEBER: Matt, she's not taking your stock. What are you going to do? 32. MATT: Turn it in. 33. WEBER: Now all of a sudden people...start losing money. Because now the 34. bank is dependent on the company and the company is dependent on the 35. bank. And you get caught in the middle.
Closing	36. AMY: Is that why it all crashed? 37. WEBER: That is a good part of why it crashed. 38. AMY: Because it was like all built on itself but nothing was really there?

Figure 6.3. Hypothetical scenario in which a factual conditional narrative (about an event that *has already happened*) resulted in recitation. Lighter to darker shading indicates progression from open question to more constrained recitation-style question-and-answer.

to guess the answer Weber was looking for. Despite their participation in the stock market simulation the day before, they had limited means of relating to the interaction between lender and investor being described. In short, though this interaction began with an open-ended, higher-order thinking (O-HOT) question—often a means of disrupting IRE/F and promoting dialogic discussion—and also included a hypothetical scenario that cast students as imagined participants, the resulting conversation bore more resemblance to a typical, teacher-led recitation than to discussion.

Closer attention to the conversational features of this interaction reveals further comparisons. Like the Invasion of Talbott/Belgium and Football/Trench warfare examples, this narrative used a conditional "if . . . then . . ." (lines 9–11, 14–16), inviting students to imagine themselves into a hypothetical situation about a stock market exchange. And like the previous examples, it began with a similar prologue and launching of the narrative using present tense and "they" before shifting into use of conditional "would." But unlike the two prior examples, which featured events known to be fictional, the situation Weber proposed was a **factual conditional narrative**, retelling events that had, in fact, taken place leading up to the stock market crash. In this narrative, although students were cast as first-person participants, they could not draw from their own experiences as investors or lenders and thus could not take up multiple, conflicting perspectives on the event. And although this narrative moved from conditional to present tense and used "you/I," those verbs and pronouns were used by Weber to narrate on behalf of students, rather than by students to provide progressively more individualized impressions of the event. Thus, although it resembled the previous two examples, this conversation's features, overall, seemed to emphasize a single, authoritative interpretation of the historical event through participation in a hypothetical reenactment of that past interaction.

I do not mean to devalue this interaction as an attempt to clarify the dynamics of the historical event. Indeed, Amy's response at the end of the hypothetical scenario suggested that she had achieved a better understanding of "why it all crashed" (lines 36–38). However, this hypothetical scenario did not answer Victoria's initial question about how stockbrokers benefited. Moreover, although it began with a student question, this interaction did not result in dialogic, whole-class discussion. While dialogic discussion is not necessarily an end in itself, the lack of it here suggested that students' inquiry was no longer the center of classroom talk during this activity. Perhaps discussion did not occur because there was little relationship between speakers and the event under study: the way students were positioned in the narrated event (as investors and lenders in the stock market exchange) did not promote their participation in the classroom interaction. That is, their participation as figures in the narrative did not encourage them to participate in whole-class discussion.

Perhaps Weber assumed that students' participation in the stock market simulation had endowed students with more first-hand expertise and insight. Or perhaps, given his prior success with using a "what if . . ." scenario, he expected students to engage differently with this hypothetical narrative. Who among us has not relied without question on a previous experience with a classroom activity genre? Yet all genres echo with multiple voices from the past that both support and constrain how participants interact.[9] Students slipped quickly into teacher-led recitation, perhaps still more used to chapter review questions than to discussion of a hypothetical scenario. But small variations in the nature of an activity over time can make a big difference, as the next example illustrates.

> **Take a turn**
> Recall a time in your own experience as a teacher or a student when an activity related to whole-class discussion failed because students were "too far" from the content under discussion. How might the activity have been recast to make the subject more present and personal?

COLLECTIVE BARGAINING: MERGING WITH THE FUTURE

During a December lesson on the Roosevelt era, Weber's goal was "for the students to gain a contextual understanding . . . of FDR's new deal," including "how everyday people would feel effects." Students had answered a series of warm-up questions about the previous night's textbook chapter, and as Weber reviewed the answers with them, he stopped to explain the 1935 Wagner Act, and the concept of collective bargaining, by calling on Mary (a student whose last name also happened to be Wagner).

As in the previous examples, this activity occurred during review of textbook questions students had answered as part of their homework the night before. Thus Weber's exchanges with Mary and Tom about collective bargaining (lines 2–11) followed the IRE/F pattern (teacher *I*nitiates a question, student *R*esponds, teacher *E*valuates or *F*ollows-up),

Developing Dialogic Discussions over Time 113

Recitation	1. MR. WEBER: ...that's something that the Mary Wagner Act helped do. Thank you, 2. Mary, for your time helping all workers like that. Now explain why the Mary 3. Wagner act was important. Besides the fact that it had your last name. 4. MARY: Because it protected the right of workers to form unions and engage 5. in collective bargaining with their employers. And also it prohibited unfair 6. labor practices. 7. MR. WEBER: This was a big effort of the second hundred days...and workers, 8. looking more at workers, trying to protect workers a little more, and um, 9. collective bargaining, do you guys know what it is? 10. TOM: Something that a union does?
Hypothetical scenario about an event likely to happen	11. MR. WEBER: There you go. Uh, it's something that a union does, quite often it's 12. why a union is so strong: they can bargain as a group. It's the reason why, like, 13. if I tell you we have a test next Thursday—
Breakdown of the classroom interactional frame	14. AMY: For real? 15. MR. WEBER: You see how I combined— 16. PENNY: Are you serious? ... [student worker delivers attendance slips] ... 18. PENNY: But we can use our notes. 19. AMY: For real? 20. WEBER: See— 21. AMY: Are we able to? 22. TOM: No. 23. WEBER: No. 24. AMY: Oh. 25. WEBER: We're going to talk more about it when we get there, but this would 26. be a perfect example of collective bargaining: Penny, you said we should be 27. able to use our notes, right? OK, I value your opinion a lot, but if you get all 28. thirty people in the room all of a sudden that voice is— 29. TOM: Let's take a vote. 30. AMY: Yeah, can we take a vote on—? 31. WEBER: (speaking in higher voice) It's not even voteable. 32. (shrugging) I'm sorry, I'm very cruel. 33. TOM: I'm going on strike. 34. STUDENTS: (laughter) ...
Closing	[Weber regains control of the class] ... 45. WEBER: Many times a company would not hear people's single voices or 46. people coming up and saying "Hey you guys should pay us more" they're like 47. "yeah yeah" but... um, you, as more people get involved with something, all 48. of a sudden the voice gets stronger, and that's something that the Mary 49. Wagner Act helped do. Thank you, Mary, for your time helping all workers like that.

Figure 6.4. Activity in which a factual conditional narrative (about an event that is *likely to happen*) resulted in breakdown of the classroom activity.

implementing a recitation-style recall of what students already knew. And as before, preliminary exchanges about an actual historical situation during this review were followed by the proposal of a hypothetical "What if . . . ?" scenario meant to clarify the event. As in previous lessons, this

"What if . . . ?" scenario proposed a transformation of the activity genre from one in which the teacher posed review questions for students to answer from their reading of the textbook to one in which a hypothetical scenario—in this case, Weber bargaining with his students about a test—would be juxtaposed with a historical event in order to explain the Wagner Act.

Students took up this proposal, animating themselves as figures in the hypothetical/historical scenario. In this case, Penny asserted that students should be able to use their notes during the test (a practice teachers at Talbott High School sometimes allowed), and thus took on the role of negotiator (line 18). Details that participants contributed to this hypothetical scenario conditioned and constrained subsequent contributions. Penny's negotiation led to Weber's response about strength in numbers (lines 26–28) and Tom's call for a vote (line 29). In this way, some details of the emergent narrative interaction exerted influence on its subsequent elaboration, illustrating the historical concept of collective bargaining. In contrast with the previous example, the narrated interaction empowered students in the classroom interaction: in their roles as union workers, students continued to attempt to bargain even after Weber tried to postpone (line 25) and discourage (lines 31–32) negotiation.

At the end of the narrative, Weber's comments made explicit this connection between the present negotiation over the guidelines for the test and a generic past event made possible by the establishment of the Wagner Act. So this interaction, in which Weber's "what if . . . ?" proposal was taken up by students and elaborated with details that illustrated collective bargaining, referred simultaneously to both a hypothetical event and a generic historical one. The resulting interaction was emergent: it could not be attributed solely to Weber's proposal, Penny's negotiation, or Tom's resistance.

As in the previous examples, the features of this collective bargaining conversation included shifts in verb tense and pronoun use that implied changes in the participants' relationships to the historical event. From the past tense (lines 1–8) and "workers" (lines 7–8) to the conditional "if . . . " (lines 13, 27) and the pronoun "we" (line 13), the scenario quickly shifted to one in which Weber and students were positioned as "you" and "I" (lines 26–27, 33) in a present-tense negotiation about whether students would be able to use their notes during the test. And at the end of the narrative, Weber transitioned back to the use of past tense and "they" (line 46).

These shifts in verb tense and pronoun use resembled the genre patterns in the preceding examples. However, the collective bargaining conversation ended quickly and, like the stock market conversation, did not result in dialogic, whole-class discussion. And though conflicting perspectives appeared on the issue of whether students could use their notes, the conflict seemed less like productive disagreement over interpretations of the past event (as in the Invasion of Talbott/Belgium and Football/Trench Warfare examples), and more like a breakdown of the classroom activity. Though the narrative event and the classroom activity were related, as in previous examples, that relationship did not promote dialogic, whole-class discussion.

The failure of this activity about collective bargaining to produce dialogic, whole-class discussion may have been affected by the fact that, unlike the previous example, the proposed hypothetical scenario concerned an actual, future event: the class *did*, in fact, have a test scheduled for next Thursday. Amy's repeated "for real?" (lines 14, 19) and Penny's "are you serious?" (line 16) suggested that they were not sure initially about the relationship between hypothetical and actual events. Indeed, Weber's response (line 15) may have been an attempt to explain how he was combining past and present. This uncertainty regarding the relationship between the hypothetical event and actual classroom events is unlike the previous example, in which students seemed to understand and accept the stock market exchange as a hypothetical reenactment of a past event. This uncertainty may be explained by the fact that this narrative sequenced events that, though hypothetical because they had not yet taken place, were also *likely to happen* in the context of Weber's classroom. In this way, the collective bargaining narrative was another factual conditional narrative like the one generated about the stock market crash, in which the events under discussion had *already happened*.

Further parallels between the narrative figures and students' actual roles may also have contributed to overlap between narrative interaction (collective bargaining about a test) and classroom interaction (explanation of collective bargaining). For example, though student Mary Wagner has no actual relation to the senator, Robert F. Wagner, who originated the National Labor Relations Act (or "Wagner" Act), her name was used in association with the legislation. Penny Novak, who took on the role of negotiator, was not only an obvious choice because she is an outspoken student and because she had already made an assertion (not a question!) on behalf of the students ("But you can use your notes"), but also because she is the daughter of the superintendent of schools for Weber's district (a fact that Weber mentioned in a post-lesson interview). In short, both students had roles in the narrative that also reflected, to a greater or lesser degree, aspects of their actual identities in Weber's class.

In this respect, the factual conditional narrative in this collective bargaining example differed from the one about the stock market. In the stock market narrative, the hypothetical scenario seemed to collapse into a past event that *had* actually happened; that is, the explanation of the crash became little more than a reenactment of the past. In contrast, the collective bargaining narrative's hypothetical scenario merged with a future event that *would* actually happen: that is, the illustration of collective bargaining became an actual negotiation about the future. Both activities differed from the examples about the Invasion of Talbott/Belgium and about Football/Trench Warfare, which seemed to balance past with present (and narrated event with classroom interaction) in a way that allowed for dialogic, whole-class discussion. Regardless of their result, these two conversations seemed to depend on the nature of the narrated events being addressed—and how those narratives constructed students' relationships to past events and to class members. Moreover, these two "failed" attempts to generate dialogic, whole-class discussion also suggested explorations of the boundaries of a developing genre.

> **Take a turn**
> Recall a time in your own experience as a teacher or a student when an activity related to whole-class discussion failed because students were "too close" to the content under discussion. How might the activity have been recast to allow them more distance on the objective?

THE BERLIN/CAPITAL CITY AIRLIFT: HYPOTHETICAL NARRATIVE AND THE BALANCE OF PAST AND PRESENT

A final example of the development of this dialogic, whole-class discussion genre took place during a lesson in March. The lesson addressed the post–WWII division of Germany and Berlin that led to Stalin's blockade of the Western part of the city and forced the Allies to fly in supplies. Weber's lesson plan called for students to "open up their books to 'The Berlin

Airlift,' . . . read the page out of the book, and summarize it in three to four sentences. Ask students to volunteer to read their sentences. Discuss. Move onto the smartboard note packet that was worked on the day before. Pick back up on the Berlin Airlift." Thus, Weber's lesson plan, as in the preceding examples, proposed the activity as a recitation-style review of textbook information. A complete transcript appears in Figure 6.5, below.

Present tense and "They"/ "We"	1. SHIRIN: So. Um does are--Why <u>are</u> **we** there? 2. Since it's like Communist and everything? 3. WEBER: Why <u>were</u> **we** in Germany to start with? 4. SHIRIN: In Berlin. 5. WEBER: OK. After World War II, it <u>was</u> <u>decided</u> that the fairest way to make 6. sure that Germany wouldn't reconsolidate power and start World War III 7. would be if each Ally took a zone of Germany. And then when **they** <u>were</u> 8. <u>trying</u> to figure out who should get Berlin, it <u>was</u> <u>decided</u> it's not fair, Berlin 9. is—if
Conditional Mood and "We"	9. , if **we're** talking about [**our** state] it <u>would be</u> like [a major industrial 10. city]. Or actually I guess **we'll** say [the capital city]. It's closer. And the 11. capital. We'll say it's like [the capital city].... It's not fair, right? If one section 12. of the state…if someone <u>got</u> [the capital city].... say you, Laura, Takara, and 13. Amy <u>were</u> <u>dividing</u> up the state, right? It's not fair if just you get [the capital 14. city] right? … 26. WEBER: So **we** <u>would</u> need to supply from here to **our** [part of the city]. 27. …What if they shut off the roads? Closed the railroads? 28. LAURA: OOOH! 29. TAKARA: How <u>would</u> **we** get supplies?
Present Tense and "You"	30. WEBER: Shirin, if **you** <u>have</u> that part of--if **you** <u>have</u>, **you** <u>know</u>, this general 31. area of [the state]. What's the advantage of closing it off so that the other 32. three girls <u>can't get</u> 33. into the city? 34. SHIRIN: That **you** <u>have</u> it. They <u>can't get</u> in. …. 47. AMY: Why <u>can't</u> **you** fly? 48. DAVE: So. What's **our** one solution, Amy? 49. AMY: Fly. 50. DAVE: **You** <u>have to fly</u> supplies in. Berlin airlift? Alright.
Past tense and "They"	51. PENNY: That's what **they** <u>did</u>, didn't **they**? 52. DAVE: That's exactly what **they** <u>did</u>.

Figure 6.5. Shifts in verb tense and pronoun use during dialogic, whole-class discussion of the Berlin/Capital City Airlift. (Verbs are underlined and pronouns bolded; shading indicates progression toward more present, personal uses of language.)

During the explanation of the division of Berlin, a student, Shirin, asked for clarification about why a city that was clearly located in the Eastern (Soviet) half of the country would also need to be divided between East and West (lines 1, 4). In response to Shirin's question, Weber proposed a "what if . . . ?" scenario that compared the past event to a hypothetical situation set in a fantastical, contemporary context (lines 9–14). This proposal transformed the sharing of textbook summaries into an activity that animated students as figures in a hypothetical scenario. That hypothetical scenario paralleled post–WWII events in Germany.

As in previous examples, students took up the proposed hypothetical scenario, elaborating it with details that enabled and constrained subsequent responses. Some of the proposed details became established features of the scenario: for instance, Takara's question about the desperate conditions (line 29) seemed to prompt Amy's solution (line 47). From Shirin's point of view, however, the blockade was an advantage (line 34); the narrative thus contained multiple, even conflicting perspectives on the event. And as before, comments by Weber and students at the end of the narrative suggested that these details applied simultaneously both to the present, hypothetical event and to the past, historical one. Neither Shirin's initial query, nor Weber's proposed scenario, nor Takara's question alone were solely responsible for the emergent scenario. So what began with a review of textbook summaries about the Berlin airlift emerged as a dialogic, whole-class discussion.

As in the first two examples, this conversation sequenced unrealized events that were *unlikely to happen*—a **fictional conditional narrative**. The narrative that unfolded contained a pattern of shifts in verb tense and pronoun use. As in the October narrative about an army marching through Talbott, Shirin's question, in present tense (line 1), acted as prologue. Weber's response shifted from past tense (lines 5–8) and "they" (line 7) to the conditional "would" and to "we" (lines 9–11). From Takara's "How would we get supplies?" (line 29), to Shirin's "You have it. They can't get in" (line 34), and Amy's "Why can't you fly?" (line 47), verb tense shifted from conditional to present tense, and use of pronouns shifted from "we" to "you." At the end of the narrative, Weber and Penny's comments returned to using past tense and "they" (lines 51–52). This progression from past to present to past, and from "they" to "you" to "they" resembled that of the first two dialogic, whole-class discussions. As in those prior examples, this progression suggested that the past became more present and personal for the students during the course of the activity.

Additionally, students' participation in the narrative interaction affected their participation in the interaction of the discussion, much as in the earlier examples. As figures in the narrative, students were able to contribute from their own first-person perspectives, like Takara, who wondered how they would get supplies, or Amy, who proposed flying as a solution. Participation in the narrated events thus shaped students' participation in the classroom interaction of the discussion. While this was also true of the Stock Market and Collective Bargaining examples, the way students were animated in those narratives produced resistance, perhaps because the narratives were either too far or too close with regard to the classroom interaction. In this respect, the dialogic, whole-class discussion about the Berlin/Capital City airlift most resembled those about the Invasion of Talbott/Belgium and about Football/Trench warfare: In all three, the narrated event affected the discussion, promoting participation through a balance between elaboration of a fantastical, hypothetical event and an actual, historical one.

In a post-lesson interview, Weber revealed that he had thought carefully about selecting a city with which to make this juxtaposition between actual past and hypothetical present.

> [I thought about using] the Vatican . . . just that idea of it's not fair if one person gets the Vatican. Not in a religious way, I just mean the Vatican city state. . . . But . . . I knew Vatican wasn't going to work. Then I moved to [the state capital] because . . . we had already done Washington, DC. Um, so I just had to pick something that was, that was relevant. . . . And I skipped the potential dividing of Talbott because that undermines the fact that it's a big city.

Weber first considered comparing the post–WWII division of Berlin to what it would be like to divide up Vatican City, hoping that comparison to this more familiar, contemporary example would help students to better understand the historical event. However, he discarded this idea, as well as that of using Washington, D.C., another important, contemporary city perhaps more familiar to the experiences of American students. Weber also decided not to make a comparison to the division of Talbott. From his point of view, it was important that the comparison not "undermine the fact that it's a big city." In short, the choice of a contemporary setting (and students' relationship to it) was important to the narrative of the hypothetical/historical event. Weber's reflections suggested that he, too, was aware of the delicate balance between narrated interaction and classroom interaction, and the potential impacts of selecting a comparison that was either too far or too close to students' experiences.

Here, the emergence of a dialogic, whole-class discussion about the Berlin/Capital City airlift depended on specific features of that interaction, and the relationship between the narrated event and the classroom interaction of the discussion. Unlike the November Stock Market conversation and the December Collective Bargaining conversation, whose hypothetical situations seemed to collapse into a reenactment of the past and merge with an anticipated future, respectively, the Berlin/Capital City airlift discussion appeared most like the initial October examples in overlaying a fantastical, contemporary context on a historical event. However, all the examples exhibited features whose similarities suggested variations on a developing dialogic discussion genre.

STORIED SUBJECTS IN DIALOGUE

In classrooms, activity genres—including those associated with whole-class, dialogic discussion—can develop over time, just as they do in relation to an academic discipline or an out-of-school cultural community. As dialogic discussion genres develop across time, narratives may emerge that position teachers and students in relation to the subject matter and to one another.[10] One might think of these narratives, composed collectively over time through classroom conversations as the "story/ies of the class." Indeed, each of us contributes to that collective story from our own experiences and perspectives, composed from our histories in and outside classrooms.[11] We are all stories in dialogue.

ACTIVITIES FOR DEVELOPING
DIALOGIC DISCUSSION GENRES OVER TIME

1. **Warm-Up: "Let's Do the Numbers":** Together, the class counts in order from 1 to the number of people in the classroom (e.g., 25) or

higher. There is no specified order: someone adds the next number in sequence whenever the opportunity arises. Each person who says a number cannot say another until everyone has participated. When any two people say a number at the same time, the count returns to zero.

Rationale: By practicing this warm-up at the beginning of class over time, students learn to participate by listening and building on what others have already said, rather than simply waiting to be called on or following a prespecified order. (Note: most groups suggest an order after experiencing the initial frustration of returning repeatedly to zero.)

Variations:
- Increase the challenge by asking students to avoid trying to say the same number each time (another common attempt to routinize, rather than to listen carefully).
- Invite students to close their eyes (while this sounds more challenging, it often makes the task easier by requiring heightened awareness).

2. **Warm-Up: Imaginary Painting:** Ask students to imagine a blank canvas (a blackboard works well). On this canvas, each subsequent speaker adds details to an imaginary painting (no actual drawing takes place). Additions must build on what has already been added and cannot "overwrite" previous contributions. (For example, if someone has added "clouds in a blue sky," the next person cannot say, "The sky turns dark and stormy" but can instead add "rain falling from one of the clouds.") At the end, students all imagine signing their names at the bottom of the imaginary canvas.

Rationale: As students add more details to the painting, a collective vision begins to emerge (a day at the beach, a final exam, a zombie apocalypse), and this vision invites and constrains subsequent additions. Practicing this activity over time, students learn to adapt their contributions to a collective vision.

Variations:
- Encourage students to be specific about their additions ("what kind of clouds?" or "a soft rain or a thunderstorm?").
- Begin with a prespecified scene or theme: "Chapter 6"; "Our school"; "Family."

- Instead of a prespecified order of contributors (going around the room), invite students to add a detail whenever they feel moved to do so (see "Let's Do the Numbers").
3. **Seminar:** The seminar is a genre of whole-class discussion whose purpose, according to history education researcher Dr. Walter Parker and his colleagues, is to explore different interpretations of a topic, issue, or artifact.[12] Over time, students can practice (and evaluate) how well this purpose has been accomplished during whole-class discussion.

    Variations:
    - "Socratic Seminar" (also see chapter 3): This student-led classroom discussion activity genre often includes two groups—one that engages in student-led discussion and one that watches and evaluates—with these groups periodically switching roles.
    - "Seminar Leaders": Students take turns facilitating (individually or in groups) the seminar, with participants evaluating whether and how the purpose was accomplished and how well facilitators supported accomplishing it.
4. **Deliberation/Inquiry Dialogue:** In this genre of whole-class discussion, students attempt to resolve a problem[13] or reach consensus about "the most reasonable answer" to open-ended and even controversial "big questions."[14] Over time, students can practice and evaluate how well this purpose has been accomplished during the conversation.

    Variations:
    - Elementary education researcher Dr. Alina Reznitskaya and her colleagues have developed an "Argument Rating Tool" that teachers and students might use (separately or together) during and after an inquiry dialogue lesson to evaluate their performances regarding four elements of "argument literacy": (1) consideration of multiple perspectives; (2) clarity of language and structure of arguments; (3) acceptability of premises; and (4) validity of inferences.[15]
5. **Closing: Discussion Exit Tickets:** At the end of a discussion, ask students to answer questions about the form/process of the discussion: What did they learn? Was it effective? How so? Why or why not?

Rationale: Unlike a traditional exit ticket, used by the teacher to assess what students have learned during a class period, this routine serves as a self-evaluation for students, as lesson evaluation for teachers, and as an opportunity over time for further metatalk about the development of effective classroom activity genres. Because the exit ticket is individual and can be anonymous, students may be more likely to share honest appraisals or reactions to characterizations of class members and content.

Variations:
- "Give and Get": Invite students to reflect on their contributions and the relative effectiveness of the discussion by asking, "What did you give today? What did you get today?"
- "Enjoy/Learn" graph: At the end of a discussion, provide a handout with (or invite students to draw) an X-Y axis (an L-shape) with "Enjoy" at the top left and "Learn" at the bottom right. In the space between, students can put a dot that represents their experience during the discussion and explain why beneath the graph (changes in the experiences of individuals or the class can be tracked over time).

6. **Closing: Thank-You Notes:** At the end of a discussion, students write an anonymous thank-you note to someone whose participation made a particular difference to them during that conversation and explain why; the teacher collects these notes and distributes them at the beginning of the next class period.

Rationale: Over time, students become more aware of how their own and others' participation shapes their experiences during whole-class discussion. Teachers can monitor students' notes for the purpose of their own lesson evaluation as well as to ensure that no negative comments are being made.

REFLECTIONS FOR TEACHERS

1. Reread the transcripts from Mr. Weber's class in this chapter.
    a. Pick one of the variations on the dialogic discussion genre that emerged over time. What might Mr. Weber have changed in order to achieve a different outcome? Imagine and then discuss or

write out an alternative transcript, explaining how and why it is different.
   b. Consider your own relationship to the academic discipline you (will) teach. Are there classroom conversations you recall when the academic content felt "too far" from or "too close" to your experience? What happened?
   c. Choose one classroom conversation activity genre that you've experienced regularly as either a teacher or a student during a single class over time. How, if at all, did this activity genre vary over time? What happened over the course of the semester or the year as you participated in it?
   d. Choose one classroom discussion activity genre that you've enjoyed (or hated) participating in regularly as a teacher or a student across multiple classes over time. Why do you find that activity genre especially enjoyable (or detestable)?
2. Consider a class in which you have participated as a teacher or a student:
   a. What implicit rules developed over time as you and others participated in classroom conversations? How, if at all, did those rules change from the beginning to the end of the semester or school year?
   b. Over time, certain people probably became established in particular roles (perhaps the most basic being those who participated a lot and those who didn't). What did you or others do (or not do) to contribute to the creation of those roles during classroom conversations? What might you or others have done (or not done) to construct them differently?
   c. How did the class construct your relationship to the academic discipline under study? (For example, was it a daily climb up a lonely mountain? a race to be run with a team?) How did the classroom conversations contribute to that relationship? How might that relationship have been constructed differently?
   d. How did the class construct your relationship to other class members and/or the teacher? (For example, were they co-conspirators? competitors? guides? fellow prisoners?) How did the classroom conversations contribute to that relationship? How might that relationship have been constructed differently?

e. What kinds of responses did you come to understand were possible/impossible or appropriate/inappropriate in classroom conversations over time? (For example, could you disagree? make a personal observation? express confusion? make a joke?) How did you come to that understanding about how to participate? What might you or others have done differently to encourage other kinds of responses?

EXPLORATIONS WITH STUDENTS

1. Ask students (individually or in groups) to describe, draw, or enact how whole-class discussions position them in relation to the subject matter of a class.
2. Ask students (individually or in groups) to describe, draw, or enact how whole-class discussions position them in relation to other class members and the teacher.
3. Invite students to describe the *explicit* and *implicit* rules, roles, relationships, and possible responses available to them during whole-class discussions in your classroom:

Activity Elements	Explicit	Implicit
Rules		
Roles		
Relationships		
Responses		

4. Invite students to choose one classroom conversation activity routine that they've experienced regularly during your class over time and write, draw, or enact the "story of that activity routine." How, if at all, has this activity genre changed over time? What happened over the course of the semester or the year as they participated in it?
5. Ask students to articulate the purposes of the different kinds of classroom conversations you engage in during a semester or year. What is one move they can make to accomplish each purpose? How

well has each purpose been accomplished during a lesson/week/semester/year?

CHAPTER SUMMARY

- Classroom discussion activity genres are flexible: even the same activity can change over time as participants become more familiar with the rules, roles, relationships, and available responses (and with one another).
- Whole-class discussions often include narrative talk (sequencing of related events) that can explicitly or implicitly characterize students and position them with regard to the subject matter and to other class members.
- Attempts at whole-class discussion may fail when they position students as "too far" from or "too close to" the subject under study.
- Opportunities to fail may be important for teachers and students as they engage in, explore, and discover variations on whole-class discussion genres that emerge in a particular classroom culture over time.

NOTES

1. William Labov, *Language in the Inner City: Studies in the Black English Vernacular* (Philadelphia: University of Pennsylvania Press, 1972).

2. S. Wortham, *Learning Identity: The Joint Emergence of Social Identification and Academic Learning* (Cambridge and New York: Cambridge University Press, 2006); S. Wortham, *Narratives in Action: A Strategy for Research and Analysis* (New York: Teachers College Press, 2001); S. Wortham and A. Reyes, *Discourse Analysis beyond the Speech Event* (New York: Routledge, 2015).

3. M. B. Sherry, "Indirect Challenges and Provocative Paraphrases: Using Cultural Conflict-Talk Practices to Promote Students' Dialogic Participation in Whole-Class Discussions," *Research in the Teaching of English* 49, no. 2 (2014): 141–67.

4. Wortham, *Narratives in Action*; Wortham, *Learning Identity*; Wortham and Reyes, *Discourse Analysis*.

5. Elinor Ochs and Lisa Capps, *Living Narrative: Creating Lives in Everyday Storytelling* (Cambridge, MA: Harvard University Press, 2001).

6. R. Keith Sawyer, "Improvisation and Narrative," *Narrative Inquiry* 12, no. 2 (2002): 319–49; R. Keith Sawyer, "Emergence in Sociology: Contemporary Philosophy of Mind and Some Implications for Sociological Theory," *The American Journal of Sociology* 107, no. 3 (2001): 551; R. Keith Sawyer, *Improvised Dialogues: Emergence and Creativity in Conversation* (Westport, CT: Ablex Pub., 2003).

7. G. S. Morson, *Narrative and Freedom: The Shadows of Time* (New Haven: Yale University Press, 1994); G. S. Morson, "Sideshadowing and Tempics," *New Literary History* 29, no. 4 (1998): 599–624; Simone Schweber, *Making Sense of the Holocaust* (New York: Teachers College Press, 2004); Ochs and Capps, *Living Narrative*.

8. M. Nystrand et al., *Opening Dialogue: Understanding the Dynamics of Language and Learning in the English Classroom* (New York: Teachers College Press, 1997); M. Nystrand et al., "Questions in Time: Investigating the Unfolding Structure of Classroom Discourse" (Albany: National Research Center on English Learning and Achievement, 2003).

9. James V. Wertsch, "Narratives as Cultural Tools in Sociocultural Analysis: Official History in Soviet and Post-Soviet Russia," *Ethos* 28, no. 4, History and Subjectivity (2000): 511–33; James V. Wertsch, *Voices of Collective Remembering* (Cambridge and New York: Cambridge University Press, 2002).

10. Wortham, *Narratives in Action*; Wortham, *Learning Identity*; Wortham and Reyes, *Discourse Analysis*.

11. D. Holland et al., *Identity and Agency in Cultural Worlds* (Cambridge, MA: Harvard University Press, 1998).

12. W. C. Parker, "Classroom Discussion: Models for Leading Seminars and Deliberations," *Social Education* 65, no. 2 (2001): 111–15; W. C. Parker and D. Hess, "Teaching with and for Discussion," *Teaching and Teacher Education* 17, no. April (2001): 273–89.

13. Parker, "Classroom Discussion"; Parker and Hess, "Teaching with and for Discussion."

14. A. Reznitskaya and I. A. G. Wilkinson, *The Most Reasonable Answer: Helping Students Build Better Arguments Together* (Cambridge, MA: Harvard Education Press, 2017).

15. Reznitskaya and Wilkinson, *The Most Reasonable Answer*; I. A. G. Wilkinson et al., "Toward a More Dialogic Pedagogy: Changing Teachers' Beliefs and Practices through Professional Development in Language Arts Classrooms," *Language and Education* 31, no. 1 (2017): 65–82.

7

Designing Dialogic Online Discussions

I circled the room, checking in with each group. "This is your two-minute warning," I said, flashing two fingers at each pair of students.

Then, raising my voice I called the partner pairs back to whole-group discussion. "So you've been discussing with a partner about times when you and someone else felt like you were talking past each other. I see that some of you also posted about this to our class's online forum: that both Romeo and Juliet were misunderstood by their parents and even their friends. Does anyone want to comment?"

"Hashtag My Life!" said someone from the back of the room. Laughter rippled through the class.

"Wait, where was that post?" asked Miriam. "I didn't even see that!"

Chapter 5 suggested that students' affiliation with cultural communities beyond school spaces could shape their participation in whole-class discussions. Those out-of-school groups might have (largely implicit) shared values, attitudes, and practices regarding certain interactions, like disagreement, that could align or conflict with academic or disciplinary conventions. So some students might find it easy to participate in whole-class discussions, while others might feel unwelcome or uncertain about how to voice their contributions. Chapter 6 addressed time as a factor in the development of dialogic discussion genres. This chapter considers the influence on students' participation in dialogic, whole-class discussions of another contextual factor associated with space and time: online discussion forums.

NEW POSSIBILITIES?

In schools, online discussions allow teachers and students to interact with the curriculum and with one another outside the space and time of the classroom. This possibility has led web developers and course management systems to offer secondary schools a variety of platforms for facilitating online discussions. Evaluations of these platforms have appeared in prior research on facilitating online discussions: some studies have addressed the benefits and challenges of using digital tools to invite discussions.[1] As the vignette above suggests, digital discussion tools have the potential for students to contribute image and video, as well as voices and text, to a shared online space. Other researchers have found that specific spatial and temporal features of online discussion forums, like anonymity and asynchronicity, can change the way students interact, offering new possibilities for self-presentation and reflection.[2]

OLD WINE?

Analyses of more conventional conversational moves like types of questions and uptake have also appeared in studies of online discussions. In online forums, teacher questions can encourage participation from multiple students when those open-ended questions spark higher-order thinking; teachers' closed, lower-order thinking discussion prompts can likewise block student participation in online discussions.[3]

Consider the following example from an online discussion among US ninth-grade English language arts students. The teacher had organized "online Literature Circles" composed of groups of students who had chosen the same book from a list of options. Each group had its own online discussion forum—and group name—for conversations about the book in a private online network moderated by a prospective teacher (one of several assigned to this host teacher's virtual classroom). In her first post to one of these groups, prospective teacher Ms. Kelly wrote:

> What does our group name mean?? Without looking up the actual definition, I want you to define the word "sesquipedalian" (sehs-kwih-ped-al-ee-ehn), what YOU think it means.
>
> - Provide a "dictionary-like" definition.
> - Use the word in a creative, fun, comical sentence (you may use complementary sentences to give us context clues).
> - Post your answers as discussion entries under this topic.
> - Most of all—HAVE FUN with this! This assignment is completely yours, it's all about what YOU think. (The more of YOU that you put into it, the better it will be!) Be creative, have fun, and just be you!
>
> After you all have replied, I will post the actual definition to the discussion board and you can see how close you were! (So please, please, please don't look up the definition until we're done!)
> Thank you all for your participation!

Despite Ms. Kelly's exhortations to "be you" and her assurances that the assignment was "completely yours," students were not fooled, as Figure 7.1 illustrates.

Students recognized in this prompt a closed, lower-order thinking (C-LOT) question: why put more of oneself into a task if the teacher would just post the "actual definition" at the end?

Despite their apparent convenience and popular appeal, online forums can easily reproduce the patterns of familiar off-line activity genres, like recitation. But whereas that pitfall of classroom conversation and student resistance to typical patterns of teacher-led Q&A are not new, the example above also hints at some important differences about the affordances and constraints of online discussions.

ONLINE DISCUSSIONS AND DIGITAL WRITING

First, online discussions typically occur in writing. Written responses in cyberspace lack verbal resources like tone and facial expression. Instead,

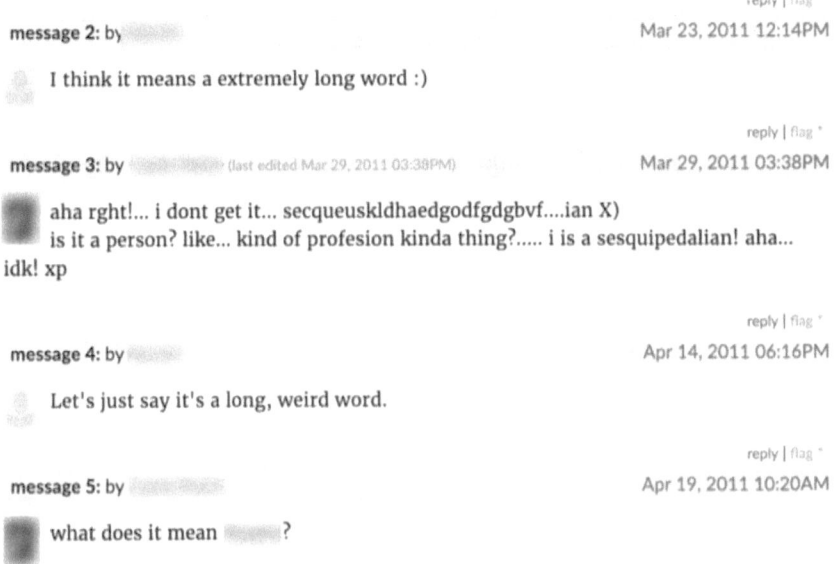

Figure 7.1. Student resistance to recitation in an online discussion.

the first student to reply in Figure 7.1, above, used a digital facial expression—:)—to subtly convey her ironic resistance to the prospective teacher's C-LOT question. Although such nonverbal moves can lead to miscommunication, students can also include other media—links, images, and video—in their posts to online discussion forums, which may open new possibilities for self-expression and relevance beyond the classroom.[4]

You may also have noticed apparent "errors" in students' written responses above. Though the written quality of online discussions may be a deterrent for struggling readers and writers, it can also increase participation from less outspoken students[5] and allow contributors more time to thoughtfully compose responses without interruption.[6] And as in most face-to-face discussions, regulating word choice and syntax is less important than encouraging participation, so unless the purpose of the online discussion is to generate academic text for a subsequent assignment, we might consider letting go of the impulse to require and evaluate the use of formal language and grammar. In fact, the use of informal language and other visual features (like emojis) may be one way writers attempt to build rapport with one another in the absence of verbal resources like tone of voice and facial expressions.[7]

The example above also illustrates how time and space in online (written) discussions can function differently from face-to-face conversations. Student four's response was quite similar to student two's, as if the writer had not read the previous posts. Although online discussions can extend beyond the bounds of a single class period and classroom, responding asynchronously may mean that students are less likely to read through the volume of other posts.[8] Indeed, because written responses over time must also be organized in space within online discussion forums, the design of such forums, and how they represent the connections among participants' posts, is paramount.[9]

ONLINE GENRES AND VISUAL PRINCIPLES

In online spaces, as in other social situations, patterns of communication emerge and become types, or genres. For example, researchers have identified at least two types of online discussions. The genre of **threaded discussions** organizes contributors' posts into a vertical list, or "thread," related by the same topic (see Figure 7.2).

Topic
- *Response1*
  - Reply1.1
  - Reply1.2
- *Response2*
  - Reply2.1
  - Reply2.2

Figure 7.2. A model of threaded discussion.

In a threaded discussion, responses to a topic and subsequent replies are often organized into a linear hierarchy. The resulting conversation thus begins to resemble a list/outline.

A second genre, **anchored discussions**, locates or "anchors" participants' posts near particular moments of the text on which the discussion focuses (see Figure 7.3).

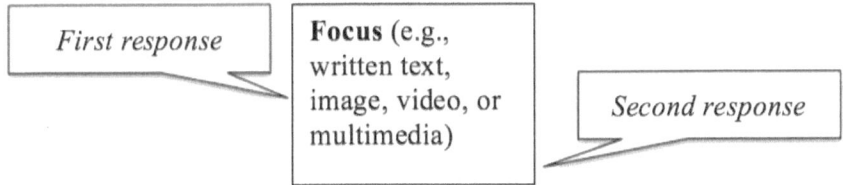

Figure 7.3. A model of anchored discussion.

In an anchored discussion, responses and replies cluster around parts of a text, image, or video. An anchored discussion thus comes to resemble annotations of the focal text.

Of course, not all online forums look alike, and web designers and users may adapt/repurpose them in combination with other genres. As in the classroom, participants shape online genres through their contributions, and genres also support and constrain users' participation in online spaces.[10]

One way in which online genres shape users' participation is through their visual features. Because online genres change quickly, the examples that follow focus not only on broad types (like threaded or anchored discussions), but also on principles of visual design that may apply across online genres and their variations.

For example, **contrast** is a principle of visual rhetoric that relates elements through differences in size, color, font, format, or style. In Figures 7.2 and 7.3, bold formatting creates contrast that distinguishes the central topic/focus from other responses in both online discussion genres. A second principle, **repetition**, relates elements through similarity of size, color, font, format, or style. In Figures 7.2 and 7.3 above, the use of italics for all responses relates them as a category. A third principle, **alignment**, relates elements in space by using lines and indents. In Figure 7.2 above, all responses to an overarching topic are aligned, and replies to those responses are further indented to show hierarchy. Finally, **proximity** relates elements in space by arranging them near others that are relevant. In Figure 7.3 above, responses are arranged in proximity to the moment of the text/focus to which they relate.

*C*ontrast, *R*epetition, *A*lignment, and *P*roximity are not superficial "window-dressings," despite the unfortunate acronym;[11] these principles of visual design allow users to see connections across multiple elements and thus to discern and participate in emerging patterns of meaning, much as one must do during a face-to-face discussion.

The examples below focus in particular on moments when these two strands (conversational techniques and visual features) intersect: when do typical features of dialogic discourse in face-to-face discussions (O-HOT questions and uptake) complement or conflict with the visual rhetoric of the online platform (contrast, repetition, alignment, and proximity)? How do these intersections allow and inhibit participation in online discussions?

UNRAVELING THREADED DISCUSSIONS

The next excerpt came from the same popular, school-friendly social network introduced above, in which users post reviews and responses about literature, including recently published young adult novels. Posts and responses appear in the vertical list characteristic of threaded discussions. One feature of this online forum allowed users to form public or private groups dedicated to discussion of certain books (or types of books), rather like online book clubs or Literature Circles. One such small-group conversation is the focus of the example that follows, in which another prospective secondary English teacher, Ms. Jenkins, collaborated with the host teacher to facilitate online exchanges among a group of ninth graders over a two-month period about the book they had chosen to read together. The ten students in this group had chosen *Breaking Point* by Alex Flinn. *Breaking Point* describes the experiences of Paul Richmond at a private school where he falls under the spell of charismatic and unscrupulous Charlie Good.

Figure 7.4, below, depicts an excerpt from this online book club's conversation. As in prior chapters, analysis of this excerpt first attends to the classic moves that characterize dialogic discussions: types of questions and follow-ups used by participants.

Following some initial introductions, explanations, and general instructions, Ms. Jenkins (whose icon includes the label "Mod" for "moderator") responded to a student's post (message 18), affirming his reaction and asking a follow-up question. Her response (message 19) used uptake, referring to the student's initial post and quoting his evaluative phrase

message 18: by   Apr 20, 2011 05:43PM

At first I thought the book was going to be bad, but ever since I got into it, I REALLY got into it. I think the weird things in the book that make it good.

reply | flag *
message 19: by   Apr 20, 2011 06:18PM

wrote: "At first I thought the book was going to be bad, but ever since I got into it, I REALLY got into it. I think the weird things in the book that make it good."

I'm glad to hear that! I agree, things definitely started to get crazier as the book progressed. What about the book helped you to get into it/make it good?

reply | flag *
message 20: by   Apr 21, 2011 05:29AM

wrote: ". wrote: "At first I thought the book was going to be bad, but ever since I got into it, I REALLY got into it. I think the weird things in the book that make it good."

I'm glad to hear that! ..."

I think davids dog is decapitated

Figure 7.4. An excerpt from a threaded discussion.

"make it good." Her follow-up on his evaluation posed an open-ended, higher-order thinking (O-HOT) question that invited this student (and others) to elaborate, and this question produced a subsequent response from the same student (message 20) about the grisly details of the mystery that had made it engaging for an adolescent audience. An analysis using types of questions and uptake thus explains the success of this initial exchange.

However, in this next sequence (Figure 7.5, below), the visual features of this online discussion forum began to intrude on the interaction.

Following Ms. Jenkins' exchange with one student (messages 18–20), two others posted questions. In her next post (message 25), the teacher attempted to respond to all three students, taking up aspects of their posts and asking provocative follow-up questions like "Do you agree?" and "What do you think will happen?" Despite the presence of student questions, O-HOT teacher questions, and teacher uptake, subsequent speakers (e.g., message 26) did not respond to one another, thereby sustaining a whole-class, dialogic discussion. Instead, each new post became increasingly disconnected from the preceding ones.

An analysis of visual features of the forum in which this excerpt occurred begins to explain this breakdown. In this forum, when a user responded to a previous post, that previous post was quoted in italics

I'm glad to hear that! ..."

I think davids dog is decapitated

---

message 21: by   Apr 23, 2011 05:47PM

i wondered y St. John didn"t hang out with them anymore?

message 22: by   Apr 23, 2011 05:48PM

I also wondered how sent the note to Paul?

message 23: by   Apr 23, 2011 05:50PM

wrote: " wrote: "I have read the entire book and thought it was quite interesting
I have no life"

Haha that doesn't mean you have no life! I liked it too! Now that you've finished it..what did you ..."

I thought why charlie or the other guy didn't get in trouble for the bomb?

message 24: by   Apr 25, 2011 01:06PM

After the mailbox scene will the guys at Paul's school stop bullying him?

message 25: by   Apr 25, 2011 01:13PM

, yep..you're right. I thought that scene was terrifying. Do you agree?

Mod , good questions. Neither of those are really clarified in the book. The author is probably leaving them open for a suspenseful effect. From your knowledge of the characters, what do you think the answers are? And both are punished for the bomb..but are they given equal punishments?

, that's a good question. If you had to take a guess, what do you think will happen?

message 26: by   Apr 25, 2011 02:46PM

i wonder why the main character decided to go along with charlie and his friends.... i guess he had no other choice

Figure 7.5. A threaded discussion begins to unravel.

above the response. While this repetition of the previous post would seem to emphasize and perhaps even promote uptake, the italics did not provide enough contrast to distinguish the repeated material from the new response. Moreover, this repetition had the effect of visually pushing the respondent's comment further down the page, distancing that comment from the one to which it responded. This decrease in proximity between the two responses was exacerbated when other, unrelated posts intervened.

So a user like the first student who posted would have had to read down through four subsequent posts by other students to recapture the "thread" of connection between his post and the teacher's uptake and follow-up question. In addition, he would have had to distinguish the quoted material of previous posts from the new material of another user's response. Other, similar discussion-forum platforms address this problem by using the visual principle of alignment.

Unlike those in this platform, responses to an earlier post are indented from, as well as grouped in proximity to, a previous comment in order to create a clear "thread" of related responses. Despite Ms. Jenkins' exemplary use of open-ended, higher-order thinking questions and uptake in her responses to students' posts, this threaded discussion unraveled because of the repetition of prior posts without adequate contrast to distinguish new material from old, and the lack of proximity and alignment to show connection among a post and subsequent responses.

WEIGHING ANCHORED DISCUSSIONS

A second example focuses on a conversation that took place on a commercial website that allows users to comment on uploaded videos. Posts in this anchored discussion connected to specific moments of the video, appearing as white dots on the video timeline below the viewing window. Below this timeline, posts also appeared in a blog-style list to which users could respond in threads to others' contributions. For graduate students in a teacher education course, this online forum served as a means to share and reflect on videos of teaching, attending to specific interactions in a classroom, without having to visit the school where the lesson transpired. In this particular online discussion, the video under review depicted a teacher leading an activity about story elements using a plot diagram written on the white board (the same excerpt from Mr. Schulz's class that appears in chapter 2).

Figure 7.6, below, shows an excerpt from this online discussion of the video. The first response appears as a white dot on the timeline below the video. This response also evoked a reply from a subsequent user.

Figure 7.6. An excerpt from an anchored discussion.

In her response to the video, a graduate student commented on the teacher's use of a plot diagram, and his question to the class in the video, "What does this remind you of?" She posted, "I like the simple diagram he drew first, however, when a student said that the diagram reminds him of a mountain, I thought 'what does a mountain have to do with this lesson?' I feel the teacher should have explained the purpose of this diagram and how it connects to story elements." Although this respondent posed a question, it did not appear to be O-HOT: on its own it seems rhetorical—not requiring a response—and simply a report of what she had already thought.

However, when combined with her imagined alternative for what the teacher might have done, it evoked a reply. That reply also took up the first respondent's use of an imagined alternative, offering another possibility for what the teacher in the video might have done: "Or perhaps he could have somehow built on the idea of a mountain to talk about the action rising to a climax, then descending to a resolution." In terms of types of questions and uptake, this first exchange was successful at promoting dialogue.

Below the video timeline, posts also appeared in this forum as a vertical list (see Figure 7.7, below). However, unlike the previous example, in this discussion forum the most recent posts (or replies to a post) appeared at the top of the list, regardless of the moment of the video to which they

Designing Dialogic Online Discussions 139

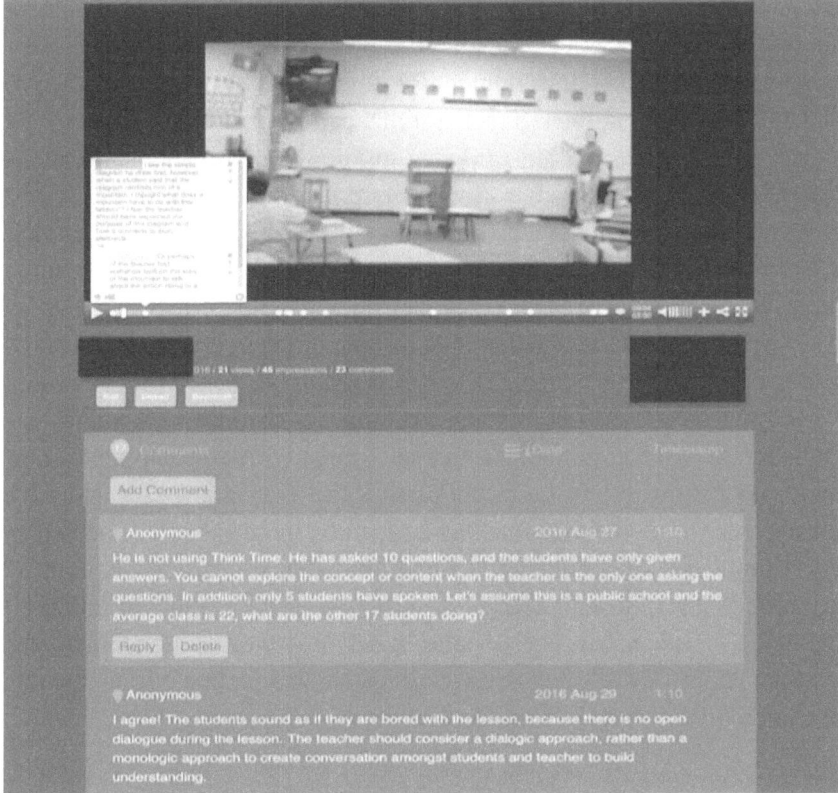

Figure 7.7. An anchored discussion fails to launch.

pertained (though a time-code appears in the post's top right corner). Thus this initial exchange was relegated to the end of the list and at the top appeared a more recent response and reply from later in the video.

Despite the obvious clustering of responses around certain moments, these and other exchanges all stopped after two turns (one response and one reply). Across twenty-three comments, this activity never resulted in dialogic exchanges among three or more people.

An analysis of visual features of this online forum using the principles of contrast, repetition, alignment, and proximity begins to explain this pattern. In the first exchange (Figure 7.6), although the reply appeared directly under and indented from the response it addressed, it did not appear as a separate dot on the timeline, nor did it modify the original dot in any way (e.g., by turning it a different color). Put differently, while the response and reply appeared in proximity and their relative alignment showed hierarchical connection, there was no repetition or contrast on the timeline to distinguish this moment for other users.

So unless they put their cursors on this particular dot (see Figure 7.6), subsequent users would have no way to know that this moment had already generated an exchange. And while promoting the most recent post to the top of the list below the video timeline highlighted recent activity, this organization also meant that subsequent users would likely see posts made later in the video before they had watched that far themselves.

Other sites have attempted to address this problem by causing posts to open or appear as each new user moves through the "text," thus revealing visually the accumulation of comments at particular moments as they become relevant. That is, moments that have already received multiple comments contrast with less annotated parts of the text. In this case, although the opportunity to anchor comments to specific moments of the video produced multiple, student-generated questions that were each taken up by a subsequent respondent, neither of these conversational moves produced dialogic discussion. The lack of contrast and repetition, to set off moments at which multiple users had already responded and replied, meant that this anchored discussion never quite found its moorings.

A NOTABLE ALTERNATIVE

Analysis of a third example addresses a discussion that occurred on a platform that allowed users to generate online "sticky-notes," to type into those notes, to arrange them on a limitless canvas, and to change their color and size. Although not originally intended for that purpose, the platform resembles an emerging online genre of "mapped" discussion forums that allow users to add notes, icons, and even drawings and images to a "landscape" or "mind map."[12]

When class cancellations due to weather made it impossible for them to meet face-to-face, freshman composition students used this forum to dialogue about their research projects, as well as two related readings: (1) an ethnography called *My Freshman Year* about anthropology professor Cathy Small who enrolled as a student in her own university to study college life; and (2) Shirley Brice Heath and Brian V. Street's *On Ethnog-*

raphy, a guide for researchers learning this methodology. An initial note instructed students to use a different color each time they introduced a topic and to choose the same color (and arrange their notes next to a related post) when responding to an existing topic. The resulting discussion (see Figure 7.8, below) resembled a collage of comments about students' reactions to the readings and concerns about conducting research.

The discussion began with the prompts in yellow at the top left. ("So what would you like to discuss about the readings so far? Do you have questions? Comments? A personal experience to relate? Agree? Disagree?") These questions invited students to agree or disagree by bringing their own experiences into relationship with the readings, an O-HOT invitation that many of the respondents took up in their posts. Indeed, phrases like "I agree," "I have to agree," "I completely agree," and "I felt the same way," appear in fourteen of the twenty-seven posts in this discussion. Students also disagreed: the orange notes at the bottom left emerged when

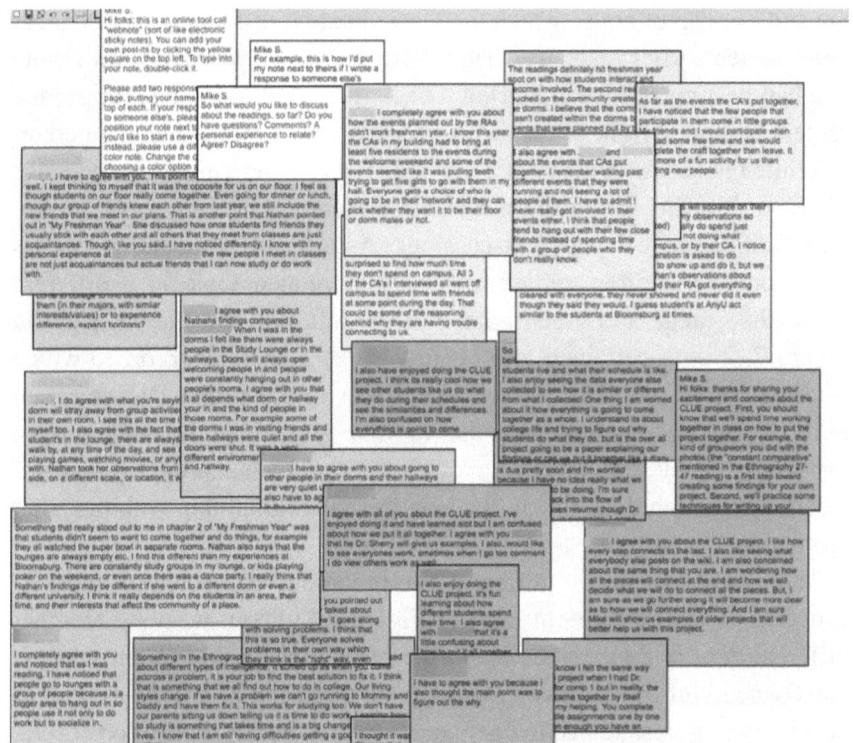

Figure 7.8. A mapped discussion using online sticky notes.

one student took issue with findings in *My Freshman Year*, writing that "I find this different than my experiences. . . ." Subsequent replies added additional anecdotes about students' own lives at Hillside University.

Moreover, students posed questions that provoked multiple responses: for example, the purple notes at the bottom right featured questions about students' research projects, particularly "how we will decide what we will do to connect all the pieces" once they had collected surveys, observations, and interviews about their own and others' freshman experiences, inspired by *My Freshman Year*. Conversational features like O-HOT questions and uptake thus contributed to the success of this dialogic discussion.

Visual features also explain the success of this online discussion, despite some drawbacks of this forum. Contrast and repetition made it easy for students to distinguish among topics of different colors and to connect their replies to other responses by using the same color. Proximity to other related notes also encouraged students to connect replies to earlier responses. One drawback to this use of proximity was the eventual crowding and overlap of notes, which may have made it difficult for subsequent users to see earlier responses. However, they could also click on a note that had become hidden and bring it back to the top of the pile, or use the "filter" at the top right of the forum to show only notes of a certain color.

While the lack of alignment made it difficult to determine the sequence of responses, this forum did not create a hierarchy among posts and replies, unlike most threaded discussions. As a result, students' responses about one topic often verged into another related topic in a different color: the orange and green notes (on the left side and the top right in Figure 7.8) both pertained to moments of *My Freshman Year*, to which students connected their own experiences with dorm life. Disagreement in the orange notes sparked another topic in gray about the reading from *On Ethnography,* and how "everyone solves problems in their own way" when interpreting data, much like new freshmen grappling with the adult problems of college life.

These exchanges about different interpretations connected to students' concerns in purple (bottom right in Figure 7.8) about weaving together different data in their research. So the discussion in this forum was the most successful of the three: contrast and repetition of colors, as well as proximity of notes, helped to distinguish and connect responses on several topics. Though proximity and a lack of alignment made for a less orderly discussion, the lack of hierarchical threads or chronologic anchors made it easier for students to connect their responses to multiple responses/topics. This difference from the other online genres addressed here is especially notable, given that this forum was not designed for online discussions.

NEW DIRECTIONS FOR ONLINE DISCUSSIONS

The visual design of online forums may complement or conflict with conversational features like questions and uptake, affecting the success of online discussions. Like those features, the visual rhetoric of threaded and anchored discussions can shape participation by implying the rules, roles, relationships, and possible responses available within those genres of activity. Put differently, the visual rhetoric of online discussion forums, like teacher questions and uptake, implicitly teaches students how to participate, though teachers may have considerably less control over the design of online forums.

The examples in this chapter affirm what you may have begun to realize since chapter 2: it is not the nature of the question or follow-up per se that produces dialogue,[13] but rather the context in which that turn in the conversation occurs and what both context and conversational turn imply about the genre of activity. Features that contextualize responses during whole-class discussions, like the visual rhetoric of online forums, may be relatively independent of the teacher's "stance,"[14] or indeed of any participant in the activity: even teachers and students with the best of intentions can struggle to hold a discussion because of the mediating technological tools.

This is not to imply that teachers and students are at the mercy of such tools, nor that these online genres are stable and independent of participants. Genres remain open to adaptation.[15] Researchers[16] have suggested that teachers attend to how genres can promote and discourage discussion, "exercising an influence on their participation that operates somewhat independently of teachers' and students' awareness, compliance, and resistance" (p. 7). Educators using threaded and anchored discussion genres might explicitly discuss with their students these genres' possibilities and limitations and set additional guidelines regarding their use.

Beyond online discussion forums, visual rhetorical principles of *contrast*, *repetition*, *alignment*, and *proximity* may help to describe dialogic (dis)connections among texts/turns in conversation. Educators may wish to explore how non-print "texts" (including not only the design of online forums, but also images, videos, gestures, and other multimodal elements that can be mobilized by students in their responses) can promote and discourage participation in whole-class, dialogic discussions.

ACTIVITIES FOR PROMOTING DIALOGIC DISCUSSIONS IN ONLINE FORUMS

1. **Name-Dropping:** Encourage students to use names when referring to what others have already written.
   Rationale: Students can reference more than one contributor, and seeing one's own name while scrolling through a page may stand out and make a writer want to respond.
   Variations:
   - "Dear Abby-Style": If contributors prefer to remain anonymous, invite students to sign their posts with a characterization of their position in the style of the well-known advice column (e.g., "Anxious about Assignments" or "Definitely Disagreeing").
   - Have students reference another person's post by using the first few words or a key line of that prior turn in the conversation.
2. **Font-Styling:** Invent a system with students for indicating a type of response or a change in topic using font styles.
   Rationale: Contrast and repetition created by *italicizing disagreement* or **bolding a new argument** (in the title of a post, or at different moments within a post) can draw attention to those moments and invite responses.
   Variations:
   - If the discussion forum allows color-coding, the class can agree on colors for different types of responses.
   - If the discussion forum does not allow formatting, type a single, class-defined word in CAPITAL LETTERS (as the title or at particular moments in a post) to point out moves like example/coun-

terexample, agreement/disagreement, new argument, procedural question, and so on.
3. **Symbol-fying:** Students may have their own symbol systems for creating connections, thanks to social media discussion forums (e.g., @name for citing a previous speaker or #topic for indicating a new/existing idea).
Rationale: "If you can't beat 'em, join 'em." :) This strategy capitalizes on students' prior experience with other kinds of discussion forums, thereby making it easier for them to apply those strategies and perhaps also making the school forum more engaging and accessible by association.
Variations:
- If the discussion forum allows, students can use emojis or other keyboard/punctuation icons, such as :), :[, :0, <3, ?, and ! to signal the nature of their responses.

REFLECTIONS FOR TEACHERS

1. For many teachers, online discussion forums may be associated with out-of-school platforms, purposes, audiences, and genres of communication (like social media). What assumptions or attitudes might you and/or students have about those kinds of forums? How might the rules, roles, relationships, and possible responses in a school online discussion forum be similar and different from one that you and/or students use outside of school?
2. Schools' decisions to purchase access to an online discussion forum or course management system are often connected to other decisions about curriculum, politics, price, and technology. Investigate and reflect on (or discuss with a trusted partner) your institution's choices regarding online discussion forums. Why have they chosen a particular platform? How do you (and others, including students) feel about this choice? What other options, if any, were or are available? What are the stakes of (re)evaluating those options?
3. The following chart summarizes the visual principles used to evaluate online discussion forums. Apply these prompts to an on-

Contrast	Identify how the forum uses *differences* in size, color, font, format, and/or style to create connections among multiple students' contributions. (Example: italicizing replies to previous responses)
Repetition	Notice how the forum uses *similarities* in size, color, font, format, and/or style to create connections among multiple students' contributions. (Example: color-coding related responses)
Alignment	Attend to how the forum uses *lines and indents* to create connections among multiple students' contributions. (Example: indented replies)
Proximity	Interrogate how the forum *spatially arranges* multiple students' contributions to show their connections. (Example: responses grouped by topic or focus)

line discussion forum to gauge how well its visual design supports dialogue.

EXPLORATIONS WITH STUDENTS

1. Discuss with students the rules, roles, relationships, and possible responses for online discussions in your class:
   a. What is the purpose of the online discussion? How do the rules, roles, relationships, and possible responses relate to that purpose? How might that purpose differ from the functions of out-of-school discussion forums (e.g., social media)?
   b. Who are the audiences for the online discussion? How do the rules, roles, relationships, and possible responses relate to who might be reading our posts? What "online etiquette" might we need to establish?
   c. What is the genre of the online discussion? How do the rules, roles, relationships, and possible responses relate to the type of discussion (see chapters 3, 4, 5, and 6 for more on student-led, disciplinary, cultural, and emergent genres)?
      i. If this is a student-led discussion, how will it be similar and different from that genre when we implement it face-to-face?

ii. If this is a disciplinary discussion, how will the online forum support or inhibit the use of evidence, organization, and language appropriate to the academic subject matter?
iii. If this discussion will include cultural conventions from communities outside the classroom, how might the online forum encourage or limit understanding of those cultural conventions (e.g., through use of multimedia, or through lack of resources like facial expression and tone)?
iv. If these discussions will continue to take place over time, what opportunities will we have for metatalk about how and why they are working and developing?
2. Researchers disagree about the value of anonymity for online discussions. Do anonymous online forums allow for more equitable participation from all participants because differences of age, gender, ethnicity, race, or social class are less apparent?[17] Does anonymity make impoliteness (and worse) more likely or does it allow for freer discussion of sensitive issues?[18] Discuss with your class their feelings about the benefits and challenges of posting anonymously to an online discussion forum. What do they think your class should do? What rules, roles, relationships, and possible responses should your class establish, given the potential for anonymous posting?
3. Researchers disagree about the effects of asynchronicity for online discussions. Do asynchronous online forums create more disconnection because there may be lag time between posts and responses?[19] Do they allow more time for participants to read/write and carefully consider their responses?[20] Discuss with your class their feelings about the possibilities and pitfalls of posting asynchronously to an online discussion forum. What guidelines for the timing of posts might your class create, and why?
4. Practice with students for online discussions by engaging in a combination of "silent discussion" (see chapter 2) and a "gallery walk" (see chapter 3) using sticky notes and one or more sheets of giant chart paper.
    a. To practice for threaded discussions, have students indent and align their responses under a topic or another note.
    b. To practice for anchored discussions, have students attach their responses near particular moments of the discussion focus.

c. Afterward, ask students to reflect (individually or in groups) on the benefits and challenges of using these genres of online discussion forums.
    i. What is easy or hard about how this type of discussion forum allows you to respond over time?
    ii. What is easy or hard about how this type of discussion forum organizes your responses in space?

CHAPTER SUMMARY

- Online discussion forums allow teachers and students to participate in discussions beyond the space and time of a typical class meeting.
- However, space and time also operate differently in such forums: for example, participants can remain anonymous or participate asynchronously.
- One reason they may operate differently is that most online discussion forums require writing.
- Participation in, and guidelines for participation in, online discussion forums may be influenced by participants' prior experience with other oral and written genres (e.g., student use of emojis or teacher evaluation of spelling).
- Visual design of online discussion forums (including features like contrast, repetition, alignment, and proximity) can support or inhibit participation, even when other features that typically promote dialogic discussion are present.

NOTES

1. S. Ruday, "Expanding the Possibilities of Discussion: A Strategic Approach to Using Online Discussion Boards in the Middle and High School English Classroom," *Contemporary Issues in Technology and Teacher Education* 11, no. 4 (2011); D. Wu and S. R. Hiltz, "Predicting Learning from Asynchronous Online Discussions," *Journal of Asynchronous Learning Networks* 8, no. 2 (2004); E. Zhu, "Interaction and Cognitive Engagement: An Analysis of Four Asynchronous Online Discussions," *Instructional Science* 34 (2006): 451–80; H. K. Kim

and B. Bateman, "Student Participation Patterns in Online Discussion: Incorporating Constructivist Discussion into Online Courses," *International Journal on E-Learning* 9, no. 1 (2010): 79–98; A. P. Rovai, "Facilitating Online Discussions Effectively," *Internet and Higher Education* 10 (2007): 77–88.

2. E.g., D. G. Beeghly, "It's About Time: Using Electronic Literature Discussion Groups with Adult Learners," *Journal of Adolescent & Adult Literacy* 49, no. 1 (2005): 12–21; Ruday, "Expanding the Possibilities"; Wu and Hiltz, "Predicting Learning."

3. S. L. Groenke, "Missed Opportunities in Cyberspace: Preparing Preservice Teachers to Facilitate Critical Talk about Literature through Computer-Mediated Communication," *Journal of Adolescent & Adult Literacy* 52, no. 3 (2008): 224–33; Kim and Bateman, "Student Participation Patterns"; Zhu, "Interaction and Cognitive Engagement."

4. Ruday, "Expanding the Possibilities."

5. B. E. Larson and T. A. Keiper, "Classroom Discussion and Threaded Electronic Discussion: Learning in Two Arenas," *Contemporary Issues in Technology and Teacher Education* 2, no. 1 (2002): 45–62.

6. Beeghly, "It's About Time."

7. J. C. Dunlap et. al, "What Sunshine Is to Flowers: A Literature Review on the Use of Emoticons to Support Online Learning," in *Emotion, Technology, Design, and Learning*, Emotions and Technology (London: Academic Press, 2016), 163–82.

8. K. A. Meyer, "Face-to-Face versus Threaded Discussions: The Role of Time and Higher-Order Thinking." *Journal of Asynchronous Learning Networks* 7, no. 3 (2003): 55–65.

9. F. Gao, "Designing a Discussion Environment to Promote Connected and Sustained Online Discussion," *Journal of Educational Media and Hypermedia* 20, no. 1 (2011): 43–59.

10. M. B. Sherry and R. Tremmel, "English Education 2.0: An Analysis of Sites That Contain Videos of English Teaching," *English Education* 45, no. 1 (2012): 35–70.

11. Robin Williams, *The Non-Designers Design Book: Design and Typographic Principles for the Visual Novice*, vol. 2 (Berkeley, CA: Peachpit Press, 2004).

12. M. Scardamalia, "CSILE/Knowledge Forum," in *Education and Technology: An Encyclopedia* (Santa Barbara, CA: ABC-CLIO, 2004), 183–92.

13. M. P. Boyd and D. Rubin, "How Contingent Questioning Promotes Extended Student Talk: A Function of Display Questions," *Journal of Literacy Research* 38, no. 2 (June 1, 2006): 141–69; M. P. Boyd and D. L. Rubin, "Elaborated Student Talk in an Elementary ESoL Classroom," *Research in the Teaching*

of English 36, no. 4 (May 1, 2002): 495–530; M. B. Sherry, "Indirect Challenges and Provocative Paraphrases: Using Cultural Conflict-Talk Practices to Promote Students' Dialogic Participation in Whole-Class Discussions," *Research in the Teaching of English* 49, no. 2 (2014): 141–67.

14. Cf. M. P. Boyd and W. C. Markarian, "Dialogic Teaching and Dialogic Stance: Moving beyond Interactional Form," *Research in the Teaching of English* 49, no. 3 (2015): 272–96.

15. M. Bakhtin, *Speech Genres and Other Late Essays*, vol. 1, trans. M. Holquist and C. Emerson, University of Texas Press Slavic Series, no. 8 (Austin: University of Texas Press, 1986), 126–27.

16. A. M. Lawrence and S. Crespo, "IRE/F as a Cross-Curricular Collaborative Genre of Implicit Argumentation," *Theory into Practice* 55, no. 4 (2016): 1–12.

17. Rovai, "Facilitating Online Discussions Effectively"; S. Kiesler, J. Siegel, and T. W. McGuire, "Social Psychological Aspects of Computer-Mediated Communication," *American Psychologist* 39 (1984): 1123–34; T. Postmes and R. Spears, "Behavior Online: Does Anonymous Computer Communication Reduce Gender Inequality?" *Personality & Social Psychology Bulletin* 28, no. 7 (2002): 1073–83.

18. G. Coleman, "Anonymity Online Serves Us All," *New York Times*, August 20, 2014, Opinion Pages edition, sec. Room for Debate.

19. F. Gao, T. Zhang, and T. Franklin, "Designing Asynchronous Online Discussion Environments: Recent Progress and Future Directions," *British Journal of Educational Technology* 44, no. 3 (2013): 469–83; W. Journell, "Facilitating Historical Discussions Using Asynchronous Communication: The Role of the Teacher," *Theory & Research in Social Education* 36, no. 4 (2008): 317–55.

20. Meyer, "Face-to-Face versus Threaded Discussions."

8

Listening to the Silence in Difficult Dialogic Discussions

"So you've been discussing with a partner about times when you and someone else felt like you were talking past each other. I see that some of you also posted about this to our class's online forum: that both Romeo and Juliet were misunderstood by their parents and even their friends. Does anyone want to comment?"

"Hashtag My Life!" said someone from the back of the room. Laughter rippled through the class.

"Wait, where was that post?" asked Miriam. "I didn't even see that!"

I waited for others to comment. After a long moment of silence, I said, "I know when I was in school, I felt like my parents didn't get me. They were divorced, and both had remarried. My sister was a lot younger. They were always busy. Now that I'm a dad, I worry that I'm not listening because I'm caught up in . . . busy-ness."

"Yeah, I get that," said Miriam. "I feel like my parents don't always listen when I want them to, but I guess I don't listen that well to my little sister, either."

John looked grim. "So my dad doesn't listen to me and I don't listen to him. Is that supposed to make it ok that people don't listen because—what? Because nobody listens? What am I supposed to do with that?" Silence followed as John subsided back into his seat, shaking his head.

Finally, from the back of the room, someone muttered, "I hear you." Looking around, I saw others nodding.

"*I wonder the same thing sometimes, John,*" *I said.* "*Let's take a moment of silence to honor John's comment and think about listening.*"

The previous chapters have suggested that, over time, students' participation in whole-class discussions could be encouraged or inhibited by the nature of the activity genre, by the expectations of the academic discipline, by cultural conventions for participation in conversations outside of school, by classroom conventions that emerge collectively over time, and by the design of technological tools like online discussion forums. The dimensions of Genre, Academic discipline, Culture, and Tool—or G, A, C, T—form what I have called the "DNA of Discussions" because they can lead not only to the success or failure of whole-class dialogic discussions, but also to positioning students vis-à-vis classroom discussion topics and school subject matters.

So what happens when whole-class discussions broach topics that are controversial, personal, and perhaps even traumatic? For example, in the vignette that begins this and the previous chapters, the activity has emerged in part as a result of John's initial resistance. (Recall his provocative paraphrase of Miriam's response in answer to the question, "So if a monologue is one person talking by themselves, a dialogue is . . . ?" "Two people talking by themselves?") That same activity now seems to compel his participation, for better or for worse, about a personal and painful topic. Likewise for Miriam, whose response suggests her reluctant and revelatory uptake of a story about parents and sisters. In this scene, even silence may have multiple meanings, both coercive and testimonial. In conversations like these, how might teachers invite and respond to students' participation? How might stories, silence, and listening figure in whole-class, dialogic discussions, particularly those that address sensitive personal topics?

ROUTINE BREAKING: DISCUSSING TEACHING ON THE DAY AFTER PARKLAND

Consider the following example from a lesson in a US English teacher education course that included both prospective and practicing teachers. On this sixth session of a weekly three-hour class, for which I served as teacher, the class was scheduled to talk about creating routines as a core task of teaching: how might we teach students to participate in recurring class activities like journaling or whole-class discussion?

But dark silence lurked at the edges of our conversations. The day before our class, a student at a local high school had gunned down seventeen people and wounded seventeen more in one of the deadliest school shootings in US history. Though none of us had visited that school on the other side of our state, I heard prospective teachers talking about the event during our ten-minute break halfway through class. They sat in clusters, some on the floor in the hallway outside our room. "I'm not sure this is what I signed up for," said one. I had not planned to discuss the shooting, perhaps because of my own shock or maybe out of a need to compartmentalize the pain, anger, and grief in a safe and separate cell. But as I followed the last person back into the classroom, I realized I would have to depart from our class routine to address this issue.

To open discussion, I reached for a story I had told many times in the seventeen years since I began teaching. During my first winter as a high school teacher, one of my eleventh graders had tried to commit suicide by throwing himself out of the third-story window of his home. Though he survived and would eventually recover—at least physically—after several days in the hospital, the morning after his leap there was no certainty about his condition. So I had left instructions for my students taped under their desks, encouraging them to go to a safe place on the high school campus, read Robert Frost's poem "Mending Wall," and then write about positive and negative walls in their own lives.

Back then, I did not hesitate to offer students this freedom. Back then, there were no locks on our classroom doors. Students sprawled on benches and curbs between bells, and teachers sometimes held classes outside. I trusted that all of my students would return by the appointed time, meeting in the woods behind our portable classroom. There, I invited them to share their compositions about positive walls or to burn what they had written about the negative ones.

That day, as we stood in a circle at the edge of the woods, one of my eleventh graders turned to me. "Is this supposed to make it all better?" she asked.

"Maybe not," I said. "But it's a start."

But on that Thursday evening in the teaching-methods class, the heroic tale I had told before was not what emerged. Instead, I backtracked to an autumn morning during that same first year when the principal visited my tenth-grade class, on the opening day of our poetry unit, to report that one of my students had died, along with her parents, in a plane crash the night before.

1. MR. SHERRY: I'll never forget that moment when the principal came in

2. and he stood there in that portable classroom

3. and told us that the plane had malfunctioned.

> **Take a turn**
> Vivid details like this take listeners closer to the experience. In your opinion, is this positively engaging? negatively triggering?

4. He said that she and her parents died instantly.

5. And one of my students, her best friend, she gasped

6. and then put her head down on the desk.

7. After the principal left, I just felt overwhelmed.

8. I had no idea what to do.

9. So instead of asking students to share how they felt,

10. I went back to the poetry lesson.

11. I handed out these poetry templates,

12. and I think I said that,

13. "Poetry is a good way to express your feelings."

14. But over the next few days, I knew that I had failed them.

15. Because no one wrote about it.

16. I hadn't been willing to talk about it, to face it.

17. To feel it.

18. So they didn't either.

19. Even if I had tried. If I had said to them,

20. "You know, this is so awful, I don't even know what to say.

21. It hurts so much that words fail."

22. Because they do sometimes. Words fail.

23. But I didn't say anything.

24. Just went home and wondered

25. if I should even be a teacher.

26. So I want to invite you to talk about what happened yesterday.

27. I know that I feel shocked and sad and frightened.

28. And you might be feeling things too.

29. Like, "Is this really what I signed up for?

30. What does this mean about . . . being a teacher?"

The story I initially reached for was one that described a teacher's response to a traumatic event. It was dialogic, responding to the news of the school shooting and the accompanying reactions that had seeped into our lesson. But it was not responsive to the group's need for shared vulnerability. What emerged instead was a story that surprised me as much as it did the other class members. At times, whole-class discussions can evoke this kind of a **narrative ambush**, eliciting stories that either the teller or the listeners (or both) have not anticipated, but that can open discussion to subsequent, perhaps equally unexpected, possibilities.

In the methods course classroom, a deep quiet descended, the kind that rarely happened, even during our usual journaling or individual reflection times. Had I made the situation worse by telling a confessional story of my own failure as a teacher, thereby silencing others, or worse, compelling students in their time of need to take care of me? In the silence, I began to wonder if I would be getting a phone call from my department chair the next day asking why there had been a sudden exodus from our English teacher preparation program.

Then, one by one, the prospective and practicing teachers in the room began to share their own stories.

31. RON: So we went to *[our field placement school]* today

32. and there was a lockdown drill.

33. STUDENTS: *(Sounds of disbelief)* No way!

34. RON: Yeah, seriously!

35. And Carrie and I,

36. we had gone down to the office.

37. And they made us get down on the floor behind the desks

38. in the dark.

39. And no one even told us it was a drill.

40. STUDENTS: *(Silence)*

41. CARRIE: There was a TV over our heads,

42. and they kept playing news about it.

43. That little tape running at the bottom of the screen.

44. And I got so panicked

45. because I remembered being in a lockdown drill

46. when I was in high school

47. and I started crying in class

48. and the other kids all laughed

49. and made fun of me.

50. I just don't know if I can go through that again.

51. STUDENTS: *(Silence)*

In response to my story, Ron and Carrie narrated their experience with a terrifying lockdown drill, and Carrie shared a painful memory of a similar drill from high school. My story may have created an opening for these **second stories**:[1] narratives that follow an initial story and include uptake of similar events, characters, themes, or stances, like Miriam's in the opening vignette. This sequencing of stories suggests

> **Take a turn**
> Second stories appeal to/rely on first stories for their legitimacy. What did this first story enable? What did it prohibit or require?

that, like questions that are open-ended and invite higher-order thinking—O-HOT or "authentic" questions[2]—stories that are authentic, "resonant,"[3] or "testimonial"[4] can also promote dialogic discussion.[5] In whole-class discussions of personal and even traumatic events, such stories may accomplish this by paving the way for other speakers, acting as a pivot to a genre of classroom activity in which it is acceptable to share narratives that express emotion and vulnerability. Or perhaps they simply make an experience narratable for others.[6]

Ron and Carrie's second stories dispelled my fear of silencing other speakers. Silence can have multiple meanings beyond awkwardness, boredom, confusion, and disdain (among other reactions to the breakdown of the social situation)—it can also express empathy, forgiveness, and gratitude (as well as other responses to moments when words become irrelevant).[7] Though it is typically associated with student-centeredness in whole-class discussions, teacher silence can also be dominating even when it is dialogic: consider the expectant pause that follows a question, or the famous teacher move, "I'll wait." Here, the class's silence after line 33 seemed instead to be witnessing:[8] they did not respond the same way at lines 40 or 51, though in both cases the speaker's surprising and emotional statement might well have prompted various reactions.

TRANSFORMING STORIES

In fact, the stories told by undergraduate teacher candidates Ron and Carrie were followed by three subsequent stories from practicing teachers:

52. JOSEPH: You know, I have this student in my eighth-grade class.

53. He's kind of a goofball.

54. Doesn't usually do his work, got himself suspended.

55. He's . . . struggling.

56. But he talks to me.

57. And he turned something in the other day

58. and I was like, "I'm proud of you."

59. And I had to tell my fiancée,

60. "You know, if I had to,

61. I think I would take a bullet for that kid."

62. STUDENTS: *(Silence)*

63. MARIE: Yeah, I think about it

64. driving to work.

65. I have some students,

66. they're just really . . . angry.

67. But when I see them in class

68. I just try to . . . see them.

69. You know, like, "Hey, you got a haircut?"

70. Or like, make a joke,

71. just be with them.

72. STUDENTS: *(Silence)*

73. KAT: I have this one girl,

74. she told me today . . . *(Voice shaking)*

75. *Pause)*

76. She handed in her project, and she was like,

77. "This is the first time I felt like I was good at something."

78. STUDENTS: *(Silence)*

79. MARK: Okay, is someone cutting onions in here?

80. STUDENTS: *(Laughter)*

While these second stories, like Ron's and Carrie's, similarly expressed the teachers' pain and vulnerability regarding the reality of school shootings, their narratives took up the situation (and the previous stories) in different ways. First Joseph and then Marie also told stories of teacher responses to struggling students in (potentially) life-threatening situations, but their stories revealed that a teacher could countenance these harsh realities, something Kat's emotional narrative about her student's project also tried to do.

These examples suggested that second stories can also dialogically take up those that came before in ways that may open new possibilities for listeners. Likewise, witnessing silence may evoke participation,[9] as it did throughout this activity. These examples remind us that whole-class dialogic discussions, especially those that address sensitive, personal issues, may depend not only on what is said, and the linguistic, social, cultural, and technological contexts in which it is expressed, but also on how we listen.

ACTIVITIES FOR INVITING DIALOGIC DISCUSSIONS OF SENSITIVE, PERSONAL, OR TRAUMATIC TOPICS

1. **Journaling:** Invite students to write about their personal experiences in a journal that will be read only by the teacher (and in which students may fold over pages they do not wish the teacher to read). If you plan to invite discussion based on a particular journal entry, notify students before they begin writing; call only on volunteers, or if students will talk with peers (see #2), offer them the option to discuss the *experience* of writing (rather than the specifics of the content).
   Rationale: Though it might seem obvious, journaling remains an effective and widely accepted way to make official space for students' personal reflections in school curricula, across disciplines. Giving students the option to keep some or all entries private, warning them before sharing will be invited, and making sharing voluntary or avoidable are all ways to establish trust while welcoming sensitive personal experiences into dialogic discussion.
   Variations:
   - Have students write regular responses (to prompts or to carefully selected "mentor texts") that encourage testimony and witnessing.[10]

- Invite students to compose or respond in a variety of media and genres (e.g., collage, poetry) that might be more suited to their preferences or to the emotional content of their journaling.
- Match students with trusted partner(s)—in or outside the class—with whom they can regularly and safely share their journal entries.

2. **Think-Pair-Share:** (See chapter 2.) Have students stop and write a response (or prepare one for homework and bring it to class); students then pair with a partner and discuss what they wrote before engaging in a whole-class discussion.
Rationale: The opportunity to first articulate their thoughts and then share with a trusted partner may make participating in whole-class discussion seem safer and less intimidating.
Variations:
- Carefully match pairs of students to ensure their safety.
- Carefully switch pairs over the course of a semester or year in order to foster community and trust.

3. **The Four Windows:**[11] Invite students to write and/or talk about an experience using the "four windows" of thinking, feeling, sensing, and imagining.
Rationale: Certain modes may come more easily for some speakers; for most, it is easy to consider an experience through thinking, but may be more difficult to access the feelings, sensory perceptions, and other imaginative intuitions evoked by that experience.
Variations:
- Go around the room or invite (but do not require) students to write or to talk about the four windows one by one (i.e., first everyone writes/talks about "thinking" then "feeling" and so on).
- Invite students to write or talk with a partner about all four windows, in whatever order makes the most sense to them; then, invite sharing and/or reflections on the process in whole-group discussion.

4. **Way of Council:**[12] Speakers sit in a circle with a central focus that may also serve as a means of creating the "container" (e.g., a candle that is lit at the beginning of the session and extinguished at the end; a drum that is struck at the beginning/end of the session). A

"talking stick" or other ceremonial object passes from one speaker to another; participants are free to pass but must not interrupt or comment, instead responding with a chorused "I hear you." All participants are invited to (1) speak from the heart; (2) listen from the heart; (3) be spontaneous; and (4) be concise, or "lean of expression."
Rationale: Versions of council, in which a group of people share stories in a ceremonial circle, appear across ages, continents, and societies, but are especially associated with the wisdom traditions of First Nations and indigenous cultures. In this practice, participants speak their own truths and bear witness, rather than attempting to interpret, fix, or transform what others have said.
Variations:
- Begin council with a "status update" or "personal weather report" that all members are invited to share as the talking stick passes in order around the circle.
- Begin council with a prompt (a question, poem, image, etc.) to which all participants are invited to respond, if and when they feel moved to do so.
- Have each speaker end his or her turn with a question that can be taken up by the next speaker (e.g., "What is most alive for you right now?").

5. **The Spiral:**[13] Ask students to write/speak to each of four (potentially recursive) steps: (1) Coming from Gratitude; (2) Honoring the Pain of the World; (3) Seeing with New Eyes; (4) Going Forth.
Rationale: Based on over forty years of "Despair and Empowerment Work" with a particular focus on climate justice, the Spiral is a central practice to Dr. Joanna Macy's "The Work That Reconnects." Macy suggests that beginning with gratitude makes it easier to first admit what is precious and precarious before attempting to countenance the "pain of the world" (anxiety, fear, anger, pain, trauma). While we often avoid these emotions in contemporary societies, they hold important understandings about our personal and collective situations. Accessing the pain and the accompanying understanding are important precursors to activism—seeing anew and going forth.

Variations:
- Instead of asking students to address each step in order, place four objects in the circle that represent each step of the spiral (e.g., a flower, a stone, a piece of glass, a feather) and invite speakers to step into the circle and take up the object as they speak.
- Invite students to imagine an audience for their contributions, beyond the circle (a past or future generation).
- Invite students to prepare and speak on behalf of others who cannot speak or have been silenced (e.g., a family member who has died or another member of the "more-than human world,"[14] such as an animal, stone, or tree).

REFLECTIONS FOR TEACHERS

1. Make a list of topics that you feel (un)comfortable talking about with students during whole-class discussions in your class. What patterns do you notice in this list? Which topics are central or "off limits"? Why?
2. Make a list of topics that you feel are important but about which you have noticed (as teacher or student) that others have trouble discussing. What experiences made these topics more accessible for you? What rules, roles, relationships, and possible responses were established (implicit or explicit) that made these topics difficult to discuss in classrooms?
3. What story from your own experience might you tell about one of the topics you listed above that might set others at ease, opening the possibility of further conversation on that topic?
4. What aspects of the curriculum in your discipline (e.g., texts, events, images, phenomena) might you or students find sensitive, personal, and even traumatic? What might you do to allow these curricular aspects to be addressed in a balanced way (neither "too far" nor "too close" with regard to students' experiences)? Consider whether, how, and why (or why not) you will communicate to students your own emotional response to this sensitive content.
5. Consider a whole-class discussion in which you have participated as a teacher or a student that touched on sensitive, personal, or even

traumatic topics. What made that discussion succeed or fail? How did you know?
    a. What role, if any, did stories play in that success or failure?
    b. What role, if any, did silence play in that success or failure?
6. Given your answer to #5, consider that same discussion from the point of view of another participant. Would that person have the same perspective on the conversation's success or failure? How do you know?
7. What, if anything, do #5 and #6 add to your thinking about preparing for dialogic, whole-class discussions of sensitive, personal, and even traumatic topics in your classroom?
8. Consider the role of silence in a discussion in which you have participated as a teacher or a student. What did the silence seem to mean? How did silence affect the way you or others responded?

EXPLORATIONS WITH STUDENTS

1. On your own or with students, generate a list of guidelines for sharing and responding during whole-class discussion of sensitive, personal, and even traumatic issues. What rules, roles, relationships, and possible responses must be established for all students to feel safe enough to share? What, if anything, is "off limits" for personal, logistical, or legal reasons?
2. Discuss with students the idea that emotions like anger, disgust, fear, and sadness are often viewed as negative and avoided in our society, but that these emotions (as well as the more general one, "stress") often hold important, positive understandings for us about our individual and collective situation that suppressing them prevents us from accessing. Ask students to choose one emotion and consider how a recent experience with it gave them a new understanding about themselves or their communities.
3. Using the following broad list of emotions, have students list topics (individually or in groups) evoked for them by each one (e.g., they might consider life events like graduation, current events like war, or world events like disease or climate change). Which of these might be associated with school? with your subject matter? with your class?

Affect/Emotion	Topics
Anger	
Disgust	
Fear	
Sadness	
Joy	

4. Given the list generated above, ask students whether they would feel comfortable addressing one or more of these topics during whole-class discussion. Why or why not? What rules, roles, relationships, and guidelines for responding make it harder or easier to discuss these topics?
5. Talk to students about our listening habits: what is the effect of listening with divided attention (for example, while checking a portable device) or with the well-intentioned habits of minimizing, placating, or fixing? Have students practice active listening or "mirroring" moves like asking specific questions, noticing important moments in the speaker's contribution, and repeating back what they heard.
6. Invite students to consider their responses to silence. What does it mean during a classroom conversation? Can it mean different things? When? Why?

CHAPTER SUMMARY

- Classrooms conversations (including whole-class, dialogic discussions) about sensitive, personal, and even traumatic experiences can invite and/or compel students to share.
- Like other moves that evoke participation during whole-class, dialogic discussions (e.g., O-HOT questions or uptake), stories can invite students to respond with "second stories" that address similar characters, events, themes, or stances.

- Silence during whole-class discussions can have multiple meanings and can interpret and influence prior and subsequent participation.

NOTES

1. Harvey Sacks, *Lectures on Conversation* (Cambridge: Blackwell, 1992).

2. M. Nystrand et al., *Opening Dialogue: Understanding the Dynamics of Language and Learning in the English Classroom* (New York: Teachers College Press, 1997); M. Nystrand et al., "Questions in Time: Investigating the Unfolding Structure of Classroom Discourse" (Albany, NY: National Research Center on English Learning and Achievement, 2003).

3. J. W. Du Bois, "The Stance Triangle," in *Stancetaking in Discourse: Subjectivity, Evaluation, Interaction*, ed. R. Englebretson (Amsterdam, Netherlands: John Benjamins, 2007), 139–82; J. W. Du Bois, "Towards a Dialogic Syntax," *Cognitive Linguistics* 25, no. 3 (2014): 359–410; M. Siromaa, "Resonance in Conversational Second Stories: A Dialogic Resource for Stance Taking," *Text and Talk* 4, no. 4 (2012): 525–45.

4. E. Dutro, *The Vulnerable Heart of Literacy: Centering Trauma as Powerful Pedagogy* (New York: Teachers College Press, 2019).

5. M. M. Juzwik et al., "Oral Narrative Genres as Dialogic Resources for Classroom Literature Study," *American Educational Research Journal* 45, no.4 (2008): 1111–54.

6. A. W. Frank, *Letting Stories Breathe: A Socio-Narratology* (Chicago: University of Chicago Press, 2010).

7. C. Glenn, *Unspoken: A Rhetoric of Silence* (Carbondale, IL: Southern Illinois University Press, 2004); R. L. Johannessen, "The Functions of Silence: A Plea for Communication Research," *Western Speech* 38 (1974): 24–35; S. J. Baker, "The Theory of Silence," *Journal of General Psychiatry* 52 (1955): 145–67.

8. Dutro, *The Vulnerable Heart of Literacy*.

9. K. Ratcliffe, *Rhetorical Listening: Identification, Gender, Whiteness* (Carbondale, IL: Southern Illinois University Press, 2005); Glenn, *Unspoken*.

10. Dutro, *The Vulnerable Heart of Literacy*.

11. E. S. Gallegos, *Animals of the Four Windows* (Embudo, NM: Moon Bear Press, 1991).

12. J. Zimmerman and V. Coyle, *The Way of Council*, 2nd ed. (North Bergen, NJ: Bramble Books, 1996); J. Zimmerman and V. Coyle, "Ways of Council," Ways of Council, 2020, https://waysofcouncil.net/.

13. J. Macy and M. Y. Brown, *Coming Back to Life: The Updated Guide to the Work That Reconnects* (Gabriola Island, BC Canada: New Society Publishers, 1989); J. Macy and C. Johnstone, *Active Hope: How to Face the Mess We're in without Going Crazy* (Novato, CA: New World Library, 2012).

14. D. Abram, *The Spell of the Sensuous: Perception and Language in a More-Than-Human World* (New York: Pantheon, 1996).

Appendix A

Key Terms

Academic discipline (p. 7): a school or professional subject matter, or the community of people who study that subject matter, with some shared values, expectations, and practices related to communication and behavior.

Alignment (p. 133): a principle of visual rhetoric that relates elements in space by using lines and indents.[1]

Anchored discussions (p. 132): a genre of online discussions that locates or "anchors" participants' posts near particular moments of the text on which the discussion focuses, creating clusters of annotations:

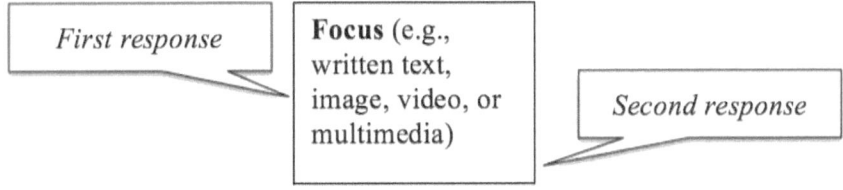

Animation (p. 61): characterizing other speakers by describing their words and actions.[2]

C-LOT questions (p. 19): questions that are closed-ended, lower-order thinking[3]—that is, questions for which the teacher has an answer in mind, and students are only expected to recall or apply what they already know.

Collaborative disagreement (p. 83): speakers reference others' contributions while disagreeing with those positions.

Contrast (p. 133): a principle of visual rhetoric that relates elements through differences in size, color, font, format, or style.[4]

Culture (p. 7): a community in which people participate whose shared values, expectations, and practices regarding communication and behavior can shape interactions in ways that may not be apparent from the immediate social situation.

Dialogic (p. 2): all language in use is dialogic because previous uses of language echo in every word; however, communication may seem unrelated when speakers/writers do not address others and respond to what they have already written or said.[5]

Discussion (p. 2): a type of talk in which participants engage in a shared inquiry, using others' contributions to build meanings together (even if they disagree).

Emergent (p. 27): arising from collective action, when no one person is responsible for defining the rules, roles, relationships, and responses that are possible.

Factual conditional narrative (p. 118): sequencing events that have taken place or are likely to happen.

Fictional conditional narrative (p. 118): sequencing events that are unrealized and unlikely to happen.

Genre (p. 22): a type of communication appropriate to a social situation, and the rules, roles, relationships, and possible responses it entails; genres are flexible: they can shape and be shaped by participation over time.

Genre contact (p. 45): aspects of another, related genre appear during an activity that may evoke a different, even contradictory set of rules, roles, relationships, and available responses.[6]

Imaginative entry (p. 67): When teacher and students imagine themselves into a hypothetical situation based on past events.

Indirect challenge (p. 86): a participant invites response from the audience by referring ironically to another's words in the third person.

IRE/F (p. 18): also called recitation, this acronym identifies a recurring, three-part pattern that typically appears in that genre of classroom talk across disciplines and grade levels:[7] (1) The teacher asks or *initiates* a question, (2) a student *responds*, and (3) the teacher *evaluates* or *follows-up* on that student's response.

> Initiation—TEACHER: What did Romeo do that was impulsive in Act I?
>
> Response—STUDENT: Went to the party of his family's enemy?
>
> Evaluation/Follow-Up—TEACHER: Right.

Metatalk (p. 62): talk about dialogue as it unfolds.[8]

Narrative (p. 104): sequencing related events over time.[9]

Narrative ambush (p. 155): story that either the teller or the listeners (or both) have not anticipated, but that can open discussion to subsequent, perhaps equally unexpected, possibilities.[10]

Non-collaborative disagreement (p. 82): speakers do not engage directly with differing perspectives voiced by other participants.[11]

O-HOT questions (p. 19): questions that are *o*pen-ended and require "*h*igher-*o*rder *t*hinking"—that is, questions that invite multiple answers and encourage students to analyze, synthesize, or evaluate.

Pivot (p. 24): a signal that can help people shift from one genre or context to another.[12]

Provocative paraphrase (p. 87): a technique in which speakers turn others' words back on them through wordplay.

Proximity (p. 133): a principle of visual rhetoric that relates elements in space by arranging them near others that are relevant.[13]

Recitation (p. 7): A prevalent and persistent classroom question-and-answer routine in which the teacher asks rapid-fire "test" questions to which he or she already knows the one right answer, and then evaluates a student's response.

> TEACHER: What did Romeo do that was impulsive in Act I?
>
> STUDENT: Went to the party of his family's enemy?
>
> TEACHER: Right.

Repetition (p. 133): a principle of visual rhetoric that relates elements through similarity of size, color, font, format, or style.[14]

Revoicing (p. 61): a particular kind of uptake that not only repeats but also connects another's assertion to an inference,[15] often through a phrase like, "So you're saying that . . ."

Second stories (p. 156): narratives that follow an initial story and include uptake of similar events, characters, themes, or stances.[16]

Threaded discussions (p. 132): a genre of online discussions that organizes contributors' posts into a vertical list, or "thread," related by the same topic, with responses and replies nested hierarchically:

> **Topic**
> - *Response 1*
>   ◦ Reply 1.1
>   ◦ Reply 1.2
> - *Response 2*
>   ◦ Reply 2.1
>   ◦ Reply 2.2

Tool (p. 3): a medium, device, platform, or other technology used by participants to accomplish a (communicative) purpose.

Uptake (p. 20): when a subsequent speaker quotes or refers back to what someone has already said.[17]

NOTES

1. Robin Williams, *The Non-Designers Design Book: Design and Typographic Principles for the Visual Novice,* vol. 2 (Berkeley, CA: Peachpit Press, 2004).

2. Erving Goffman, "Footing," in *Forms of Talk* (Philadelphia: University of Pennsylvania Press, 1981); Erving Goffman, *Frame Analysis: An Essay on the Organization of Experience* (Boston: Northeastern University Press, 1986).

3. M. Nystrand et al., *Opening Dialogue: Understanding the Dynamics of Language and Learning in the English Classroom* (New York: Teachers College Press, 1997); M. Nystrand et al., "Questions in Time: Investigating the Unfolding Structure of Classroom Discourse" (Albany, NY: National Reseach Center on English Learning and Achievement, 2003).

4. Williams, *The Non-Designers Design Book.*

5. M. Bakhtin, *Speech Genres and Other Late Essays,* trans. M. Holquist and C. Emerson, vol. 1, University of Texas Press Slavic Series, no. 8 (Austin: University of Texas Press, 1986); M. Bakhtin, *Problems of Dostoevsky's Poetics,* trans. C. Emerson, *Theory and History of Literature,* vol. 8 (Minneapolis: University of Minnesota Press, 1984); M. Bakhtin, *The Dialogic Imagination: Four Essays,* trans. M. Holquist, University of Texas Press Slavic Series, no. 1 (Austin: University of Texas Press, 1981).

6. G. S. Morson and C. Emerson, *Mikhail Bakhtin: Creation of a Prosaics* (Stanford: Stanford University Press, 1990); Bakhtin, *Problems of Dostoevsky's Poetics.*

7. Courtney B. Cazden, "Classroom Discourse," in *Handbook of Research on Teaching,* vol. 3 (New York and London: Macmillan; Collier Macmillan, 1986), xi, 1037; H. Mehan, "'What Time Is It, Denise?': Asking Known Information Questions in Classroom Discourse," *Theory into Practice* 18, no. 4 (1979): 285–94; J. Sinclair and M. Coulthard, *Towards an Analysis of Discourse: The English Used by Teachers and Pupils* (Oxford, UK: Oxford University Press, 1975); G. Wells, *Dialogic Inquiry* (Cambridge: Cambridge University Press, 1999).

8. C. Edwards-Groves and C. Davidson, "Metatalk for a Dialogic Turn in the First Years of Schooling," in *Routledge International Handbook of Research on Dialogic Education* (New York: Routledge, 2020), 125–38.

9. William Labov, *Language in the Inner City: Studies in the Black English Vernacular* (Philadelphia: University of Pennsylvania Press, 1972).

10. A. W. Frank, *Letting Stories Breathe: A Socio-Narratology* (Chicago: University of Chicago Press, 2010).

11. A. D. Grimshaw, *Conflict Talk* (Cambridge: Cambridge University Press, 1990); D. Tannen, *The Argument Culture* (Virago, 1998).

12. D. Holland et al., *Identity and Agency in Cultural Worlds* (Cambridge, MA: Harvard University Press, 1998).

13. Williams, *The Non-Designers Design Book*.

14. Williams, *The Non-Designers Design Book*.

15. M. C. O'Connor and S. Michaels, "Aligning Academic Task and Participation Status through Revoicing: Analysis of a Classroom Discourse Strategy," *Anthropology & Education Quarterly* 24, no. 4 (1993): 318–35.

16. Harvey Sacks, *Lectures on Conversation* (Cambridge: Blackwell, 1992).

17. J. Collins, "Discourse Style, Classroom Interaction, and Differential Treatment," *Journal of Reading Behavior* 14 (1982): 429–37; Nystrand et al., *Opening Dialogue*.

Appendix B

Classroom Examples

Chapter	Topic/*Genre*	Grade Level	Academic Discipline
1 (p. 3)	Guillermo's wrestling practice (*author's chair/editing*)	(Elementary) 1st grade: Ms. Davis	English Language Arts
1 (p. 5)	Hunter's hockey game (*author's chair/editing*)	(Elementary) 1st grade: Ms. Davis	English Language Arts
2 (p. 17)	Plot diagram (*recitation*)	(High) 10th grade: Mr. Schulz	English Language Arts
2 (p. 23)	Invasion of Belgium/Talbott (*imaginative entry*)	(High) 9th grade: Mr. Weber	History
3 (p. 41)	*The Outsiders* (*Literature Circle*)	(Middle) 7th grade: student-led	English Language Arts
3 (p. 49)	Personal narrative introductions (*peer review*)	(Undergraduate) Frosh: student-led	Composition
4 (p. 61)	Lemonade ratios (*science lab*)	(Middle) 6th grade: Ms. Lynne	Science
4 (p. 62)	Geometric shapes (*recitation*)	(Elementary) 1st grade: Ms. Kohl	Math

Appendix B

Chapter	Topic/Genre	Grade Level	Academic Discipline
4 (p. 67)	Trench warfare/football (*imaginative entry*)	(High) 9th grade: Mr. Weber	History
5 (p. 81)	Pulling the plug (*journaling responses*)	(High) 10th grade: Ms. Jefferson	English Language Arts
5 (p. 85)	*Hiroshima (debate)*	(High) 10th grade: Ms. Jefferson	English Language Arts
6 (p. 110)	Stock market crash (*imaginative entry*)	(High) 9th grade: Mr. Weber	History
6 (p. 113)	Collective bargaining (*imaginative entry*)	(High) 9th grade: Mr. Weber	History
6 (p. 117)	Berlin/capital city airlift (*imaginative entry*)	(High) 9th grade: Mr. Weber	History
7 (p. 130)	Our group name (*online threaded discussion*)	(High) 9th grade: Ms. Kelly	English Language Arts
7 (p. 134)	*Breaking Point* (*online threaded discussion*)	(High) 9th grade: Ms. Jenkins	English Language Arts
7 (p. 138)	Lesson video (*online anchored discussion*)	(Graduate) MA: Student-led	English Teacher Education
7 (p. 141)	Ethnographic research (*online mapped discussion*)	(Undergraduate) Frosh: Mr. Sherry	Composition
8 (p. 154)	School shooting (*way of council*)	(Undergraduate/ Graduate) Senior/ MA: Mr. Sherry	English Teacher Education

I stood before my 8th graders, a dog-eared copy of Shakespeare's Romeo and Juliet *in hand. The students, seated in a horseshoe of desks around the perimeter of the room, waited quietly, some leaning forward attentively, others slumped in their seats.*

"So yesterday we were talking about monologue," I said. "What did we say a monologue was?"

Miriam shot a hand into the air. I nodded to her. "One person talking by themselves?" she responded.

"Right!" I smiled, and Miriam sat back in her seat contentedly. "So today we're going to talk about dialogue. What is a dialogue?" I looked around the room expectantly. When no one volunteered, I call on one of the slumpers, leaning on his hand and trying not to make eye contact. "John?" Without lifting his head, John swiveled toward me. Seconds passed. Finally, I prompted him. "If a monologue is one person talking by themselves, then a dia*logue is . . . ?"*

"Two people talking by themselves?" As John's retort hung in the air, students looked at me to see how I would respond. I laughed. "That's a good point, John! Sometimes when people are supposed to be having a dialogue, it seems like they're talking by themselves." As I spoke, I walked across the room toward two other students who were whispering and giggling. "In fact, we saw that happen in the play when Juliet talks to her parents. Have any of you ever felt like that? Turn to your partners and talk about a time when you were trying to have a dialogue with someone, and you felt like you were talking past each other."

In response to my question, students erupted into conversation. I walked around the room, past each group of four with their desks squared against each other so that two facing pairs are seated side-by-side. Reaching Miriam and John's group, I paused to listen.

"So what are we supposed to be doing?" asked John.

Miriam repeated to John the question I had posed to the class, "When you were talking with someone, have you ever felt like you were talking past each other?"

"With my dad. I'm like 'Dad, check this out,' and he's like "Yeah, that's great.' But I can tell he's not really listening. But then he tells me to do something, and he's like, 'Why don't you listen to me?'" John sighed, slumping back in his seat.

Miriam nodded, "Yeah, that's a good example." Turning away from John, she cast a sidelong glance at me where I stood listening nearby. "Is that right?"

"What do you think?" I asked Miriam.

"C'mon," said John, "You know nothing's ever really 'right' in this class." He laughed ruefully, "I wish that were true in my next class."

"Not me," said Miriam. "I like when you know if it's right. If you show your work, of course."

From where I stood listening, I asked John and Miriam, "So are you saying that people often talk past each other in families?"

Miriam nodded, "Yeah, in my family, sometimes everyone talks at once and it's hard to—"

John interrupted, "Yeah, when my older brothers are home and everyone's talking at the dinner table—forget about it! I can't get a word in edgewise!"

"Speaking of that, have you both had time to share?" I asked, raising my eyebrows and looking meaningfully at John.

"Oh, sorry," he said, turning back to Miriam.

I circled the room, checking in with each group. "This is your two-minute warning," I said, flashing two fingers at each pair of students.

Then, raising my voice I called the partner pairs back to whole-group discussion. "So you've been discussing with a partner about times when you and someone else felt like you were talking past each other. I see that some of you also posted about this to our class's online forum: that both Romeo and Juliet were misunderstood by their parents and even their friends. Does anyone want to comment?"

"Hashtag My Life!" said someone from the back of the room. Laughter rippled through the class.

"Wait, where was that post?" asked Miriam. "I didn't even see that!"

I waited for others to comment. After a long moment of silence, I said, "I know when I was in school, I felt like my parents didn't get me. They were divorced, and both had remarried. My sister was a lot younger. They were always busy. Now that I'm a dad, I worry that I'm not listening because I'm caught up in . . . busy-ness."

"Yeah, I get that," said Miriam. "I feel like my parents don't always listen when I want them to, but I guess I don't listen that well to my little sister, either."

John looks grim. "So my dad doesn't listen to me and I don't listen to him. Is that supposed to make it ok that people don't listen because—what? Because nobody listens? What am I supposed to do with that?" Silence followed, as John subsided back into his seat, shaking his head.

Finally, from the back of the room, someone muttered, "I hear you." Looking around, I saw others nodding.

"I wonder the same thing sometimes, John," I said. "Let's take a moment of silence to honor John's comment and think about listening."

GUILLERMO'S WRESTLING PRACTICE
(1ST GRADE ENGLISH LANGUAGE ARTS)

US first-grader Guillermo had just recounted his story about wrestling practice to teacher Jessica Davis, who knelt by the easel where she had written it on a large piece of chart paper. Guillermo's classmates, seated in a semicircle on the floor in front of the easel in their suburban Midwestern elementary classroom, offered revision suggestions for a sentence about doing warm-up neck rotations.

1. TONISHA: What does "like this" mean?

2. MS. DAVIS: Oh, so you're saying a reader might not know what "this" refers to?

3. GUILLERMO: Well, I did say we go side to side.

4. TONISHA: You already said it up here,

5. but down here. *(Points to the end of the sentence)*

6. JOEY: Maybe you could make it longer.

7. MS. DAVIS: So we're saying we don't know how you go "side to side."

8. I wonder if he could cross out "like this" and add a detail to explain.

9. GUILLERMO: Okay. *(Picking up pen)*

10. JOEY: Hey, maybe he could put an arrow!

HUNTER'S HOCKEY GAME
(ELEMENTARY, FIRST GRADE ENGLISH LANGUAGE ARTS)

In a Midwestern suburban first-grade class, teacher Jessica Davis had just written Hunter's story about his hockey game on chart paper and invited students seated on the floor around the author's chair to offer their revision suggestions. Adriana, a student who was also an English Language Learner, raised her hand.

1. MS. DAVIS: Adriana, what do you think?

2. ADRIANA: The "i" has to be capitalized?

3. MS. DAVIS: Come and point to what "i" needs to be capitalized.

4. ADRIANA: *(Stands up, walks to the chart paper,*

5. *points to "i" in "it" at the beginning of the second line)*

6. MS. DAVIS: *(Reading the whole sentence aloud)* Oh.

7. "I am at my hockey game and it is almost time for me to play."

8. *(Standing to address the class)* When do we have capital letters in our writing?

9. *(Various students raise their hands.)*

10. MACKENZIE: *(Leaning forward with her hand raised high)* OH!

11. MS. DAVIS: Remember, what's one place that we need to have a capital letter?

12. Mackenzie?

13. MACKENZIE: Beginning and the end of a sentence,

14. when you start a new sentence.

15. MS. DAVIS: Okay, is this the beginning of a sentence?

16. CLASS: NOOO!

PLOT DIAGRAM
(HIGH SCHOOL, TENTH-GRADE ENGLISH LANGUAGE ARTS)

US tenth-grade teacher Mr. Schulz had planned to review story elements like Exposition, Rising Action, Climax, Falling Action, and Resolution with a class of twenty-two tenth graders at a rural Midwestern high school. The desks were arranged in a horseshoe and the diagram below was written on the board.

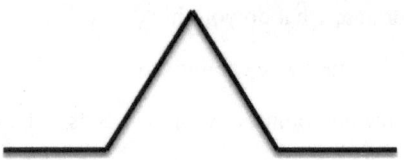

1. MR. SCHULZ: So . . . what does this remind you of?

2. ASHLEY: A mountain.

3. MR. SCHULZ: A mountain. Alrighty . . .

4. So could someone tell me what is the first part of a story?

5. Like what starts out a story usually?

6. From here to here to here. *(Points to diagram on board)*

7. Yes?

8. KEN: A problem?

9. MR. SCHULZ: A problem? Okay . . . *(Writes on board)* Yes?

10. DIANA: A climax.

11. MR. SCHULZ: Climax. *(Writes on board)* That would be right up there.

12. JAMIE: The characters?

13. MR. SCHULZ: Okay. *(Writes on board)* The characters and problems and stuff—

14. what is that called . . . ? At the beginning of a story?

15. KELSEY: Introduction?

16. MR. SCHULZ: Introduction? Introduction's a word for it.

17. There's another word that starts with an "E." . . .
18. The "ex_____" . . . Go ahead?
19. ASHLEY: Exposition?
20. MR. SCHULZ: It's an exposition.
21. It's this thing when you're introducing the characters and other stuff,
22. so you're right when you say "introduction,"
23. but "exposition" is a better word for it if you want to get technical.

THE INVASION OF BELGIUM/TALBOTT
(HIGH SCHOOL, NINTH-GRADE US HISTORY)

In a US Midwestern ninth-grade suburban history classroom, teacher Dave Weber reviewed the textbook questions assigned for homework regarding the WWI invasion of Belgium.

1. MR. WEBER: What was the Schlieffen plan?

2. BECCA: Um . . .

3. MR. WEBER: Yeah, Becca?

4. BECCA: *(Reading from book)* "It called for holding action against Russia."

5. PENNY: I didn't really understand that.

6. AMY: Yeah, I didn't remember that at all.

7. MR. WEBER: Okay, that's what it says in the book, right?

8. And then, while they're holding action,

9. just holding the line against Russia. On the East.

10. They've got this. *(Drawing on board)* There's Russia.

11. We've got Germany here, and we've got Belgium here.

12. Alright, and they decide they want to hold this line against Russia.

13. But while they're doing it, they want to start marching into Paris, France.

14. After that they go over and attack Russia. Does that help?

15. BECCA: No.

16. PENNY: Well, yes.

17. AMY: But what are the three . . . ?

18. OLIVIA: Yeah, what are the three little bubbles?

19. PENNY: Yeah, what are the rocks?

20. STUDENTS: *(Laughing)*

21. MR. WEBER: Rocks? *(Pointing to map)* Germany, Belgium, France.

22. SHIRIN: Question: when they go through all those places,

23. do they, like, try to get them to go with them?

24. Or are they, like—?

25. MR. WEBER: Are they trying to ask people to go with them? Is that what you're—?

26. SHIRIN: Kind of, yeah.

27. MR. WEBER: I don't know if they were necessarily trying to gain military strength

28. through grabbing people up as they went.

29. But say there was another country's army marching through Talbott.

30. What impact would that have on Talbott if tens of thousands of soldiers

31. . . . it'd be kind of weird?

37. CHASE: They'd screw everything up.

38. MR. WEBER: I couldn't even imagine how bad Glen Road would be.

39. STUDENTS: *(Laughing)*

40. ELLA: Oh my god!

41. AMY: We'd have to, like, walk everywhere.

42. MR. WEBER: They'd have to eat something, right?

43. LAURA: Yeah, they'd take all our food!

44. MR. WEBER: They'd take all our food. They'd take a lot of our stuff . . .

45. And here they are, just marching through.

46. And say they were trying to get to *[the neighboring town of]* Burch:

47. would it be our fault that we were in between?

48. GARY: Yeah, I would—

49. BECCA: No, because we just happen to be there.

50. WEBER: And what impact would it have on all of us if these people were violent?

51. Would you want to stay here?

52. STUDENTS: No!

53. TOM: I'd fight them.

54. MR. WEBER: So it did have a very profound impact on the people of Belgium,

55. a very important impact. That will later factor into the war.

LITERATURE CIRCLE ON *THE OUTSIDERS* (MIDDLE SCHOOL, SEVENTH-GRADE ENGLISH LANGUAGE ARTS)

In a US Midwestern rural middle school, four seventh-grade ELA students discussed *The Outsiders* by S. E. Hinton, in which rival gangs clash, resulting in tragedy for the main characters. During this student-led discussion, students sat with their desks facing each other in a small Literature Circle group separate from the rest of the class.

1. KATIE: Okay. Had Johnny not died,

2. do you think he would still continue to be a Greaser after all that happened?

3. RICK: Okay. I think Johnny would have gone on to be someone,

4. and he would have traveled.

5. Because when he was talking to Pony in the hospital,

6. he just said that he didn't want to die, there was so much he hadn't seen.

7. So I think he would have traveled and become something.

8. ASHLEY: Yeah, he didn't realize what he didn't have when he was a Greaser,

9. but I think he would still be a Greaser just because of his situation.

10. He couldn't not be a Greaser,

11. but I think the whole experience would have changed him.

12. KATIE: He was loyal to his buddies.

13. So he would still be a Greaser,

14. he just wouldn't be as violent.

15. JEN: Yeah, and also it was him and Pony who were always saying,

16. "Will we still have time to make something of ourselves?"

17. So I think he would go out and do something

18. because his family wasn't very caring.

19. So I think he would help himself do something.

20. KATIE: It's been said that Darry wanted to die,

21. but do you think he robbed the store so that—

22. ASHLEY: Oh! *(Raises hand)*

23. KATIE: —he would die?

24. ASHLEY: No, I think he robbed the store out of grief that Johnny was dead.

25. So I don't think he robbed the store because he wanted to die.

26. RICK: Yeah, I think so much was going on at that moment that he had to do

27. something to take his mind off it: so robbing the store. But it was said way

28. earlier in the book that Greasers weren't supposed to get caught, if they got

29. caught they were on their own. But I'm not sure if he wanted to get caught on

30. purpose or if he just slipped up . . .

Literature Circles Handout

Literature Circles Role (during discussion)	Purpose and Participation Stems
Discussion director	Managing <u>participation</u> in discussion
—makes sure everyone contributes —makes sure class norms are upheld —makes sure that all ideas are both supported and challenged	"I'd like to hear from _____ on this topic." "Is that really the best way for us to _____?" "Does anyone want to agree/disagree?"
Questioner	Managing the <u>quality</u> of discussion
—asks follow-up questions that help elaborate and deepen interpretations of the text —makes sure the group sets goals for reading and manages time during discussion activities	"Can you give us an example?" ("Take it to the text!") "How much should we read for next time?" "Are we ready to move on to the next step?"

Classroom Examples

Literature Circles Role (during discussion)	Purpose and Participation Stems
Summarizer	Managing the <u>direction</u> of the discussion
—keeps a record of the group's discussion —points out connections among group members' comments	"Like last week, today we've talked about _____." "How does what _____ just said relate to what you've been saying?"
Citation Manager	Managing the <u>possibilities</u> for discussion
—makes sure that all members of the group are prepared with notes/responses —points out particular moments of the text (or related materials to support or provoke further discussion)	"What was one part of the text you marked for us to talk about?" "What did you think of this: _____?"

PEER REVIEW OF A PERSONAL NARRATIVE (UNDERGRADUATE—COLLEGE COMPOSITION)

In a college-level writing classroom at a US Northeastern rural university, three students sat facing each other to discuss one writer's draft of a personal narrative assignment, based on guidelines furnished in a handout.

1. MARK: So what are we supposed to do?

2. KELSEY: We're each supposed to read our paper

3. and get comments from the other people.

4. And then talk about it.

5. TINA: Yeah, the author reads

6. and then stays quiet while the other two talk,

7. and then she gets to talk again at the end.

8. MARK: Okay, so who goes first?

9. TINA: I will if you want.

10. KELSEY: Okay.

11. TINA: "Sometimes a lesson takes a long time to learn. When I was a freshman—"

12. MARK: Wait, aren't you supposed to tell us what you want us to look for?

13. TINA: Oh yeah! Um, I'm not sure.

14. I guess when I wrote it I had one story in my mind

15. but towards the end I kind of ran out of gas.

16. So if you have any ideas about that.

17. And whatever else you notice. Organization. Grammar.

18. Really anything is fine.

19. KELSEY: Okay.

20. TINA: Okay, so I'll start over. *(Reads)* So now I'll be quiet and you two can talk.

21. MARK: Well, I have a comment, but it's not about the end.

22. KELSEY: Go ahead. I think that's okay.

23. MARK: I think the first sentence should be taken out.

24. It sounds like a cliché.

25. KELSEY: I agree, but then you can't just start with "When I was a freshman . . ."

26. MARK: Why not?

27. KELSEY: Well, aren't we supposed to start with the action?

28. MARK: I guess.

29. KELSEY: I mean a lot of the examples we looked at started in the middle of action.

30. MARK: Well, it could start when she gets to the professor's office.

31. TINA: But do you need the background?

32. Sorry, I know I'm not supposed to—

33. I just thought a reader would need to know what happened earlier in the—

34. MARK: —Well could she—you—could you put some of that stuff into the first scene,

35. kind of like a flashback?

36. TINA: I guess so.

37. KELSEY: I kind of disagree—

38. MARK: But you were the one arguing for starting with the action!

39. KELSEY: —because, yeah, but I think that might be confusing for—

40. TINA: —So I guess I'm going to cut the first line,

41. but leave the background?

42. MARK: Whatever.

TINA'S PERSONAL NARRATIVE

Sometimes a lesson takes a long time to learn. When I was in college, I took a creative writing course with Professor V. Each week, I dutifully turned in writing, wrote comments on the writing of my classmates, and contributed to the discussion of the each writer's work. Toward the end of the fall semester, Professor V arranged to conference with each of us individually in her office. I arrived on the day of my conference, brushing snow off my sleeves, secure in the knowledge that I had fulfilled all the requirements of the course.

Professor V, an elegant African American woman with long braids who often wore crisp, brightly colored suits, watched me from behind her desk as I sat down facing her in a hard wooden chair. Never one for pleasantries, she came right to the point. "Michael, I was watching the Olympics the other day, watching figure skating. And it struck me that you're a silver medalist."

I shifted in my chair. "What do you mean?"

"I mean when it comes to writing, I think you're a silver medalist." She leaned forward, put her elbow on the desk, and extended her hand toward me. "You always turn in your work. It tells a clear and vivid story that anyone can relate to. You make insightful comments. As it is, you'll always be better than most of the other writers in the class. . . ."

Smiling tightly at this praise, I waited, sensing the ax about to fall.

"But if you want to be a *writer*," she said, tapping the desk with her fingers, "that's not good enough. If you want to be a gold medalist, you have to do more than that. So the question is, are you content to be a silver? Or do you want to be a gold?"

Walking back to my dorm from Professor V's office that day, I watched, dazed, as the snow quietly covered the familiar landscape of the campus, transforming it into a cold, lunar landscape. Back in front of my computer, I reread the piece I had written for tomorrow's creative writing class. Was it the work of a silver medalist? I wasn't sure.

That spring, I signed up for another creative writing course. This time, the teacher, Professor O, asked us to read and discuss short stories by published authors, as well as whatever had been turned in by our peers for that week. As a result, there was sometimes a stack of writing to read, and sometimes almost none. Sometimes we spent an hour on one person's writing, then discussed three other pieces in the next fifteen minutes. Frustrated, I stopped submitting my own work. At the end of the semester, I applied to the next stage of the creative writing program, which would mean meeting for regular one-on-one tutorial with a professor. The news that my application had been rejected only seemed to confirm what Professor V had said: as a silver medalist, I was missing some part of what it took to be a real writer.

Only now, as I begin to write creative pieces again and to teach writing to high school students, am I beginning to understand Professor V's advice. My students' writing is excellent, full of good vocabulary, personal examples, and varied sentence structure. Much of it is "A" work. But does it matter to them? And if not, will it matter to anyone else?

Appendix B

PEER REVIEW HANDOUT

Expectations:	What is it you hope to gain from peer review today?
Plans:	What practices might help you/your classmates attain those expectations?
Procedure:	For this peer review, groups of three will follow these steps:

1. Author: sets expectations; reads/explains narrative aloud
2. Peers: write comments using rubric; share *praise/questions*
3. Author: asks *questions/responds* to peer comments
4. Peers: make *suggestions/respond* to author questions

Have you received comments about . . . ?	Member 1 ☑	Member 2 ☑	Summarize those comments for yourself below
Focused: includes events and interpretations that together relate to the purpose of the story			
Active, Vivid: uses active verbs, concrete nouns, and vivid details to convey the "scenes" of the story			
Voice: selection of purpose, details, and words creates consistent and relateable narrator and is appropriate to purpose			
Coherent: events and interpretations are related in an authentic, well-paced order consistent with the purpose and voice of the story			

Reflection:	Now that you've received some comments, how will you address them when you revise your work?
Evaluation:	Were your expectations met today? Why or why not?

LEMONADE RATIOS
(MIDDLE SCHOOL, SIXTH-GRADE SCIENCE)

In an urban sixth-grade UK science classroom,[1] students were studying ratios by creating lemonade concentrates. Each student made one, recording the ratio of sugar and lemon juice, in preparation for adding them into a class graph. One student, Paulina, lost her concentrate ratio, recalling only that she had used two spoonfuls of sugar, and between ten and twenty-two spoonfuls of lemon juice. With the teacher Ms. Lynne's guidance, the class discussed what Paulina should do. Should she create a completely new concentrate or enter into the graph a ratio with her known sugar amount and an average of the possible missing lemon juice values? Some students argued that neither option would be Paulina's "real" first concentrate, but then Steven made the following comment:

1. STEVEN: . . . Um, but if she kept her, um, sugar

2. and used that

3. and then took her thing of ten to twenty-two

4. and then picked another number like halfway,

5. like Allison said,

6. and then made that her concentrate . . .

7. MS. LYNNE: So then you don't agree with Sarita that

8. if she *[Paulina]* picks a number halfway between

9. then that's not really making her first concentrate either?

GEOMETRIC SHAPES (ELEMENTARY, FIRST-GRADE MATH)

During a first-grade geometry lesson in a US Southern suburban school, Ms. Kohl and her students discussed geometric shapes. The original transcript is followed by an imagined revision:[1]

1. MS. KOHL: Think of one of the shapes that we talked about this week.

2. Who can think of a shape?

3. Student A?

4. STUDENT A: A Granny Smith.

5. MS. KOHL: *(Laughing)* A Granny Smith?

6. Is that a shape?

7. STUDENTS: No!

8. MS. KOHL: That's an apple.

1. MS. KOHL: Think of one of the shapes that we talked about this week.

2. Who can think of a shape?

3. Student A?

4. STUDENT A: A Granny Smith.

5. MS. KOHL: *(Laughing)* A Granny Smith?

6. Are you saying that you see angles and curves—

7. maybe even symmetry—

8. in an apple,

9. which is something that we find in our everyday lives?

10. STUDENT A: Yeah, round,

11. kind of like a circle.

12. MS. KOHL: You're saying that a Granny Smith is kind of like a circle.

13. What about a Granny Smith is not like a circle?

14. STUDENT A: It has lumps.

15. MS. KOHL: Okay, so a Granny Smith apple may not be perfectly round.

16. "Perfectly round" is one of the defining features of a circle

17. listed on our chart.

18. So even when we're not in school, we're thinking like mathematicians

19. when we compare geometric shapes, like circles,

20. with ordinary things, like apples.

21. Can you remember a time when you thought like a mathematician

22. outside of school

23. by seeing a geometric shape in an ordinary thing?

TRENCH WARFARE/FOOTBALL
(HIGH SCHOOL, NINTH-GRADE US HISTORY)

After reviewing homework questions, teacher Dave Weber's US Midwestern suburban ninth-grade history class discussed trench warfare through an imagined scenario involving a competition with another class.

64. MR. WEBER: So when they are—they have the Schlieffen plan—

65. they start setting up these wars, battles.

66. And they decide on . . . on a different type of battle.

67. What's that type?

68. TOM: Trench warfare.

69. MR. WEBER: Trench warfare.

70. So this is—what if all of a sudden

71. we decided we were going to take it out to the football field and

72. we were going to get into a battle with Mr. Abbott's fourth hour?

78. MR. WEBER: What would it be like when we're in there?

79. ERICA: Wouldn't they like see, if they're running, wouldn't they like see there's a hole?

80. MR. WEBER: Okay, they would see the hole, but how would they get over to us?

81. ERICA: Um run.

82. CHELSEA: Run and climb.

83. LAURA: Jump.

84. TOM: Dig.

85. MR. WEBER: Would there be any—

86. AMY: Couldn't we just shoot them before they got over anyways?

87. STUDENTS: *(Laughter)*

88. AMY: I'm dead serious.

89. MR. WEBER: No, Amy, you are dead serious, go ahead and say it again.

90. STUDENTS: *(Laughter)*

91. AMY: They probably wouldn't be able to get over anyways

92. because if we're just like sitting there

93. we could probably just like shoot them before they could get over a fence.

94. TOM: What if they had guns too?

106. MR. WEBER: So let's think about it: what would it be like if we're in the trenches?

107. How would it feel?

108. TOM: Boring.

109. MR. WEBER: Boring.

110. BECCA: I would feel claustrophobic. Because they're like right on top of you.

111. MR. WEBER: Alright.

112. PENNY: Yeah but they're—

113. AMY: But you'd kind of feel powerful.

114. PENNY: —because they couldn't get to you.

115. AMY: Yeah, I'd feel safe.

116. MR. WEBER: Okay, you would kind of feel safe, sometimes.

117. BECCA: Hiding in a hole?

PULLING THE PLUG
(HIGH SCHOOL, TENTH-GRADE ENGLISH LANGUAGE ARTS)

During a US tenth-grade English Language Arts lesson in an urban Midwestern school, teacher Tamara Jefferson had asked students in her fourth-hour class to compose entries in their writing journals in preparation for reading Sophocles' *Antigone*. In this Greek tragedy, the title character decides to bury her brother, despite the fact that Theban law decreed by her uncle, King Creon, forbids the interment of traitors. Ms. Jefferson asked students to relate the events of the story to a present-day dilemma: Should a doctor or nurse remove life support from a suffering or terminally ill patient, despite possible legal consequences?

1. KAYLA: I don't think . . . I don't think he should

2. because then he go'n' lose his job,

3. and it's all over, and he probably never go'n' get a doctoring job again.

4. MS. JEFFERSON: Right. Okay. Okay. Go ahead.

5. GARRETT: Um, it's not like I would follow the law, but in my mind, like,

6. following the law, it's like, kind of like my own personal belief that

7. if I push my ways on other people that, like, change their beliefs,

8. maybe in their religion or something, that they can't do that or something.

9. So it would be kind of like me pushing my ways on other people.

10. MS. JEFFERSON: Okay. Good point. Montana?

11. MONTANA: Basically I would say that I would follow my conscience,

12. but it would be toward, like, rather than just up and pulling the plug,

13. I would try to go through whatever, try to find whatever loopholes I could,

14. try to find existent family members, or whatever.

15. I would basically work around the system before I made anything decisive,

16. and if that didn't work, yes, I would pull the plug just to stop the suffering.

17. MS. JEFFERSON: Okay. Derek?

ALL'S FAIR IN LOVE AND WAR
(HIGH SCHOOL, TENTH-GRADE ENGLISH LANGUAGE ARTS)

In a US Midwestern urban tenth-grade school, teacher Tamara Jefferson's sixth-hour class had read John Hersey's *Hiroshima*. The class had previously discussed the maxim "All's fair in love and war" in preparation for writing a position paper about "fairness" and the US's atomic bombing of Japan. Unsatisfied with what she had found to be simplistic reactions from students in the previous activity, Ms. Jefferson planned in this lesson to compare the bombing of Hiroshima to the terrorist attacks of September 11, 2001.

1. MS. JEFFERSON: So what did we say this idea of "All is fair in love and war" actually means?

2. What does that quote mean, Franklin? What did we say that was?

3. FRANKLIN: Like if you're in a war, you can go to any extent.

4. MS. JEFFERSON: So Franklin said if you're in a war you can go to any extent.

5. MS. JEFFERSON: If it gets to the point where you need to drop an atomic bomb,

6. then that's fair.

7. If it gets to the point, similar to 9/11 here,

8. where you take a plane and you crash into the Trade Center . . .

9. then that's also fair.

10. FRANKLIN: Well no . . . but . . . if they bomb us then—

11. RICHARD: —If they bomb us, and then we bomb them back,

12. then they can't say nothin' 'cause it's fair.

13. MS. JEFFERSON: So you're saying this is more of a retaliation.

14. If someone does something to me,

15. then I should have the right to do the same thing to them.

16. Or even if I do something bigger and better than what they did to me,

17. then that makes it right. Okay.

18. BRIAN: What's interesting is that, they bombed Pearl Harbor,

19. which was a naval base, but we bombed a city.

20. MS. JEFFERSON: No reason to kill innocent people.

21. Wait, but Kevin said they deserved it!

22. KEVIN: They did.

23. RICHARD: I just want to say something.

24. MS. JEFFERSON: Okay. Wait a minute. Let's let Kevin make his point

25. and then you can make yours.

26. Okay, Kevin. So they bombed us, they deserved it.

27. KEVIN: They shouldn't have killed Americans. For no reason.

28. RICHARD: You see how Brian was saying that we bombed a city?

29. But when we bombed them,

30. their military was underground.

31. So who else was there to bomb?

32. BRIAN: There was no point to build the bomb.

33. RICHARD: But we did build it,

34. so what's the point in making it sit there and not use it?

35. BRIAN: What's the point in using it?

36. RICHARD: To kill. So they know who's boss.

37. BRIAN: But if we bomb them,

38. we just had to rebuild them and pay them back for it.

39. GLORIA: Why? It doesn't seem to me like, and I don't understand why . . .

40. In Iraq, they kinda did mess it up, too, 'cause they were fighting us.

41. So why shouldn't they help rebuild it if we got to rebuild it?

42. EBONY: Like when they crashed into the Trade Center,

43. they didn't come and clean up our [unintelligible].

44. Why are we cleaning up their stuff?

45. GLORIA: Like, what she said, it's not like they asked for our help. . . .

46. MS. JEFFERSON: I think this debate—I think this debate is very . . . is very much needed. . . .

47. When you write this essay,

48. I want you to keep in mind this idea of "All is fair in love and war."

THE STOCK MARKET CRASH
(HIGH SCHOOL, NINTH-GRADE US HISTORY)

In a US Midwestern suburban ninth-grade history classroom, during a November lesson on the 1920s "Black Tuesday" US stock market crash, teacher Dave Weber intended to "Begin the class by reminding the students of the [stock market simulation] game that we played over the past two days. . ." and then "Begin discussing the nature of the Great Depression, and some causes/effects in brief." Then, a student asked a clarifying question.

1. VICTORIA: How are [stockbrokers] getting any money off of it? They're

2. just giving people help.

3. MR. WEBER: OK. Very good point. So it works like this. Uh, we're going to go

4. with Tom right here. . . . You owned a lot of Rylant stock [during the stock

5. market simulation game], right?

6. TOM: Yeah, me and Jon had like eight of them.

7. MR. WEBER: Eight of them? So, in the very beginning though, we're just going

8. to start in the beginning. Say you guys together, you had most of the Rylant

9. stock. Now in a real company, a big company like Rylant, if you own the

10. majority of the stocks, in a situation like that, all of a sudden they start-

11. they're very interested in what you think, because when you own stock,

12. like, that certificate proves that you own part of that company. I—I think

13. you guys understood that as we went through it, right? You are buying

14. into that company. So if all of a sudden if you guys combined had like

15. fifty-one percent of it they're really interested in what you have in what

16. you have to say about Rylant Motors.

17. OK. So the problem we have here is that Tom starts taking partial

18. money from Matt because . . . Whitney is lending money to Matt. . . . Now,

19. Matt, you still have like zero dollars to your name, right? You don't have any

20. money, you just own that stock and the stock keeps going up, and you're

21. pretty happy about it. Now all of a sudden, Whitney, you need your money,

22. right? Because he owes you money. So what do you do?

23. WHITNEY: Ask him to turn it in?

24. MR. WEBER: You ask him for it. And Matt, Whitney comes up to you and says,

25. Can I have my money please?" And what do you pay her with?

26. MATT: The stock?

27. MR. WEBER: You could. Maybe. Whitney, do you want stock? You're a bank.

28. WHITNEY: No?

29. MR. WEBER: You want money right?

30. WHITNEY: Yeah.

31. MR. WEBER: Matt, she's not taking your stock. What are you going to do?

32. MATT: Turn it in.

33. MR. WEBER: Now all of a sudden people . . . start losing money. Because now the

34. bank is dependent on the company and the company is dependent on the

35. bank. And you get caught in the middle.

36. AMY: Is that why it all crashed?

37. MR WEBER: That is a good part of why it crashed.

38. AMY: Because it was like all built on itself but nothing was really there?

Appendix B

COLLECTIVE BARGAINING
(HIGH SCHOOL, NINTH-GRADE US HISTORY)

In a US Midwestern suburban ninth-grade history classroom, during a December lesson on the Roosevelt era, teacher Dave Weber's goal was "for the students to gain a contextual understanding . . . of FDR's new deal," including "how everyday people would feel effects." Students had answered a series of warm-up questions about the previous night's textbook chapter, and as Weber reviewed the answers with them, he stopped to explain the 1935 Wagner Act, and the concept of collective bargaining, by calling on Mary (a student whose last name also happened to be Wagner).

1. MR. WEBER: . . . that's something that the Mary Wagner Act helped do. Thank you,

2. Mary, for your time helping all workers like that. Now explain why the Mary

3. Wagner Act was important. Besides the fact that it had your last name.

4. MARY: Because it protected the right of workers to form unions and engage

5. in collective bargaining with their employers. And also it prohibited unfair

6. labor practices.

7. MR. WEBER: This was a big effort of the second hundred days . . . and workers,

8. looking more at workers, trying to protect workers a little more, and um,

9. collective bargaining, do you guys know what it is?

10. TOM: Something that a union does?

11. MR. WEBER: There you go. Uh, it's something that a union does, quite often it's

12. why a union is so strong: they can bargain as a group. It's the reason why, like,

13. if I tell you we have a test next Thursday—

14. AMY: For real?

15. MR. WEBER: You see how I combined—

16. PENNY: Are you serious?

. . .

[student worker delivers attendance slips]

. . .

18. PENNY: But we can use our notes.

19. AMY: For real?

20. MR. WEBER: See—

21. AMY: Are we able to?

22. TOM: No.

23. MR. WEBER: No.

24. AMY: Oh.

25. MR. WEBER: We're going to talk more about it when we get there, but this would

26. be a perfect example of collective bargaining: Penny, you said we should be

27. able to use our notes, right? OK, I value your opinion a lot, but if you get all

28. thirty people in the room all of a sudden that voice is—

29. TOM: Let's take a vote.

30. AMY: Yeah, can we take a vote on—?

31. MR. WEBER: (speaking in higher voice) It's not even votable.

32. (shrugging) I'm sorry, I'm very cruel.

33. TOM: I'm going on strike.

34. STUDENTS: (laughter)

. . .

[Weber regains control of the class]

. . .

45. MR. WEBER: Many times a company would not hear people's single voices or

46. people coming up and saying "Hey you guys should pay us more" they're like

47. "yeah yeah" but . . . um, you, as more people get involved with something, all

48. of a sudden the voice gets stronger, and that's something that the Mary

49. Wagner Act helped do. Thank you, Mary, for your time helping all workers like that.

THE BERLIN/CAPITAL CITY AIRLIFT
(HIGH SCHOOL—NINTH GRADE ENGLISH LANGUAGE ARTS)

In March, teacher Dave Weber addressed the post–WWII division of Germany and Berlin that led to Stalin's blockade of the Western part of the city and forced the Allies to fly in supplies. During this lesson in a US Midwestern suburban ninth-grade history class, Weber's plan called for students to "open up their books to 'The Berlin Airlift,'... read the page out of the book, and summarize it in three to four sentences. Ask students to volunteer to read their sentences. Discuss. Move onto the smart board note packet that was worked on the day before. Pick back up on the Berlin Airlift."

1. SHIRIN: So. Um does are—Why *are* **we** there?

2. Since it's like Communist and everything?

3. MR. WEBER: Why *were* **we** in Germany to start with?

4. SHIRIN: In Berlin.

5. MR. WEBER: OK. After World War II, it *was decided* that the fairest way to make

6. sure that Germany wouldn't reconsolidate power and start World War III

7. would be if each Ally took a zone of Germany. And then when **they** *were*

8. *trying* to figure out who should get Berlin, it *was decided* it's not fair, Berlin

9. is—if

10. if **we**'re talking about [**our** state] it *would be* like [a major industrial

11. city]. Or actually I guess **we**'ll say [the capital city]. It's closer. And the

12. capital. We'll say it's like [the capital city]. . . . It's not fair, right? If one section

13. of the state . . . if someone *got* [the capital city]. . . . say you, Laura, Takara, and

14. Amy *were dividing* up the state, right? It's not fair if just you get [the capital

. . .

26. MR. WEBER: So **we** *would* need to supply from here to **our** [part of the city].

27. . . . What if they shut off the roads? Closed the railroads?

28. LAURA: OOOH!

29. TAKARA: How *would* **we** get supplies?

30. MR. WEBER: Shirin, if you *have* that part of—if **you** have, **you** *know*, this general

31. area of [the state]. What's the advantage of closing it off so that the other

32. three girls *can't get*

33. into the city?

34. SHIRIN: That **you** *have* it. They *can't get* in.

. . . .

47. AMY: Why *can't* **you** fly?

48. MR. WEBER: So. What's our one solution, Amy?

49. AMY: Fly.

50. MR. WEBER: **You** *have to fly* supplies in. Berlin airlift? Alright.

51. PENNY: That's what **they** *did*, didn't **they**?

52. MR. WEBER: That's exactly what **they** *did*.

OUR GROUP NAME
(HIGH SCHOOL, NINTH-GRADE ENGLISH LANGUAGE ARTS)

Students in a US Midwestern suburban ninth-grade English Language Arts classroom corresponded with prospective teachers in a Northeastern rural university teacher education course via a private online social network. The host teacher had organized "online literature circles" composed of groups of students who had chosen the same book from a list of options. Each group had its own online discussion forum—and group name—for conversations about the book moderated by a prospective teacher. In her first post to one of these groups, prospective teacher Dara Kelly wrote:

> What does our group name mean?? Without looking up the actual definition, I want you to define the word "sesquipedalian" (sehs-kwih-ped-al-ee-ehn), what YOU think it means.
>
> - Provide a "dictionary-like" definition.
> - Write the word in a creative, fun, comical sentence (you may use complementary sentences to give us context clues).
> - Post your answers as discussion entries under this topic.
> - Most of all—HAVE FUN with this! This assignment is completely yours, it's all about what YOU think. (The more of YOU that you put into it, the better it will be!) Be creative, have fun, and just be you!
>
> After you all have replied, I will post the actual definition to the discussion board and you can see how close you were! (So please, please, please don't look up the definition until we're done!)
> Thank you all for your participation!

BREAKING POINT
(HIGH SCHOOL, NINTH-GRADE ENGLISH LANGUAGE ARTS)

A prospective secondary English teacher in a US Northeastern university teacher education course, Janae Jenkins (labeled "Mod," below), collaborated with her host teacher to facilitate online exchanges among a group of US Midwestern suburban ninth-graders over a two-month period about the book they had chosen to read together. The ten students in this group had chosen *Breaking Point*, by Alex Flinn. *Breaking Point* describes the experiences of Paul Richmond at a private school, where he falls under the spell of charismatic and unscrupulous Charlie Good.

message 18: by _____   Apr 20, 2011 05:43PM

At first I thought the book was going to be bad, but ever since I got into it, I REALLY got into it. I think the weird things in the book that make it good.

reply | flag •

message 19: by _____   Apr 20, 2011 06:18PM

_____ wrote: *"At first I thought the book was going to be bad, but ever since I got into it, I REALLY got into it. I think the weird things in the book that make it good."*

I'm glad to hear that! I agree, things definitely started to get crazier as the book progressed. What about the book helped you to get into it/make it good?

reply | flag •

message 20: by _____   Apr 21, 2011 05:29AM

_____ wrote: "_____ wrote: *"At first I thought the book was going to be bad, but ever since I got into it, I REALLY got into it. I think the weird things in the book that make it good."*

I'm glad to hear that! ..."

I think davids dog is decapitated

I'm glad to hear that! ..."

I think davids dog is decapitated

message 21: by   Apr 23, 2011 05:47PM

    i wondered y St. John didn"t hang out with them anymore?

message 22: by   Apr 23, 2011 05:48PM

    I also wondered how sent the note to Paul?

message 23: by   Apr 23, 2011 05:50PM

    wrote: ":   wrote: "I have read the entire book and thought it was quite interesting
    I have no life"

Haha that doesn't mean you have no life! I liked it too! Now that you've finished it..what did you ..."

    I thought why charlie or the other guy didn't get in trouble for the bomb?

message 24: by   Apr 25, 2011 01:06PM

    After the mailbox scene will the guys at Paul's school stop bullying him?

message 25: by   Apr 25, 2011 01:13PM

    , yep..you're right. I thought that scene was terrifying. Do you agree?

    [Mod] :   , good questions. Neither of those are really clarified in the book. The author is probably leaving them open for a suspenseful effect. From your knowledge of the characters, what do you think the answers are? And both are punished for the bomb..but are they given equal punishments?

    , that's a good question. If you had to take a guess, what do you think will happen?

message 26: by   Apr 25, 2011 02:46PM

    i wonder why the main character decided to go along with charlie and his friends.... i guess he had no other choice

Appendix B

LESSON VIDEO
(GRADUATE MA, ENGLISH TEACHER EDUCATION)

Graduate students in a US Southern urban university teacher education course used an online forum to share and reflect on videos of teaching, attending to specific interactions in a classroom, without having to visit the school where the lesson transpired. In this particular online discussion, the video under review depicted a teacher leading an activity about story elements using a plot diagram written on the white board.

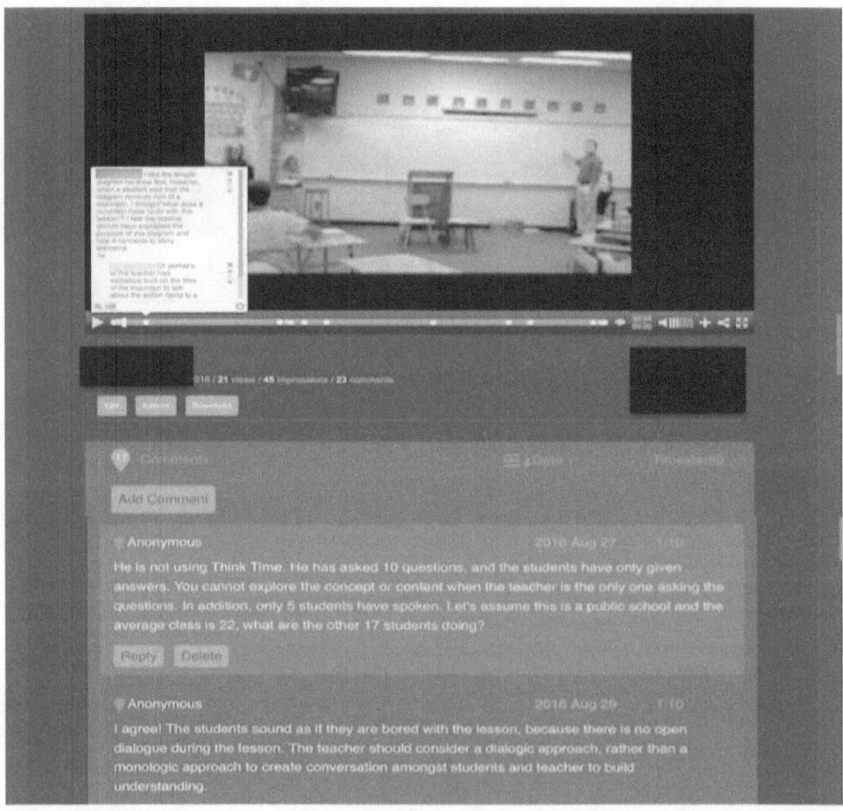

ETHNOGRAPHIC RESEARCH
(UNDERGRADUATE, COLLEGE COMPOSITION)

When class cancellations due to weather made it impossible for them to meet face-to-face, freshman composition students in a US Northeastern rural university course used this forum to dialogue about their research projects, as well as two related readings: an ethnography called *My Freshman Year*, about an anthropology professor who enrolled as a student in her own university to study college life; and Heath and Street's *On Ethnography*, a guide for researchers learning this methodology. An initial note instructed students to use a different color each time they introduced a topic and to choose the same color (and arrange their notes next to a related post) when responding to an existing topic.

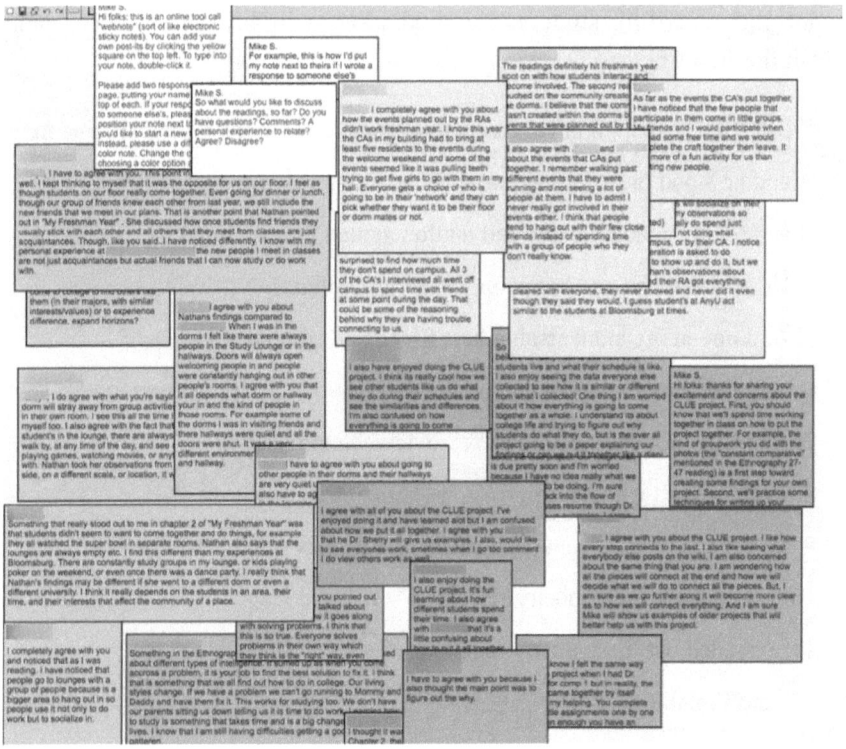

Appendix B

ROUTINE BREAKING (UNDERGRADUATE/GRADUATE, ENGLISH TEACHER EDUCATION)

At a US Southern urban university, on this sixth session of a weekly three-hour English teacher education course that included both prospective and practicing teachers, the class was scheduled to talk about creating routines as a core task of teaching: how might we teach students to participate in recurring class activities like journaling or whole-class discussion? But the day before the class, a student at a local high school had gunned down seventeen people and wounded seventeen more in one of the deadliest school shootings in US history. To open discussion of this event, teacher Michael Sherry told the story of how, as a first-year teacher, the principal visited his tenth-grade class, on the opening day of our poetry unit, to report that one of his students had died, along with her parents, in a plane crash the night before.

1. MR. SHERRY: I'll never forget that moment when the principal came in

2. and he stood there in that portable classroom

3. and told us that the plane had malfunctioned.

4. He said that she and her parents died instantly.

5. And one of my students, her best friend, she gasped

6. and then put her head down on the desk.

7. After the principal left, I just felt overwhelmed.

8. I had no idea what to do.

9. So instead of asking students to share how they felt,

10. I went back to the poetry lesson.

11. I handed out these poetry templates,

12. and I think I said that,

13. "Poetry is a good way to express your feelings."

14. But over the next few days, I knew that I had failed them.

15. Because no one wrote about it.

16. I hadn't been willing to talk about it, to face it.

17. To feel it.

18. So they didn't either.

19. Even if I had tried. If I had said to them,

20. "You know, this is so awful, I don't even know what to say.

21. It hurts so much that words fail."

22. Because they do sometimes. Words fail.

23. But I didn't say anything.

24. Just went home and wondered

25. if I should even be a teacher.

26. So I want to invite you to talk about what happened yesterday.

27. I know that I feel shocked and sad and frightened.

28. And you might be feeling things too.

29. Like, "Is this really what I signed up for?

30. What does this mean about . . . being a teacher?"

31. RON: So we went to *[our field placement school]* today

32. and there was a lockdown drill.

33. STUDENTS: *(Sounds of disbelief)* No way!

34. RON: Yeah, seriously!

35. And Carrie and I,

36. we had gone down to the office.

37. And they made us get down on the floor behind the desks

38. in the dark.

39. And no one even told us it was a drill.

40. STUDENTS: *(Silence)*

41. CARRIE: There was a TV over our heads,

42. and they kept playing news about it.

43. That little tape running at the bottom of the screen.

44. And I got so panicked

45. because I remembered being in a lockdown drill

46. when I was in high school

47. and I started crying in class

48. and the other kids all laughed

49. and made fun of me.

50. I just don't know if I can go through that again.

51. STUDENTS: *(Silence)*

52. JOSEPH: You know, I have this student in my eighth-grade class.

53. He's kind of a goofball.

54. Doesn't usually do his work, got himself suspended.

55. He's . . . struggling.

56. But he talks to me.

57. And he turned something in the other day

58. and I was like, "I'm proud of you."

59. And I had to tell my fiancée,

60. "You know, if I had to,

61. I think I would take a bullet for that kid."

62. STUDENTS: *(Silence)*

63. MARIE: Yeah, I think about it

64. driving to work.

65. I have some students,

66. they're just really . . . angry.

67. But when I see them in class

68. I just try to . . . see them.

69. You know, like, "Hey, you got a haircut?"

70. Or like, make a joke,

71. just be with them.

72. STUDENTS: *(Silence)*

73. KAT: I have this one girl,

74. she told me today . . . *(Voice shaking)*

75. *(Pause)*

76. She handed in her project, and she was like,

77. "This is the first time I felt like I was good at something."

78. STUDENTS: *(Silence)*

79. MARK: Okay, is someone cutting onions in here?

80. STUDENTS: *(Laughter)*

Appendix C

Activities for Promoting Dialogic Discussions

Alternate Endings: On their own, or in small groups, students compose alternate endings to a story. Afterward, they discuss how and why their endings are different from, yet still justified by, the original text.

Audience Participation: During whole-class discussion, invite students to speak to audiences (real or imagined) beyond their immediate classroom community.

Complex Instruction:[1] Students receive a "group task" that asks them to create something in response to a problem, question, or other prompt. Creating this product requires all students' input, but students each have different responsibilities associated with a role detailed in advance and in the "group task" materials: Team Captain, Resource Manager, Recorder/Reporter, Facilitator.

Discussion Channels: During a discussion, students are encouraged to switch between different "channels" with explicitly different expectations about when and how to participate: for example, whole-class discussion with certain formal constraints and pair or small-group conversations in which informal language practices are welcome.

Discussion Mapping: Students write down ideas (on a note card or sticky note) and then post them on a wall or board. During or after this posting process, students can begin to group their responses next to other, similar ideas (e.g., about the same topic, character, event, or passage).

Draw from the Basket: Having read and responded to a text, students each write on a slip of paper one topic or question that they would like to pursue further (they may also list one vocabulary word or one idea about which they felt confused or uncertain). These slips of paper are collected in a "basket"; teacher(s) draw them out one-by-one (or sort through and choose) to generate discussion.

Experiences/Patterns/Explanations: Having encountered a scientific phenomenon (e.g., how shadows form or how cold soda can freeze after being opened), students first share *experiences* (verifiable observations about the phenomenon), then identify *patterns* (repetitions and contrasts in those observations), and finally generate *explanations* (theories and models that account for the patterns in their observations).

Fishbowl: Having read and responded to a text, at least three (or more) designated students start a conversation about the text; others listen and take notes, generating questions. At the end of time, a new group (or the other half of the class) replaces the old one. Repeat as necessary.

Font-Styling: Invent a system with students for indicating a type of response or a change in topic using font styles during online discussions.

"Four Corners" Discussion: In response to a question or statement about a text they have read, or another shared focus, students decide where to position themselves on a scaled response (e.g., strongly disagree/disagree/agree/strongly agree; or always/often/sometimes/never), writing down an explanation for why they have chosen this position for now. Then students raise hands to show who shares the same position before discussing what they chose and why.

Four Windows:[2] Invite students to write and/or talk about an experience using the "four windows" of thinking, feeling, sensing, and imagining.

"How (Else) Do You Know?": Given a math problem, students first solve and then discuss the answer to the problem. However, rather than simply evaluating their solutions, a teacher can invite students to discuss how they know if an answer is correct, whether the problem could be solved differently, and why one procedure might be preferable to another.

Imaginary Painting: Ask students to imagine a blank canvas (a blackboard works well). On this canvas, each subsequent speaker adds details to an imaginary painting (no actual drawing takes place). Additions must build on what has already been added and cannot "overwrite" previous contributions (for example, if someone has added "clouds in a blue sky" the next person cannot say, "The sky turns dark and stormy" but can instead add "rain falling from one of the clouds." At the end, students all imagine signing their names at the bottom of the imaginary canvas.

Imagined Dialogue: Having read and responded to a text, students imagine a dialogue between that text (or the author of that text, or a character from the text) and other stakeholders (these could be other texts/authors already read in class, other characters, or other generic roles—teacher, parent, student, etc.). This dialogue can be elaborated with a group and even enacted; voice of the original text/author must be tied to specific evidence from the original text.

Journaling: Invite students to write about their personal experiences in a journal that will only be read by the teacher (and in which students may fold over pages they do not wish the teacher to read). If you plan to invite discussion based on a particular journal entry, notify students before they begin writing; call only on volunteers, or if students will talk with peers, offer them the option to discuss the *experience* of writing (rather than the specifics of the content).

"Let's Do the Numbers": Together, the class counts in order from one to the number of people in the classroom (e.g., twenty-five) or higher. There is no specified order: someone adds the next number in sequence whenever the opportunity arises. Each person who says a number cannot say another until everyone has participated. When any two people say a number at the same time, the count returns to zero.

Literature Circles:[3] This is a routine, or recurring activity genre, in which small groups of students who are reading the same text (that might be different from the one read by another group) take turns playing roles with particular responsibilities as they participate in regular conversations about the section of the text they have agreed to read for that meeting.

Most Important Passage/Idea: Having read a text (and/or written about it), students choose what was for them the most important passage or idea from that text; in the margin next to this passage/idea, they write why they chose it. Students can then share with a partner and/or the class.

Multi-Genre Discussion: On their own or in groups, students can contribute to a discussion using a variety of modes, including nonverbal (e.g., write a comment on a sticky note, draw a picture, create a skit or human tableau).

Name-Dropping: Encourage students to use names when referring to what others have already written during online discussions.

Notice/Question/Interpret: Having read and responded to a text, students answer three rounds of questions. (What is one thing you notice? What is one question you have? What is one interpretation you can make?) These can be answered individually and/or with partner(s). After each round, students can share answers with a partner or the class.

Panel Interview/Town Hall: In groups or as a class, students choose characters (real or fictional) with different voices (e.g., of different backgrounds or perspectives) to participate in a panel interview or "town hall" discussion of a particular topic.

Participation Stems: Either before or after reading and responding to a text, students receive a list of question/response stems (as a handout or bookmark) that they can use during discussion (e.g., "I'd like to respectfully disagree with ____ because . . ." and "I have an example of what we're talking about: it's ____").

Poems for Multiple Voices: Using models from Paul Fleischman's *Joyful Noise*[4] (or other examples), students work on their own or in groups to create "dialogue poems" in which two or more different voices appear in parallel columns that can be read together. Parallel lines are meant to sound in unison, while others go back and forth in complement or counterpoint. After writing their poems, students share and discuss.

Response Roles:[5] Before or during a discussion, students receive assigned response roles with accompanying participation practices and/or conversation stems: for example, Problem Poser, Devil's Advocate, Theme Spotter, Evidence Assessor, Synthesizer.

Scaled Response Discussion: In response to a question or statement about a text they have read, or another shared focus, students decide where to position themselves on a scaled response (e.g., strongly disagree/disagree/agree/strongly agree; or always/often/sometimes/never), writing down an explanation for why they have chosen this position for now. Then students raise hands to show who shares the same position before discussing what they chose and why.

Silent Discussion: Having written a response (or brought a written response to class), students pass their responses to the right. After reading a classmate's response, they write back to that person underneath it. Repeat as many times as necessary, then return to original author for review and discussion.

Socratic Seminar: Having prepared in advance, one or more student leaders pose O-HOT discussion questions to a group; other students respond in ways that may correspond to particular roles or agreed-upon class norms (e.g., talk to one another, not just to the discussion leader; don't interrupt; use examples and evidence; ask follow-up questions).

Speed-Dating: After reading a text and writing responses, teacher (or each student) selects line or passage from each writer's response (these can be printed in advance or written on a note card at beginning of class). Each class member chooses one of these lines/passages (not his or her own). Arrange desks in two rows facing each other (if the classroom is already in rows, this can easily be done with students in front/behind or across the aisle). Pairs read their lines/passages to each other and discuss, attempting to bring them into relationship, for one to two minutes. At the end of time, place lines/passages face down on desk, then shift seats to face a new partner (e.g., all students in a row move down one seat; the last person moves to the front of the line).

The Spiral:[6] Ask students to write/speak to each of four (potentially recursive) steps: (1) Coming from Gratitude; (2) Honoring the Pain of the World; (3) Seeing with New Eyes; and (4) Going Forth.

Structured Debate: Students choose or are assigned to different positions on a debatable topic; having prepared to defend that position, one or more students present their ideas to the opposing side (and/or to other evaluators) in a sequence that may include parts like opening arguments, rebuttals, cross-examinations, and closing statements.

Symbol-fying: Encourage students to develop or apply their own symbol systems for creating connections during online discussions, based on their experiences with other forums, including social media (e.g., @name for citing a previous speaker or #topic for indicating a new/existing idea).

Think-Pair-Share: Have students stop and write a response (or prepare one for homework and bring it to class); students then pair with a partner and discuss what they wrote before engaging in a whole-class discussion.

Time Travel Tickets: Students each receive contextual information (e.g., a role-card, letter, ticket, passport, picture, or other cultural artifact) about a historical figure and that person's role in an event (e.g., the sinking of the RMS *Titanic*—see https://titanicorlando.com/visit). During and after a detailed review or reenactment of the event, students contribute to discussions about how their characters experienced the event differently, and why.

Way of Council:[7] Speakers sit in a circle with a central focus that may also serve as a means of creating the "container" (e.g., a candle that is lit at the beginning of the session and extinguished at the end; a drum that is struck at the beginning/end of the session); a "talking stick" or other ceremonial object passes from one speaker to another; participants are free to pass but must not interrupt or comment, instead responding with a chorused "I hear you"; all participants are invited to (1) speak from the heart; (2) listen from the heart; (3) be spontaneous; and (4) be lean of expression.

NOTES

1. Elizabeth G. Cohen, *Designing Groupwork: Strategies for the Heterogeneous Classroom* (New York: Teachers College Press, 1986).

2. E. S. Gallegos, *Animals of the Four Windows* (Embudo, NM: Moon Bear Press, 1991).

3. Harvey Daniels, *Literature Circles: Voice and Choice in the Student-Centered Classroom* (York, ME: Stenhouse Publishers, 1994).

4. P. Fleischman, *Joyful Noise: Poems for Two Voices* (New York: HarperCollins, 2013).

5. S. D. Brookfield, *The Skillful Teacher: On Technique, Trust, and Responsiveness in the Classroom* (San Francisco, CA: Jossey-Bass, 2015); S. D. Brookfield and S. Preskill, *Discussion as a Way of Teaching: Tools and Techniques for Democratic Classrooms* (San Francisco, CA: Jossey-Bass, 2005).

6. J. Macy and M. Y. Brown, *Coming Back to Life: The Updated Guide to the Work That Reconnects* (Gabriola Island, BC Canada: New Society Publishers, 1989); J. Macy and C. Johnstone, *Active Hope: How to Face the Mess We're in without Going Crazy* (Novato, CA: New World Library, 2012).

7. J. Zimmerman and V. Coyle, *The Way of Council*, 2nd ed. (North Bergen, NJ: Bramble Books, 1996); J. Zimmerman and V. Coyle, "Ways of Council," Ways of Council, 2020, https://waysofcouncil.net/.

References

Abram, D. *The Spell of the Sensuous: Perception and Language in a More-Than-Human World.* New York: Pantheon, 1996.

Applebee, A. N. *Curriculum as Conversation: Transforming Traditions of Teaching and Learning.* Chicago: University of Chicago Press, 1996.

Applebee, A. N., J. A. Langer, M. Nystrand, and A. Gamoran. "Discussion-Based Approaches to Developing Understanding: Classroom Instruction and Student Performance in Middle and High School English." *American Educational Research Journal* 40, no. 3 (2003): 685–730.

Aukerman, M. S. "When Reading It Wrong Is Getting It Right: Shared Evaluation Pedagogy among Struggling Fifth Graders." *Research in the Teaching of English* 42, no. 1 (2007): 56–103.

Baker, S. J. "The Theory of Silence." *Journal of General Psychiatry* 52 (1955): 145–67.

Bakhtin, M. *Problems of Dostoevsky's Poetics.* Translated by C. Emerson. Theory and History of Literature, vol. 8. Minneapolis: University of Minnesota Press, 1984.

———. *Speech Genres and Other Late Essays.* Translated by M. Holquist and C. Emerson. Vol. 1. University of Texas Press Slavic Series, no. 8. Austin: University of Texas Press, 1986.

———. *The Dialogic Imagination: Four Essays.* Translated by M. Holquist. University of Texas Press Slavic Series, no. 1. Austin: University of Texas Press, 1981.

Barton, K. C. "Students' Ideas about History." In *Handbook of Research on Social Education*, edited by L. Levstik and C. A. Tyson, 239–58. New York: Routledge, 2008.

Beeghly, D. G. "It's About Time: Using Electronic Literature Discussion Groups with Adult Learners." *Journal of Adolescent & Adult Literacy* 49, no. 1 (2005): 12–21.

Bellack, A. A., H. M. Kliebard, R. T. Hyman, and F. L. Smith. *The Language of the Classroom*. New York: Teachers College Press, 1966.

Boyd, M. P., and D. Rubin. "How Contingent Questioning Promotes Extended Student Talk: A Function of Display Questions." *Journal of Literacy Research* 38, no. 2 (June 1, 2006): 141–69. https://doi.org/10.1207/s15548430jlr3802_2.

Boyd, M. P., and D. L. Rubin. "Elaborated Student Talk in an Elementary ESoL Classroom." *Research in the Teaching of English* 36, no. 4 (May 1, 2002): 495–530.

Boyd, M. P., and W. C. Markarian. "Dialogic Teaching and Dialogic Stance: Moving beyond Interactional Form." *Research in the Teaching of English* 49, no. 3 (2015): 272–96.

Brookfield, S. D. *The Skillful Teacher: On Technique, Trust, and Responsiveness in the Classroom*. San Francisco, CA: Jossey-Bass, 2015.

Brookfield, S. D., and S. Preskill. *Discussion as a Way of Teaching: Tools and Techniques for Democratic Classrooms*. San Francisco, CA: Jossey-Bass, 2005.

Brooks, Sarah. "Historical Empathy as Perspective Recognition and Care in One Secondary Social Studies Classroom." *Theory & Research in Social Education* 39, no. 2 (Spring 2011): 166–202.

Cambridge Primary Review Trust. "Dialogic Teaching." Evaluation Report and Executive Summary. London, UK: Education Endowment Foundation, 2017.

Cazden, Courtney B. "Classroom Discourse." In *Handbook of Research on Teaching*, vol. 3: xi, 1037. New York and London: Macmillan; Collier Macmillan, 1986.

Cazden, Courtney B., and E. Leggett. "Culturally Responsive Education: Recommendations for Achieving LAU Remedies II." In *Culture and the Bilingual Classroom: Studies in Classroom Ethnography*, viii, 248 p. Rowley, MA: Newbury House Publishers, 1981.

Chin, C. "Classroom Interaction in Science: Teacher Questioning and Feedback to Students' Responses." *International Journal of Science Education* 28, no. 11 (2007): 1315–46.

Chisholm, J. S., and A. J. Loretto. "Tensioning Interpretive Authority during Dialogic Discussions of Literature." *L1-Educational Studies in Language and Literature* 16 (2016): 1–32.

Cohen, Elizabeth G. *Designing Groupwork: Strategies for the Heterogeneous Classroom*. New York: Teachers College Press, 1986.

Coleman, G. "Anonymity Online Serves Us All." *New York Times*. August 20, 2014, Opinion Pages edition, sec. Room for Debate.
Collins, J. "Discourse Style, Classroom Interaction, and Differential Treatment." *Journal of Reading Behavior* 14 (1982): 429–37.
Corsaro, W. A., and T. A. Rizzo. "Disputes in the Peer Culture of American and Italian Nursery School Children." In *Conflict Talk: Sociolinguistic Investigations of Arguments in Conversation*, edited by A. D. Grimshaw. Cambridge: Cambridge University Press, 1990.
Daniels, Harvey. *Literature Circles: Voice and Choice in the Student-Centered Classroom*. York, ME: Stenhouse Publishers, 1994.
Dijk, Teun A. Van. *Discourse as Social Interaction*. London: SAGE, 1997.
Du Bois, J. W. "The Stance Triangle." In *Stancetaking in Discourse: Subjectivity, Evaluation, Interaction*, edited by R. Englebretson, 139–82. Amsterdam, Netherlands: John Benjamins, 2007.
———. "Towards a Dialogic Syntax." *Cognitive Linguistics* 25, no. 3 (2014): 359–410.
Duke, N. K., V. Purcell-Gates, L. A. Hall, and C. Tower. "Authentic Literacy Activities for Developing Comprehension and Writing." *The Reading Teacher* 60, no. 4 (2006): 344–55.
Dunlap, J. C., D. Bose, P. R. Lowenthal, C. S. York, M. Atkinson, and J. Murtagh. "What Sunshine Is to Flowers: A Literature Review on the Use of Emoticons to Support Online Learning." In *Emotion, Technology, Design, and Learning*, 163–82. Emotions and Technology. London, UK: Academic Press, 2016.
Dutro, E. *The Vulnerable Heart of Literacy: Centering Trauma as Powerful Pedagogy*. New York: Teachers College Press, 2019.
Edwards-Groves, C., and C. Davidson. "Metatalk for a Dialogic Turn in the First Years of Schooling." In *Routledge International Handbook of Research on Dialogic Education*, 125–38. New York: Routledge, 2020.
Fleischman, P. *Joyful Noise: Poems for Two Voices*. New York: HarperCollins, 2013.
Frank, A. W. *Letting Stories Breathe: A Socio-Narratology*. Chicago: University of Chicago Press, 2010.
Freedman, S. W., E. R. Simons, J. S. Kalnin, A. Casareno, and The M-Class Teams. *Inside City Schools: Investigating Literacy in Multicultural Classrooms*. New York: Teachers College Press, 1999.
Gallegos, E. S. *Animals of the Four Windows*. Embudo, NM: Moon Bear Press, 1991.
Gallimore, Ronald, Stephanie Dalton, and Roland G. Tharp. "Self-Regulation and Interactive Teaching: The Effects of Teaching Conditions on Teachers' Cognitive Activity." *The Elementary School Journal* 86, no. 5 (1986): 612.

Gao, F. "Designing a Discussion Environment to Promote Connected and Sustained Online Discussion." *Journal of Educational Media and Hypermedia* 20, no. 1 (2011): 43–59.

Gao, F., T. Zhang, and T. Franklin. "Designing Asynchronous Online Discussion Environments: Recent Progress and Future Directions." *British Journal of Educational Technology* 44, no. 3 (2013): 469–83.

Gardner, Howard. *Frames of Mind: The Theory of Multiple Intelligences*. 10th anniversary ed. New York: BasicBooks, 1993.

Gates, Henry Louis. *The Signifying Monkey: A Theory of Afro-American Literary Criticism*. New York: Oxford University Press, 1988.

Glenn, C. *Unspoken: A Rhetoric of Silence*. Carbondale, IL: Southern Illinois University Press, 2004.

Goffman, Erving. "Footing." In *Forms of Talk*. Philadelphia: University of Pennsylvania Press, 1981.

———. *Forms of Talk*. University of Pennsylvania Publications in Conduct and Communication. Philadelphia: University of Pennsylvania Press, 1981.

———. *Frame Analysis: An Essay on the Organization of Experience*. Boston: Northeastern University Press, 1986.

Grimshaw, A. D. *Conflict Talk*. Cambridge: Cambridge University Press, 1990.

Groenke, S. L. "Missed Opportunities in Cyberspace: Preparing Preservice Teachers to Facilitate Critical Talk about Literature through Computer-Mediated Communication." *Journal of Adolescent & Adult Literacy* 52, no. 3 (2008): 224–33.

Gumperz, J. J. *Discourse Strategies*. Cambridge: Cambridge University Press, 1982.

Hardman, F. "Embedding a Dialogic Pedagogy in the Classroom: What Is the Research Telling Us?" In *Routledge International Handbook of Research on Dialogic Education*, 139–51. New York: Routledge, 2020.

Heritage, John C., and Andrew L. Roth. "Grammar and Institution: Questions and Questioning in the Broadcast News Interview." *Research on Language & Social Interaction* 28, no. 1 (January 1995): 1. https://doi.org/Article.

Hess, D. *Controversy in the Classroom: The Democratic Power of Discussion*. Critical Social Thought. New York: Routledge, 2009.

Hoetker, J., and W. Jr. Albrand. "The Persistence of Recitation." *American Educational Research Journal* 6 (1969): 145–67.

Holland, D., W. Jr. Lachicotte, D. Skinner, and C. Cain. *Identity and Agency in Cultural Worlds*. Cambridge, MA: Harvard University Press, 1998.

Hurston, Z. N. *Mules and Men*. Philadelphia: J. B. Lippincott Company, 1935.

Johannessen, R. L. "The Functions of Silence: A Plea for Communication Research." *Western Speech* 38 (1974): 24–35.

Johnstone, B. "Variations in Discourse: Midwestern Narrative Style." *American Speech* 65, no. 3 (1990): 195–214.

Jordan, L. E. "Social Construction as Tradition: A Review and Reconceptualization of the Dozens." *Review of Research in Education* 10 (1983): 79–101.

Journell, W. "Facilitating Historical Discussions Using Asynchronous Communication: The Role of the Teacher." *Theory & Research in Social Education* 36, no. 4 (2008): 317–55.

Juzwik, M. M., M. Nystrand, S. Kelly, and M. B. Sherry. "Oral Narrative Genres as Dialogic Resources for Classroom Literature Study." *American Educational Research Journal* 45, no. 4 (2008): 1111–54.

Kiesler, S., J. Siegel, and T. W. McGuire. "Social Psychological Aspects of Computer-Mediated Communication." *American Psychologist* 39 (1984): 1123–34.

Kim, H. K., and B. Bateman. "Student Participation Patterns in Online Discussion: Incorporating Constructivist Discussion into Online Courses." *International Journal on E-Learning* 9, no. 1 (2010): 79–98.

Kim, M. Y., and I. A. G. Wilkinson. "What Is Dialogic Teaching? Constructing, Deconstructing, and Reconstructing a Pedagogy of Classroom Talk." *Learning, Culture, and Social Interaction* 21 (2019): 70–86.

Kohlmeier, J. "'Couldn't She Just Leave': The Relationship between Consistently Using Class Discussions and the Development of Historical Empathy in a 9th Grade World History Course." *Theory and Research in Social Education* 34, no. 1 (2006): 34–57.

Labov, William. *Language in the Inner City: Studies in the Black English Vernacular*. Philadelphia: University of Pennsylvania Press, 1972.

Ladson-Billings, G. "Toward a Theory of Culturally Relevant Pedagogy." *American Educational Research Journal* 32, no. 3 (1995): 465–91.

Langer, J. A. "Discussion as Exploration: Literature and the Horizon of Possibilities." In *Exploring Texts: The Role of Discussion and Writing in the Teaching and Learning of Literature*, edited by G. E. Newell and R. K. Durst, 23–43. Norwood, MA: Christopher Gordon, 1992.

Larson, B. E., and T. A. Keiper. "Classroom Discussion and Threaded Electronic Discussion: Learning in Two Arenas." *Contemporary Issues in Technology and Teacher Education* 2, no. 1 (2002): 45–62.

Lawrence, A. M., and S. Crespo. "IRE/F as a Cross-Curricular Collaborative Genre of Implicit Argumentation." *Theory into Practice* 55, no. 4 (2016): 1–12.

Lee, C. D. *Culture, Literacy & Learning: Taking Bloom in the Midst of the Whirlwind*. New York: Teachers College Press, 2006.

Lefstein, A. "Changing Classroom Practice through the English National Literacy Strategy: A Micro-Interactional Perspective." *American Educational Research Journal* 45, no. 3 (2008): 701–37.

Lemke, J. *Talking Science: Language, Learning and Values*. Norwood, NJ: Ablex, 1990.

Lent, R. C. *This Is Disciplinary Literacy: Reading, Writing, Thinking, and Doing . . . Content Area by Content Area*. Thousand Oaks, CA: Corwin, 2016.

Levstik, L. "Any History Is Someone's History: Listening to Multiple Voices from the Past." *Social Education* 61 (1997): 48–51.

Levstik, L., and K. C. Barton. *Doing History: Investigating with Children in Elementary and Middle Schools*. New York: Taylor & Francis, 2001.

———. *Researching History Education: Theory, Method, and Context*. New York: Routledge, 2008.

Liska, J., and V. Hazleton. "Deferential Language as a Rhetorical Strategy: The Case for Polite Disagreement." *Journal of Social Behavior & Personality* 5, no. 3 (1990): 187–98.

Losey, K. M. "Mexican American Students and Classroom Interaction: An Overview and Critique." *Review of Educational Research* 65, no. 3 (1995): 283–318.

Macy, J., and C. Johnstone. *Active Hope: How to Face the Mess We're in without Going Crazy*. Novato, CA: New World Library, 2012.

Macy, J., and M. Y. Brown. *Coming Back to Life: The Updated Guide to the Work That Reconnects*. Gabriola Island, BC Canada: New Society Publishers, 1989.

Marshall, J. D., P. Smagorinsky, and M. W. Smith. "The Language of Interpretation: Patterns of Discourse in Discussions of Literature." Urbana, IL: NCTE, 1995.

Masciarotte, G-J. "'C'mon Girl': Oprah Winfrey and the Discourse of Feminine Talk." *Genders* 11 (1991).

Matusov, E. *Journey into Dialogic Pedagogy*. New York: Nova Science Publishers, Inc., 2009.

Mehan, H. "'What Time Is It, Denise?': Asking Known Information Questions in Classroom Discourse." *Theory into Practice* 18, no. 4 (1979): 285–94.

Mercer, N., L. Dawes, and J. K. Staarman. "Dialogic Teaching in the Primary Science Classroom." *Language and Education* 23, no. 4 (2009): 353–69.

Meyer, K. A. "Face-to-Face versus Threaded Discussions: The Role of Time and Higher-Order Thinking." *Journal of Asynchronous Learning Networks* 7, no. 3 (2003): 55–65.

Michaels, S., C. O'Connor, M. W. Hall, and L. B. Resnick. *Accountable Talk Sourcebook: For Classroom Conversation That Works*. 1st ed., vol. 3. Pittsburgh, PA: Institute for Learning, University of Pittsburgh, 2012.

Mitchell-Kernan, C. "Signifying, Loud-Talking, and Marking." In *Rappin' and Stylin' out; Communication in Urban Black America*, 309–30. Urbana, IL: University of Illinois Press, 1972.

Moje, Elizabeth B. "Responsive Literacy Teaching in Secondary School Content Areas." In *Meeting the Challenge of Adolescent Literacy: Research We Have, Research We Need*, 58–80. New York: Guilford, 2008.

Morgan, M. "Conversational Signifying: Grammar and Indirectness among African American Women." In *Interaction and Grammar*, 405–34. Studies in Interactional Sociolinguistics 13. Cambridge and New York: Cambridge University Press, 1996.

Morson, G. S. *Narrative and Freedom: The Shadows of Time*. New Haven: Yale University Press, 1994.

———. "Sideshadowing and Tempics." *New Literary History* 29, no. 4 (1998): 599–624.

Morson, G. S., and C. Emerson. *Mikhail Bakhtin: Creation of a Prosaics*. Stanford: Stanford University Press, 1990.

Nassaji, H., and G. Wells. "What's the Use of 'Triadic Dialogue'? An Investigation of Teacher-Student Interaction." *Applied Linguistics* 21, no. 3 (2000): 376–406.

National Center for History in the Schools. "Historical Thinking Standards." University of California. Los Angeles: National Council for History Standards, 1996. http://nchs.ucla.edu/Standards/historical-thinking-standards-1.

Nystrand, M., A. Gamoran, R. Kachur, and C. Prendergast. *Opening Dialogue: Understanding the Dynamics of Language and Learning in the English Classroom*. New York: Teachers College Press, 1997.

Nystrand, M., L. L. Wu, A. Gamoran, S. Zeiser, and D. Long. "Questions in Time: Investigating the Unfolding Structure of Classroom Discourse." Albany, NY: National Research Center on English Learning and Achievement, 2003.

Ochs, Elinor, and Lisa Capps. *Living Narrative: Creating Lives in Everyday Storytelling*. Cambridge, MA: Harvard University Press, 2001.

O'Connor, M. C., and S. Michaels. "Aligning Academic Task and Participation Status through Revoicing: Analysis of a Classroom Discourse Strategy." *Anthropology & Education Quarterly* 24, no. 4 (1993): 318–35.

———. "When Is Dialogue 'Dialogic'?" Accessed January 2, 2010. http://proquest.umi.com.proxy1.cl.msu.edu/pqdweb?index=4&did=1339279201&SrchMode=3&sid=1&Fmt=6&VInst=PROD&VType=PQD&RQT=309&VName=PQD&TS=1262468378&clientId=3552&aid=1.

Parker, W. C. "Classroom Discussion: Models for Leading Seminars and Deliberations." *Social Education* 65, no. 2 (2001): 111–15.

———. "Listening to Strangers: Classroom Discussion in Democratic Education." *Teachers College Record* 112, no. 11 (2010): 2815–32.

Parker, W. C., and D. Hess. "Teaching with and for Discussion." *Teaching and Teacher Education* 17 (April 2001): 273–89.

Peterson, Dale E. "Response and Call: The African American Dialogue with Bakhtin." *American Literature* 65, no. 4 (1993): 761–65.

Postmes, T., and R. Spears. "Behavior Online: Does Anonymous Computer Communication Reduce Gender Inequality?" *Personality & Social Psychology Bulletin* 28, no. 7 (2002): 1073–83.

Prior, P. "A Microhistory of Mediated Authorship and Disciplinary Enculturation: Tracing Authoritative and Internally Persuasive Discourses." In *Writing/Discplinarity: A Sociohistoric Account of Literate Activity in the Academy*, 215–46. Mahwah, NJ: Lawrence Erlbaum Associates, 1998.

Purcell-Gates, V., N. K. Duke, and J. A. Martineau. "Learning to Read and Write Genre-Specific Text: Roles of Authentic Experience and Explicit Teaching." *Reading Research Quarterly* 42, no. 1 (2007): 8–45.

Pytash, K. E., and L. Ciecierski. "Teaching from a Disciplinary Literacy Stance." *Voices in the Middle* 22, no. 3 (2015): 14–18.

Ratcliffe, K. *Rhetorical Listening: Identification, Gender, Whiteness*. Carbondale, IL: Southern Illinois University Press, 2005.

Reisman, A. "Entering the Historical Problem Space: Whole-Class Text-Based Discussion in History Class." *Teachers College Record* 117, no. 2 (2015): 1–44.

Resnick, L. B., C. O'Connor, and S. Michaels. "Classroom Discourse, Mathematical Rigor, and Student Reasoning: An Accountable Talk Literature Review." Pittsburgh, PA: Pittsburgh Science of Learning Center, 2007.

Reynolds, T. "Understanding and Embracing Contradictions: An Exploration of High School English Teachers' Beliefs about Whole-Class Discussion." *Language and Education* 32, no. 4 (2018): 1–15.

Reznitskaya, A., and I. A. G. Wilkinson. *The Most Reasonable Answer: Helping Students Build Better Arguments Together*. Cambridge, MA: Harvard Education Press, 2017.

Reznitskaya, A., and M. Glina. "Comparing Student Experiences with Story Discussions in Dialogic versus Traditional Settings." *The Journal of Educational Research* 106, no. 1 (2013): 49–63.

Romano, T. *Blending Genre, Altering Style: Writing Multigenre Papers*. Portsmouth, NH: Boynton/Cook, 2000.

Roth, W.-M., and R. Gardner. "'They're Gonna Explain to Us What Makes a Cube a Cube?' Geometrical Properties as Contingent Achievement of Sequentially Ordered Child-Centered Mathematics Lessons." *Mathematics Education Research Journal* 24 (2012): 323–46.

Rovai, A. P. "Facilitating Online Discussions Effectively." *Internet and Higher Education* 10 (2007): 77–88.

Ruday, S. "Expanding the Possibilities of Discussion: A Strategic Approach to Using Online Discussion Boards in the Middle and High School English Classroom." *Contemporary Issues in Technology and Teacher Education* 11, no. 4 (2011). http://www.citejournal.org/vol11/iss4/languagearts/article2.cfm.

Sacks, Harvey. *Lectures on Conversation*. Cambridge: Blackwell, 1992.

Sawyer, R. Keith. "Emergence in Sociology: Contemporary Philosophy of Mind and Some Implications for Sociological Theory." *The American Journal of Sociology* 107, no. 3 (2001): 551.

———. "Improvisation and Narrative." *Narrative Inquiry* 12, no. 2 (2002): 319–49.

———. *Improvised Dialogues: Emergence and Creativity in Conversation*. Publications in Creativity Research. Westport, CT: Ablex Pub., 2003.

Scardamalia, M. "CSILE/Knowledge Forum." In *Education and Technology: An Encyclopedia*, 183–92. Santa Barbara, CA: ABC-CLIO, 2004.

Schiffrin, Deborah. "Jewish Argument as Sociability." *Language in Society* 13, no. 3 (September 1984): 311–35.

Schweber, Simone. *Making Sense of the Holocaust*. New York: Teachers College Press, 2004.

Segal, A., I. Pollak, and A. Lefstein. "Democracy, Voice, and Dialogic Pedagogy: The Struggle to Be Heard and Heeded." *Language and Education* 31, no. 1 (2017): 6–25.

Sherry, M. B. "Bringing Disciplinarity to Dialogic Discussions: Imaginative Entry and Disciplinary Discourse in a Ninth-Grade History Classroom." *Curriculum Inquiry* 46, no. 2 (2016): 168–95.

———. "How the Visual Rhetoric of Online Discussion Enables and Constraints Student Participation." *Journal of Adolescent & Adult Literacy* 61, no. 3 (2017): 299–310.

———. "Indirect Challenges and Provocative Paraphrases: Using Cultural Conflict-Talk Practices to Promote Students' Dialogic Participation in Whole-Class Discussions." *Research in the Teaching of English* 49, no. 2 (2014): 141–67.

Sherry, M. B., G. Dodson, and S. Sweeney. "Improvising Literate Identities: Comparing Cultural Roles and Dialogic Discourse in Two Lessons from a US Elementary Classroom." *Linguistics & Education* 50 (2019): 36–45.

Sherry, M. B., and R. Tremmel. "English Education 2.0: An Analysis of Sites That Contain Videos of English Teaching." *English Education* 45, no. 1 (2012): 35–70.

Sinclair, J., and M. Coulthard. *Towards an Analysis of Discourse: The English Used by Teachers and Pupils*. Oxford, UK: Oxford University Press, 1975.

Siromaa, M. "Resonance in Conversational Second Stories: A Dialogic Resource for Stance Taking." *Text and Talk* 4, no. 4 (2012): 525–45.

Slagle, P. "Getting Real: Authenticity in Writing Prompts." *The Quarterly* 19, no. 3 (1997).

Smitherman, Geneva. *Talkin and Testifyin: The Language of Black America*. Boston: Houghton Mifflin, 1977.

———. *Talkin That Talk : Language, Culture, and Education in African America*. New York: Routledge, 2000.

Snell, J., and A. Lefstein. "'Low Ability,' Participation and Identity in Dialogic Pedagogy." *American Educational Research Journal* 55, no. 1 (2018): 40–78.

Tannen, D. "'Don't Just Sit There—Interrupt!': Pacing and Pausing in Conversational Style." *American Speech* 75, no. 4 (2000): 393–95.

———. *Talking Voices: Repetition, Dialogue, and Imagery in Conversational Discourse*. Vol. 2. Studies in Interactional Sociolinguistics. Cambridge and New York: Cambridge University Press, 2007.

———. *The Argument Culture*. London: Virago, 1998.

Thayer, V. T. *The Passing of the Recitation*. Boston: D.C. Heath, 1928.

Voloshinov, V. N. "Reported Speech." In *Readings in Russian Poetics: Structuralist and Formalist Views*, edited by L. Matejka and K. Pomorska. Cambridge, MA: MIT Press, 1971.

Welch, N. "Sideshadowing Teacher Response." *College English* 60, no. 4 (1998): 374–95.

Wells, G. *Dialogic Inquiry*. Cambridge: Cambridge University Press, 1999.

———. "Reevaluating the IRF Sequence: A Proposal for the Articulation of Theories of Activity and Discourse for the Analysis of Teaching and Learning in the Classroom." *Linguistics and Education* 5, no. 1 (1993): 1–37.

Wertsch, James V. "Narratives as Cultural Tools in Sociocultural Analysis: Official History in Soviet and Post-Soviet Russia." *Ethos* 28, no. 4, History and Subjectivity (2000): 511–33.

———. *Voices of Collective Remembering*. Cambridge and New York: Cambridge University Press, 2002.

Whitney, A. E. "In Search of the Authentic English Classroom: Facing the Schoolishness of School." *English Education* 44, no. 1 (2011): 51–62.

Wilkinson, I. A. G., A. Reznitskaya, K. Bourdage, J. Oyler, M. Glina, R. Drewry, M. Kim, and K. Nelson. "Toward a More Dialogic Pedagogy: Changing

Teachers' Beliefs and Practices through Professional Development in Language Arts Classrooms." *Language and Education* 31, no. 1 (2017): 65–82.

Williams, Robin. *The Non-Designers Design Book: Design and Typographic Principles for the Visual Novice*. Vol. 2. Berkeley, CA: Peachpit Press, 2004.

Wineburg, S. *Historical Thinking and Other Unnatural Acts: Charting the Future of Teaching the Past*. Philadelphia: Temple University Press, 2001.

Wortham, S. *Learning Identity: The Joint Emergence of Social Identification and Academic Learning*. Cambridge and New York: Cambridge University Press, 2006.

———. *Narratives in Action: A Strategy for Research and Analysis*. New York: Teachers College Press, 2001.

Wortham, S., and A. Reyes. *Discourse Analysis beyond the Speech Event*. New York: Routledge, 2015.

Wu, D., and S. R. Hiltz. "Predicting Learning from Asynchronous Online Discussions." *Journal of Asynchronous Learning Networks* 8, no. 2 (2004). http://www.adesignmedia.com/onlineresearch/Sloan-C%C2%A0-%C2%A0Publications%C2%A0-%C2%A0Journal%20JALN%C2%A0-%C2%A0Vol82.htm.

Zhu, E. "Interaction and Cognitive Engagement: An Analysis of Four Asynchronous Online Discussions." *Instructional Science* 34 (2006): 451–80.

Zimmerman, J., and V. Coyle. *The Way of Council*. 2nd ed. North Bergen, NJ: Bramble Books, 1996.

———. "Ways of Council." Ways of Council, 2020. https://waysofcouncil.net/.

About the Author

Michael B. Sherry is associate professor of English Education at University of South Florida. He began to study discussions when he first faced crickets and tumbleweeds in his own classroom as a middle and high school teacher. Since then, he has pursued that inquiry into classroom dialogue as a teacher educator and education researcher, observing and recording discussions from different classrooms, disciplines, and grade levels in different parts of the country. He continues to be fascinated by how teacher responses can promote participation from all students, particularly those who might otherwise be marginalized by classroom conversations.

www.ingramcontent.com/pod-product-compliance
Lightning Source LLC
Chambersburg PA
CBHW020649230426
43665CB00008B/370